寻觅备选世遗佳境 1

In Search of the Places in the Preparatory List for the World Heritage I

杨永发 / 著+摄影　顾大信 / 译

Passages and photographs by Yang Yongfa

Translation by Gu Daxi

上海科学技术文献出版社

Shanghai Scientific and Technological Literature Press

图书在版编目（CIP）数据

寻觅备选世遗佳境 1 / 杨永发著；杨永发摄影；顾大僖译．—上海：
上海科学技术文献出版社，2014.8
ISBN 978-7-5439-6305-4

Ⅰ．①寻… Ⅱ．①杨…②杨…③顾… Ⅲ．①文化遗产—介绍—
中国 Ⅳ．①K203

中国版本图书馆 CIP 数据核字 (2014) 第 134548 号

责任编辑：王卓娅
特约编辑：倪 华
装帧设计：袁 力
封面题字：田文惠

寻觅备选世遗佳境 1
杨永发 著＋摄影 顾大僖 译
出版发行：上海科学技术文献出版社
地 址：上海市长乐路 746 号
邮政编码：200040
经 销：全国新华书店
印 刷：上海市印刷七厂有限公司
开 本：787×1092 1/16
印 张：18.75
版 次：2014 年 8 月第 1 版 2014 年 8 月第 1 次印刷
书 号：ISBN 978-7-5439-6305-4
定 价：118.00 元
http://www.sstlp.com

致读者

中国有一种看得见的自然之美，这是一种给人带来感官享受的美。美在九曲黄河的回肠荡气，北疆禾木的秋日盛宴，沙市古镇的鲜活灵动，闽南红厝的灿若红霞，哈尼梯田的烟波浩渺，甲居藏寨的空谷灵秀，平潭海岛的海蚀奇貌，闽浙廊桥的长虹卧波，扬州园林的大气婉约，北海银滩的碧波蓝天，和钓鱼古城的丹崖赤壁。

中国还有一种看不见的人文之美，这是一种给人带来心灵震撼的美。美在关圣遗存的忠孝仁义，党家古村的耕读传家，惠山百祠的血脉传承，赣南围屋的中原情怀，清源名山的文化共融，玉门雄关的中华意志，钓鱼古城的民族气节，梭坡碉楼的藏羌气质，白哈巴村的图瓦风情，和新市古镇的活态运河。

《保护世界文化和自然遗产公约》规定，列入联合国教科文组织《世界文化与自然遗产预备名单》是申报世界遗产的先决条件，至少每十年修订一次。为此， 国家文物局于2012年11月底发布了新版《中国世界文化遗产预备名单》，共45项，加上国家建设部前几年发布的中国国家自然遗产和自然与文化双遗产预备名录，我国目前申报世界文化遗产的点位约有上百处。这些叹为观止的人文和自然景观，代表着中国人文和审美的最高境界，彰显出中华民族对世界文明的突出贡献，不仅属于中国，更属于世界。

凑巧的是，这上百处点位与我近年来追寻的中国原生态自然和人文景观不谋而合，遂精选了部分点位汇编成书，此为首册，以飨同好。

2014年2月6日于上海竹山堂

To the Readers

China boasts a kind of visible beauty in nature, which provides people with sensual charm. This kind of beauty is to be found along the soul–stirring meandering Yellow River; in the autumn feast of Hemu in northern Xinjiang; in the old aquatic but still energetic town of Shashi; in the brilliant twilight of the dusk in Hongcuo of southern Fujian; in the terraced fields similar to mist–covered waters in Hani; in the mysterious hollow valley where the Jiaju Tibetan Village is located; in the eroded rocks on the sea near Pingtan Island; in the corridor bridges in Zhenjiang and Fujian that look like spanning rainbows above the waterways; in the gardens of Yangzhou that represent the blended style of northern and southern gardening; in the blue waves of the sea and the white clouds in the blue sky at the Silvery Beach of Beihai; and in the steep cliffs of Chibi, where people have been enjoying angling generation after generation.

China also boasts a kind of invisible beauty of humanities, which produces heart–touching effects on the viewers. This kind of beauty is to be discovered in the historic remains about Guan Yu that reflect national sentimentality; in the heritage of traditional farming and schooling in the Dangjia Village; in the family inheritance in the numerous temples of Huishan; in the circular houses in southern Fujian that reveal the complex of central China; in co–existence of different cultures in the Qingyuan Mountains; in the national ethos of the Yumen Pass that protected the country from alien invaders; in the Chinese will power of the ancient city where people have been enjoying angling; in the heroic Chinese history in stones at the Suopo Watchtowers; and in the ethnic flavor of the Tuvan people that have been living in Baihaba Village.

In accordance with the regulations of the Convention Concerning the Protection of World Cultural and Natural Heritage, it is a prerequisite for any place to apply as world heritage that it should, first and foremost, be put in the preparatory list of the World Cultural and Natural Heritage, which is subjected to revision every ten years. Therefore, the State Administration of Cultural Relics issued the preparatory list for Chinese World Heritage in November, 2012, which includes 45 items. Besides, a few years earlier, the National Ministry of Construction issued a preparatory list of national natural relics and cultural and natural heritage. Therefore, China has so far applied over 100 places for the World Heritage. These breathtaking natural spots and cultural sites, which are at the culmination of Chinese humanities and esthetics, make up the outstanding contributions to world civilization by the Chinese people. These places belong not only to China but also to the world.

These sites are coincidentally located in the ecologically unique natural and historical places that have interested me these past years. After careful selection of the sites, I would like to dedicate this book to my dear readers. It is my hope that you will enjoy the sites as much as I do.

Yang Yongfa

Shanghai, on February 6, 2014

目录
Contents

目录
Contents

目录
Contents

山海鍾靈
御書樓

01 大义秉春秋 Eternal Righteousness

关圣文化的活态传承　古代建筑的精品力作
Heritage of Guan Yu Culture and Temple Architecture

中华民族靠什么延续泱泱五千年文明史生生不息？以什么价值取向凝聚海内外炎黄子孙的人心？在山西省运城这片古称河东的土地上，兴许可以寻找到答案。

How has the Chinese nation managed to last for 5,000 years? What values do Chinese at home and abroad share? Most probably, it is on the land of Yuncheng, Shanxi Province, which used to be referred to as Hedong, meaning the east side of the Yellow River, that answers might be chanced upon.

千年古庙传忠义

Symbol of Righteousness

山西省西南部的运城盆地，黄河蜿蜒远逝，这里是中国古称“河东”的核心区域，以物华天宝、地灵人杰著称于世。

中国原始社会后期的部落联盟领袖舜和禹，都曾在这片黄土地上捭阖纵横，创建了当时社会的政治、经济和文化中心，即所谓的“舜都蒲坂”“禹都安邑”。远古时代决定炎黄民族早期文明构成、文明方向和文明进程的一次历史大决战，即黄帝与蚩尤大战于“冀州之野”，也发生在此地。其时的“冀州”，就是后世的“河东”。在众多的传说和史籍中，教人以养蚕造丝的嫘祖，授人以稼穑耕作的后稷，示人以“版筑”造墙的傅说，也都活动于河东地区。在春秋战国至宋元明清这段有确切文字记载的历史长河中，河东之地更是风起云涌、英才辈出，荀况、裴秀、郭璞、裴松之、卢纶、司空图、聂夷中、柳宗元、薛仁贵、王通、司马光、马远、杨深秀等名字耳熟能详，为创造和推动中国古代社会的灿烂文明，做出了不可磨灭的突出贡献。

在河东灿若星辰的古代圣贤中，有一颗明星分外耀眼，千古传颂，这就是被后世封为“大帝”、

相机：佳能 Canon Eos-1DX，镜头：24-70mm f/2.8，光圈：f/13，快门：1/320秒，感光度：ISO800，曝光补偿：0EV **关帝庙石牌坊**

尊为“武圣”的关公。关公姓关，名羽，字云长，生于160年，卒于219年，为今山西省运城市常平乡常平村人。相传，关公幼年喜读《左氏春秋》等儒家经典，深明大义。青年时因打抱不平，杀死乡里恶霸而避祸他乡。遇刘备、张飞后，与之结义，发誓辅佐刘备，匡扶汉室。此后跟随刘备灭董卓、破袁绍、战吕布、退曹操，屡建战功，实现了魏、蜀、吴三国鼎立的政权割据，后因大意失荆州而败走麦城，悲壮去世。蜀汉丞相诸葛亮评关公曰“绝伦逸群”。关公的义胆忠心被后人视为楷模，“温酒斩华雄”“过五关斩六将”“千里走单骑”“水淹七军”等故事被世人津津乐道，传颂至今。

解州位于运城市西关，北靠银湖（盐池），面对中条山，景色秀丽。解州大地，关圣情结无处不在。红色历来被中华民族视为赤胆忠义的象征，解州关帝庙呈现的那一道道灿如晚霞的红墙，更是令访客平添些许义胆忠魂的情愫。

作为关公的故里，关帝庙兴建的历史非常久远。据碑刻记载，远在陈隋之际，解州关帝庙已经修建。宋元到明清，随着社会各界对关公美化、圣化和神化的情形不断提升，又对解州关帝庙进行了多次大规模的修复、重建和扩建。晚清时，该庙曾数次失火，损失惨重，但在民国年间又得到修复和重建。新中国成立之后，人民政府将解州关帝庙建筑群落列为国家重点文物保护单位。

对每一位中国人来说，忠义是为人处世的基本准则，内心深处或多或少也烙上了关公情结。千百年以来，尤其在宋元明清的封建社会时期，解州关帝庙是进行中国传统道德文化感化的精神殿堂。历朝历代的封建统治者，通过加封、赐匾、祭祀等手段，对臣民灌输伦理道德和封建纲常思想，以维护其统治地位；当少数民族统治者入主中原后，也来到这里进行褒封和祭祀，力图通过对关圣文化的认同，来弥合民族之间在思想和文化方面的分歧；在

相机：佳能 Canon Eos-1DX，镜头：24-70mm f/2.8，光圈：f/13，快门：1/125秒，感光度：ISO800，曝光补偿：0EV **关帝庙春秋殿**

相机：佳能 Canon Eos-1DX，镜头：24-70mm f/2.8，光圈：f/18，快门：1/400秒，感光度：ISO800，曝光补偿：0EV **关帝庙柏树林**

国家和民族危难存亡之际，肩负民族复兴大义的英雄儿女，在这里通过对关公的祭拜，增添保家卫国兴邦的信念，毅然奔赴杀敌前线；数不清的庶民百姓，也一次又一次地来到这里参拜祭祀，虔诚地从关圣身上汲取忠、诚、信、义的精神养分；在物欲横流、世风日下之际，那些遵从中华传统道德的人们，也来到这里，从关公身上寻找恪守信义和忠诚的道德营养。

看似无声胜有声。关帝庙中每一座建筑、每一尊塑像、每一块匾额，每时每刻都以物化的形态，默默地向世人讲述着忠义的故事，传承着中华文化的脉络。

Located in the Yuncheng Basin in the southwest of Shanxi Province, through which the Yellow River flows meanderingly, this area known in ancient China as Hedong, is world famous for its precious products and talented people.

The tribal leaders, Shun and Yu, in the later years of primitive Chinese society, maneuvered, one after the other, among political groups on this vast stretch of yellow earth, making it a political, economic, and cultural center in society. And it was here that a significant battle broke out between Huang Di and Chi You, which gave rise to the birth, orientation and development of the early civilization of the Chinese people. In many legends and historical records, Lei Zu, who taught people sericulture, Hou Ji, who taught people farming, and Fu Yue, who taught people construction, once lived and worked in the Hedong area. In the history from the Spring and Autumn and Warring States Period to the Song, Yuan, Ming and Qing Dynasties, quite a number of talents emerged in this area, such as Xun Kuang, Pei Xiu, Guo Pu, Pei Songzhi, Lu Lun, Sikong Tu, Nie Yizhong, Liu Zongyuan, Xue Ren-

相机：佳能 Canon Eos-1DX，镜头：24-70mm f/2.8，光圈：f/13，快门：1/800秒，感光度：ISO800，曝光补偿：0EV **关帝庙结义园**

相机：佳能 Canon Eos-1DX，镜头：24-70mm f/2.8，光圈：f/11，快门：1/250秒，感光度：ISO800，曝光补偿：0EV **关帝庙午门**

相机：佳能 Canon Eos-1DX，镜头：24-70mm f/2.8，光圈：f/11，快门：1/800秒，感光度：ISO800，曝光补偿：0EV **气肃千秋牌楼**

壶口冬瀑

gui, Wang Tong, Sima Kuang, Ma Yuan, and Yang Shenxiu, just to name a few. Respectively in one way or another, they made extraordinary contributions to the creation and promotion of the brilliant civilization of ancient Chinese society.

Among all the historic stars in the Hedong area, one deserves special attention for his everlastingly overwhelming achievements in history. It is Guan Yu, who was born in Changping Village, Yuncheng City, Shanxi Province, in AD 160 and died in AD 219. In his boyhood, Guan Yu was fond of reading classical books, thus becoming quite aware of righteousness. With a high sense of right and wrong and with the intention to defend the weak against injustice, he killed some local despots and ran away from home. Later he ran into Liu Bei and zhang fei, and the three became sworn brothers. Determined to support Liu Bei and restore the Han Dynasty, Guan Yu fought many a glorious battle. Finally, the three kingdoms, Wei, Shu and Wu, came into being, and the Shu Kingdom belonged to Liu Bei. Unfortunately, however, Guan Yu was defeated and lost Jingzhou because of his carelessness, thus passing away tragically. Zhuge Liang, the prime minister of the Shu Kingdom, commented, "Guan Yu is exceptionally outstanding." Consequently, Guan Yu has long been worshipped as an idol of bravery and loyalty, and the anecdotes about him have been passed down from generation to generation.

Special sentimentality about Guan Yu abounds in Haizhou, which is located in the west of Yuncheng. Red has long been cherished by the Chinese people as a symbol of bravery and loyalty; therefore, the red walls of the Guan Yu Temple in Haizhou further arouse sentimental respect for

相机：佳能 Canon Eos-1DX，镜头：24-70mm f/2.8，光圈：f/11，快门：1/640秒，感光度：ISO800，曝光补偿：0EV **关帝庙崇宁殿**

相机：佳能 Canon Eos-1DX，镜头：24-70mm f/2.8，光圈：f/13，
快门：1/250秒，感光度：ISO800，曝光补偿：0EV **关帝庙石刻**

相机：佳能 Canon Eos-1DX，镜头：24-70mm f/2.8，光圈：f/16，
快门：1/100秒，感光度：ISO400，曝光补偿：0EV **关帝庙碑亭**

相机：佳能 Canon Eos-1DX，镜头：24-70mm f/2.8，光圈：f/11，
快门：1/800秒，感光度：ISO800，曝光补偿：0EV **关帝庙铸铁像**

相机：佳能 Canon Eos-1DX，镜头：24-70mm f/2.8，光圈：f/8，
快门：1/800秒，感光度：ISO400，曝光补偿：0EV **运城盐池庙太阳神祠**

Guan Yu in visitors.

As the native place of Guan Yu Temple here has a long history. As found in the records on the stone tablets, construction of the Guan Yu Temple was begun as early as the Sui Dynasty. Then, in the Song, Yuan, Ming and Qing Dynasties, it underwent large-scale renovation, reconstruction and expansion many times as a result of the ever-increasing glorification of Guan Yu by people from all walks of life. In the late Qing Dynasty, however, it caught fire, thus suffering heavy damage. In the years of the Republic of China, it was restored and reconstructed. After the founding of the People's Republic of China, it was listed as a key national protected cultural relic.

To every Chinese, loyalty is one of the basic principles of life. Deep in the subconscious, he is branded, more or less, with Guan Yu complex. For hundreds of years, the Guan Yu Temple in Haizhou has been a sacred and spiritual place where the traditional Chinese morality and culture are advocated. The feudal rulers from dynasty to dynasty tried by all means to maintain their dominance by preaching the feudal ethics. When some alien minority invaders conquered and dominated central China, they also came to worship Guan Yu, vainly attempting to make up the ideological and cultural gap between different peoples. And when the nation was confronted with mortal danger, heroic people shouldering the responsibility of defending and rejuvenating the country also came to pay homage to Guan Yu, thus boosting their morale to safeguard the country. And nowadays, countless ordinary people come here and pay heartfelt respect with the intention of learning the noble spirit of loyalty, honesty, faith and righteousness from

相机：佳能 Canon Eos-1DX，镜头：24-70mm f/2.8，光圈：f/13，快门：1/125秒，感光度：ISO400，曝光补偿：0EV **关圣父母墓**

相机：佳能 Canon Eos-1DX，镜头：24-70mm f/2.8，光圈：f/10，快门：1/250秒，感光度：ISO400，曝光补偿：0EV **关圣手植柏**

Guan Yu.

Every building, every statue and every plaque in the Guan Yu Temple is actually telling people stories of loyalty and righteousness and passing down Chinese culture from generation to generation.

炎黄子孙聚人心

Congregation of Chinese People

县县有文庙，村村有武庙。这句话形容的是宋元明清时期，关公文化在全国各地的繁盛之状。有人说，如按每县设一座文庙，清代全国孔庙也不过三千余座；而每村如建一座武庙的话，那么清代全国的关公庙可达三十余万座！清人赵翼惊叹："今且南极岭表，北极寒垣，凡儿童妇女，无不震其（关公）威灵者。香火之盛，将与天地同不朽。"明人吕子固在《谒解庙》诗中，也曾无限感慨地吟咏道："正气充盈穷宇宙，英灵烜赫几春秋。巍然庙貌环天下，不独乡关祀典修。"真实地反映了那个时代百姓对关公的崇拜和敬仰，以及关帝庙遍布天下的盛景。

岁月流逝，沧海桑田。历史的车轮不可阻挡，吕子固诗中所吟咏的情形，早已变成过眼烟云。当年万民顶礼膜拜的关公，在现代社会中，也早已不是社会各界共同崇拜的道德偶像。昔日作为道德文化教育和感化的重要场所，终年香火鼎盛的关帝庙，也早已变成了人们旅游休闲的胜地，这是社会历史的进步、文化发展的必然。

然而，这座历史悠久、气势恢宏的古老庙宇，在现今社会，却仍然有着独特的文化价值。它是中国古代道德文化发展到宋元明清时代的物质化凝结，作为珍贵的文化遗存，将永远向后人揭示着中国古代道德文化的丰富内涵；它是中国传统道德文化在社会生活中的历史见证，它用实物而非文字的形式，向后人真实而形象地述说着中国古代道德文化的发展与变迁；它也是一面镜子，能够让今世

相机：佳能 Canon Eos-1DX，镜头：24-70mm f/2.8，光圈：f/10，快门：1/100秒，感光度：ISO400，曝光补偿：0EV **关圣手植柏**

及后世的人们，从中领略中国传统道德文化中的精华和糟粕，并为未来的道德文化走向提供借鉴；同时，作为中国古代博大精深传统文化的实物宝库和载体，作为中华民族古代文明的一份宝贵遗产，无论是现在还是将来，都会成为一条维系海内外炎黄子孙、认同民族传统文化的精神纽带。

查阅各地地方志，几乎都有与关帝庙有关的记载。清代中叶，仅京城中，拜祀关公的庙宇、殿宇便多达一百一十多处。关羽葬于洛阳，洛阳关林的庙会也已有四百多年的历史。在青藏高原珠穆朗玛峰脚下，有一座世界上海拔最高的关帝庙遗址——定日县关帝庙遗址。据记载，清康熙六十年（1721年），清朝派大军进藏平乱后，驻藏清兵集资在日喀则建起了藏区第一座关帝庙，乾隆五十七年（1792年），福康安重修了该庙，并在拉萨布达拉宫以西的巴玛热山、江孜、定日、工布江达等处也建起了关帝庙。

近代以来，随着中华文化走向世界，关帝庙遍及神州内外、世界各地。以香港为例，关帝被当地百姓奉为武财神，港九新界便有十多座大大小小的关帝庙。香港最古老的关帝庙是始建于明代的大澳关帝庙，至今已有五百多年历史。澳门最著名的供奉关帝的场所，是位于玫瑰圣母堂附近的公局新市南街的三街会馆，又名关帝古庙，这里已成为澳门世界文化遗产的景点之一。三街会馆建于1750年，距今已近三百年历史。根据民间习俗，每年关公诞辰日和磨刀日，各地关帝庙都要举行各类关圣民俗活动。据不完全统计，目前世界上共有三十多个国家和地区建有关帝庙，仅日本和马来西亚就有关帝庙一千多座。

当今社会，多元文化相互激荡碰撞，如果有一种文化及其价值取向，能够被海内外广大炎黄子孙普遍接纳，并共同推崇，那是中华民族的幸事，关圣文化也许便是其中之一。

相机：佳能 Canon Eos-1DX，镜头：24-70mm f/2.8，光圈：f/22，快门：1/1600秒，感光度：ISO800，曝光补偿：0EV **永济普救寺**

As the saying goes, every county has a Confucius temple and every village has a Guan Yu temple. It is an accurate depiction of the prosperity of Guan Yu culture all over the country during the Song, Yuan, Ming and Qing Dynasties. It is said that if every county had a Confucius temple, there would have been some 3,000 Confucius temples all over China in the Qing Dynasty. Yet, if every village built a Guan Yu temple, there would have been over 300,000 Guan Yu temples all over China in the Qing Dynasty. In any case, this truthfully reflected people's respect for and worship of Guan Yu in those days.

Despite the vicissitudes of history and with the passage of time, the above-mentioned events have totally vanished into thin air. Guan Yu, who was worshipped in the past, is no longer a moral idol in modern society. And the Guan Yu Temple, which used to be an important location for moral and cultural education and enjoyed incense burning all the year round, has already turned into a scenic spot for tourism and relaxation. This is social and historical progress, and an inevitable cultural development.

Nevertheless, this old temple, which has a long history and manifests magnificence, still maintains its unique value in contemporary times. It is actually a material crystallization of ancient Chinese moral culture. As precious cultural heritage, it will forever reveal to the people of the generations to come the rich meaning of the ancient Chinese moral culture. It is the witness of the development of traditional Chinese moral culture, especially in the later years of Chinese feudal society. With artifacts, but not words, it truthfully and graphically narrates the development and changes of ancient Chinese moral culture to the people of future generations. It is also a mirror, through which people today and tomorrow will learn and understand the essence of traditional Chinese moral culture; moreover, it will provide a point of reference for the future orientation of moral culture. Meanwhile, as a treasure house and vehicle of the artifacts of traditional Chinese culture and as priceless heritage of the ancient civilization of the Chinese people, it will, at present and in the future, always be a spiritual bond for all Chinese people at home and abroad in terms of the sense of belonging to traditional Chinese culture.

Local chronicles indicate that almost all places, large and small, in China have some records about Guan Yu temples. And in recent times, with Chinese culture expanding to the outside world, Guan Yu temples can be found not only at home but overseas as well. According to incomplete statistics, more than 30 countries and regions in the world have constructed Guan Yu temples. In Japan and Malaysia alone, there are more than 1,000 Guan Yu temples.

In today's world, multiple cultures collide with each other. If there were a culture whose value orientation could be universally accepted and worshipped by the Chinese people at home and abroad, then Guan Yu culture would be it.

Tips 寻访者须知

佳境指数 Scenery Index：★★★★★

备选序列：关圣文化建筑群——中国世界文化遗产预备名单第5号（国家文物局2012年11月版）

List Number: Architectural Complex of the Guan Yu Culture — No.5 in the preparatory list for Chinese World Heritage (November 2012 Edition by the State Cultural Relics Bureau)

寻访提示：运城地处晋、秦、豫三省交界黄河大拐弯处，风陵渡素有“鸡鸣一声听三省”之誉，周边有绝美的人文和自然景观。除解州关帝庙、常平关圣家庙和运城关王庙等关圣遗迹外，还有“中国死海”——盐池、普救寺、永乐宫、蒲津渡、大禹渡、风陵渡、李家大院等景观。西渡黄河过潼关，可至陕西省华阴华山和临潼华清池；南临河南省三门峡市，冬季天鹅湾野生大天鹅成群结队，翩翩起舞；北上至临汾可至吉县壶口瀑布、洪洞大槐树、广胜寺、师家大院和王家大院等。

Location Notes: Yuncheng is located at the big bend of the Yellow River, in the area bordering on Shanxi, Shaanxi and Henan Provinces, where there are quite a number of cultural sites and scenic spots, some of them closely related to Guan Yu.

摄影提示：运城关圣文化建筑群是创作摄影活动的重点。精美绝伦的牌坊、照壁、楼阁、殿宇，雄伟大气；艺术精湛的铸铁像、石雕、塑像，比比皆是；罕见的千年古柏，苍劲有力，造型奇特。这些都是摄影创作的极好元素。在视角上宜采用45度角，更能显示古建筑的立体感。拍摄时注意观察景物的细微之处，更能突现关圣文化的历史厚度。运城日出较晚，日落较早，且中午阳光比较强烈，因此在光线的运用上要格外注意。

Tips for Photography: The Architectural Complex of the Guan Yu Culture at Yuncheng

相机：佳能 Canon Eos-1DX，镜头：24-70mm f/2.8，光圈：f/18，快门：1/250秒，感光度：ISO800，曝光补偿：0EV **蒲津渡开元铁牛**

provides excellent spots for photography. Almost everywhere can be found splendid memorial archways, screen walls, pavilions, palaces, as well as exquisite artworks such as cast iron images, stone sculptures and statues. Cypress trees that are a thousand years old look impressively vigorous and powerful and are quite unique in appearance. All these can serve as excellent objects for photography. When taking photos, the photographer should pay much attention to the subtleties of the sights so as to bring out the historical profoundness of Guan Yu culture.

民俗提示：解州当地与关圣文化有关的民俗活动主要有三项：一是农历四月初八的传统古庙会。源自汉乾祐元年（948年），是当时重要的药材和物资集散地。庙会期间举行的“关帝巡城”活动，最早始于北宋徽宗年间（1101—1119年），庆典多有“恭请神架绕境祈安降福”仪式，吸引着海内外游客纷至沓来。二是农历六月二十四关帝诞辰纪念日。关帝家庙自2000年对外开放以来，每年都要在此举行祭祀活动，让无数海内外关公信徒找到了根。三是中国运城国际关公文化旅游节。从1990年起，每年金秋时节都将在运城举办规模盛大的集旅游、文化、民俗、经贸于一体的大型国际性商旅活动——关公庙会，它已成为山西乃至全国的重要文化活动之一。

Brief Introduction to the Local Culture: The folk activities related to the Guan Yu culture in Haizhou mainly fall into three categories. The first is the traditional temple fair held on the 8th day of the 4th lunar month every year. The second is the celebration of Guan Yu's birthday on the 24th day of the 6th lunar month every year. The third is the China Yuncheng International Tourism Festival of Guan Yu Culture, which started in 1990.

美食提示：解州有四大名吃：羊肉泡馍、黍面油糕、炒面油茶和猪油葱花扯面，而其中又以羊肉

泡馍最为著名。比较有名气的是“王剑”和“一把抓”。王剑羊肉泡馍始于1989年，以甘甜的“州水”和放牧的肥嫩羊肉为主要原料，加之技艺考究，科学配制，具有独到的特色，鲜香真纯，不腥不膻。加以千层饼佐食，味道悠长。一把抓羊肉泡馍选用的羊肉是经过检验的不超过三十斤的绵羊肉。烹饪时经选骨、砸骨、泡骨、洗骨、熬汤、选肉，煮肉等七道工序。

Food Tips: Haizhou is famous for its four snacks: Hard Pies Soaked in Lamb Soup, Millet Cakes, Fried Noodles, and Noodles with Minced Green Onion. Of the four, the most important is Hard Pies Soaked in Lamb Soup.

寻觅备选世遗佳境 1
四川省阿坝州若尔盖湿地
Zoige Wetlands, Aba Prefecture, Sichuan

02 黄河的乳名
The Pet Name of the Yellow River

中国最美湿地景观　亚洲最佳天然牧场

The Prettiest Wetlands in China;
The Best Natural Pasture in Asia

喜马拉雅是你的胎盘
巴颜喀拉是你的摇篮
青藏高原遗传大爱无疆的血型
冰川雪峰承续玉洁无瑕的基因
蹒跚学步时
你叩开川西的大门
像一位发育期的孩儿
单纯，羸弱
忧郁，寡语
独自穿行于天色苍茫的无垠草原
九曲是你的乳名
如雷贯耳的大名
此刻还不为外人所知
或然有一天
你长驱直入
登上造物主铺设的壮阔舞台

With the Himalayas as your placenta and the Bayanhar as your cradle, you derived your blood type from the Qinghai-Tibetan Plateau and inherited your gene, pure and pristine, from the glaciers and Snow Mountains. Only when you were still a toddler, did you knock on the gate of Sichuan. As a child yet to go mature, you looked simple and frail and appeared gloomy and taciturn. Alone by yourself, you took strides across the boundless prairie under the vast vault of heaven.

Even though you were first called Jiuqu, meaning nine zigzags, in your infanthood, your full name, the Yellow River, is thunderously known all over the world. However, few people knew you when you were in infancy. Yet, you would, all of a sudden, dash straight forward and climb onto the broad platform set up by the Creator.

相机：佳能 Canon Eos-1DX，镜头：24-70mm f/2.8，光圈：f/7.1，快门：1/1600秒，感光度：ISO1600，曝光补偿：0EV **唐克九曲黄河落日余晖**

相机：佳能 Canon Eos-1DX，镜头：24-70mm f/2.8，光圈：f/11，快门：1/500秒，感光度：ISO320，曝光补偿：0EV **唐克九曲黄河晨雾**

相机：佳能 Canon Eos-1DX，镜头：24-70mm f/2.8，光圈：f/10，快门：1/500秒，感光度：ISO320，曝光补偿：0EV **唐克索克藏寺**

唐克九曲黄河夕照

涛涛的白河铸就挺直的脊梁
透明的海子融入仁慈的品性
瑰丽的格桑花带来吉祥的笑容
悠扬的牧歌滋润博大的胸襟
你欢快地吸吮
磨砺间长高
嗓音日渐浑厚
体格日趋健壮
宽容成为你的品格
血性是你永恒的标签

The torrential white river forms the straight backbone and the crystal lakes embody the amiable character. The charming cosmos flowers bring about benevolent smiles and the melodious pastoral songs express broad-mindedness. As an infant, you merrily sucked the milk. Just within a few years, you grew up. Gradually, you became tall; moreover, your voice turned resonant and your body became strong and robust. What's most important, you bore the characteristic of tolerance and displayed upright courage as your permanent symbol.

不经意间
你完成了成人仪式
但又迷恋乳汁的甘甜
留恋哺育的家园
几乎再也迈不开前行的步伐
然而
展翅高飞是内心的呼唤
担当未来是天赋的使命

Even without being aware, you've solemnly fulfilled the ceremony of your adulthood. Alas, still indulging yourself in the sweet milk and being nos-

相机：佳能 Canon Eos-1DX，镜头：24-70mm f/2.8，光圈：f/20，快门：1/400秒，感光度：ISO320，曝光补偿：0EV **川西高寒草原牧场**

相机：佳能 Canon Eos-1DX，镜头：24-70mm f/2.8，光圈：f/14，快门：1/500秒，感光度：ISO320，曝光补偿：0EV **阿坝青稞成熟**

相机：佳能 Canon Eos-1DX，镜头：24-70mm f/2.8，光圈：f/16，快门：1/400秒，感光度：ISO320，曝光补偿：0EV **若尔盖湿地牧场**

talgic of your home village, you seemed unable to take further strides forward. However, soaring into the skies is an internal summons, and shouldering the task for a bright future is predestined.

远方的那道地平线啊
就是生与死的界碑
挣扎，纠结
犹豫，彷徨
索性转身向西
却又一步一回眸
在大地上连续泼洒出九条巨大的弧线
映衬朝阳日落的余晖
像舞动天际的彩练
又似宇宙间庄严的幻影
这是告白天下的宣言书
昭示你义无反顾奔腾入海的誓言
恍然间
耳畔传来大海的怒吼
这是人类及所有生命的共同语言

The distant horizon is the boundary tablet between life and death. After struggle and strife, irresolution and hesitation, you changed your mind and turned westward. But you still looked backward with every step westward. Consequently, you've consecutively drawn nine huge arcs over the vast land. In the twilight of sunrise and sunset, they look like dancing ribbons at the far end of the world. Yet, they also resemble a solemn mirage in space. They serve as a declaration and an oath to the world that you are determined to run into the sea. Very soon, you hear the roaring sound of the sea, which is the common language for man and all living beings in the world.

相机：佳能 Canon Eos-1DX，镜头：24-70mm f/2.8，光圈：f/2.8，快门：1/50秒，感光度：ISO6400，曝光补偿：0EV **薄晨转寺**

相机：佳能 Canon Eos-1DX，镜头：24-70mm f/2.8，光圈：f/14，快门：1/200秒，感光度：ISO320，曝光补偿：0EV **阿坝格尔登寺**

相机：佳能 Canon Eos-1DX，镜头：24-70mm f/2.8，光圈：f/14，快门：1/320秒，感光度：ISO320，曝光补偿：0EV **阿坝贾洛寺**

Tips 寻访者须知

佳境指数 Scenery Index： ★★★★

备选序列：四川省若尔盖湿地——中国国家自然遗产预备名录（国家建设部2006年7月版）

List Number: Zoige Wetlands, Sichuan Province — in the preparatory list for Chinese World Heritage (July 2006 Edition by the State Construction Ministry)

寻访提示：若尔盖草原地处川青甘边界，被誉为中国最美湿地、天边的草原，自然和人文景观不胜枚举。唐克黄河九曲第一湾壮美多姿，水天一色；热尔大草原一马平川，绿草如茵，牛羊多如繁星；花湖碧波万顷，鸥翔鹤舞，天光云影；纳摩大峡谷怪石嶙峋，峰峦叠翠，名寺耸立；降扎温泉氤氲缭绕，林海莽莽；红军"右路军"巴西会址光芒四射；"神鹿家园"铁布"小江南"风光迷人；古潘州遗址绵亘至今。同时，周边还有青海省果洛藏族自治州的神山年保玉则和仙女湖、甘肃甘南的朗木寺和拉卜楞寺、甘南草原等景观值得游览。周边平均海拔3,000至4,200米，需做好应对高原反应的准备和措施。

Location Notes: Located in the bordering area of Sichuan, Qinghai and Gansu, Zoige Wetlands are reputed as the most beautiful wetlands in China. There can be found numerous vast prairies as well as natural and cultural landscapes. The first bend of the nine zigzags of the Yellow River at Tangke, where the sky and the earth meet, is bewitching. The Gers Prairie is a verdant carpet, far and wide, where goats, sheep and cattle are as many as stars in the sky. With gulls and cranes flying and fluttering high and low above, the Flower Lake stretches green and vast, reflecting the white clouds floating in the sky. In the Namo Grand Canyon stand surrealistic rockeries and among the mountain peaks, covered with green trees, are quite a few well-known temples. Deep amidst the forests are situated the Jiangzha Hot Springs, which seem to be veiled by a mist. Tiebu, which is often referred to as a little paradise, is home to deer and presents spellbinding scenery. The ancient ruins of Panzhou still survive even to the present. Besides, in its vicinity are some worthwhile sites in Qinghai and Gansu. Because of the average elevation of 3,000–4,200 meters above sea level, visitors are advised to take some precautionary measures against the potential altitude sickness.

摄影提示：若尔盖唐克九曲黄河和花湖为摄影创作的重点内容。唐克九曲黄河最佳拍摄时间，为夏秋两季的日落日出时分。夕阳余晖将大地和九曲黄河染成一片金黄色，景色随着光影的变化绚丽多彩。而旭日朝霞又将河谷披上一道金光，雾气蒸腾，远近景观千变万化，神秘莫测，不可言状。拍摄时须备妥三脚架、快门线等拍摄器材，同时需提前30分钟登临索克藏寺后山坡的制高点，需具备一定的体能。同时，若尔盖藏传佛教和民俗风情也为摄影创作的极好题材。

Tips for Photography: The zigzagging Yellow River and the Flower Lake in Tangke, Zoige, are, of course, a major focus for photography. The best time for taking photos is at sunrise and sunset in summer and autumn. The twilight of the setting sun dyes the earth and the river into a mass of golden yellow. Along with the changes of the light the scenery is beautiful and colorful. And the twilight of early dawn drapes the valley with a golden cape, and the vapor of fog rises. The mysterious alteration of the views, nearby and far away, is beyond description. When taking photos, photographers should have the tripod, cable release and other necessary equipment ready. What's more, one should reach the commanding height on the slope of the mountain 30 minutes ahead of time. Of course, Tibetan Buddhism and folk customs in Zoige are also excellent subjects for photography.

民俗提示：若尔盖县是一个藏民族聚居县，绝大多数民众信仰藏传佛教。宗教文化内涵丰富，全县有纳摩格尔底寺、达扎寺等二十四座寺庙。古刹纳摩格尔底寺是藏传佛教格鲁派寺院之一，寺院建筑气势恢弘，金碧辉煌，在川、甘、青三省颇具影响力。寺内供奉着活佛肉身法体，历三百多年仍栩栩如生。达扎寺创建距今已有三百多年，寺内供奉着数千尊菩萨，珍藏有大量价值连城的经书。盛大的“莫郎法会”“传昭法会”“晒佛”“燃灯”“摸顶”“跳神”等宗教活动让人感受到宗教文化的神秘和博大；神奇的酥油花和“檀城”，长长的手推转经廊、时刻不离的手摇转经筒、永不停息的水冲转经房，高高的白塔、虔诚的信徒、佛号灵郎的寺院，无不彰显着藏传佛教文化的神奇。

Brief Introduction to the Local Culture: Zoige County is a place where Tibetans live. Most of the inhabitants believe in Tibetan Buddhism. Rich in religious culture, the whole county boasts 24 Buddhist temples, where a variety of Buddhist ceremonies and activities are held every year.

美食提示：若尔盖以牦牛肉最负盛名。通常用盐卤制成，吃时切成薄片，拌上辣椒，与青稞酒一起享用最为豪爽。糌粑形似内地的炒面，可分为青稞、豌豆、燕麦糌粑等。藏民无论下地劳作、上山放牧、出门旅行，都要随身携带糌粑。吃时，往碗里倒些糌粑，另放少量的酥油，冲茶水食用。酸菜汤味道极好，可调节口味，增加食欲，还可防治感冒。荞麦面制成的荞麦馒头、荞麦面条均为粗粮，咀嚼筋道，入口清香。酸奶是纯正的牦牛酸奶，味道特别纯正。不过原味酸奶非常酸，一般人受不了，可适当放一些食糖。

Food Tips: Zoige is famous for its Yak meat,

寻访路径
Geographical location

which is usually salted. Before eating, Tibetans cut the Yak meat into thin slices and stir it with pepper. It is a great enjoyment for them to savor the meat together with their highland barley wine. The staple food for the Tibetans, zanba, is made from different grains. Their yoghurt is so sour that many people are not used to it; however, sugar could be put into it if you would like.

寻觅备选世遗佳境 1
陕西省渭南市韩城市党家村古建筑群
Dangjia Village, Hancheng, Weinan City, Shaanxi

03 人至无欲品自高
Consummation of Human Life

山陕民居的经典范例　东方聚落的艺术瑰宝

Typical Civil Residence in Shaanxi and Ancient Village as Artistic Treasure

曾到过欧、亚、美、非四大洲数十个国家的英国皇家建筑学会教授查理、日本建筑学会青木正夫博士在此感叹道：“从没有见过布局如此紧凑，做工如此精湛，风貌如此古朴典雅，历史文化气息如此悠久浓厚，保存如此完好的古代传统居民村寨。不愧为东方人类古代传统居住村寨的活化石。”他们赞美的这个村落，就是陕西省韩城市党家村。

Professor Charlie, a member of the Royal Institute of British Architects, and Aoki Masao, a member of Architectural Institute of Japan, who have been to scores of countries in Europe, Asia, the Americas and Africa, marveled at the views in front of them. They could not but say, "Never have we seen such a well-kept ancient village! It is compactly laid out. It shows exquisitely superb craftsmanship and simple but elegant style. It demonstrates a long and profound historical and cultural flavor. It is perfect for civil residence. It deserves the reputation of Living Fossil of the Traditional Ancient Village of the Orient." The village that they were eulogizing is Dangjia Village, Hancheng, Shaanxi Province.

一

九曲黄河，奔腾不息，行至晋陕交界的禹门口（龙门），“鲤鱼跃龙门”“大禹治水凿龙门”的千古传说，至今仍在关中地区流传。这里是中华民族发祥地之一，西周、秦、汉、隋、唐等十余个朝代都曾在此建都；这里地处秦东黄河之滨，古有“关中四塞之国”“秦塞雄都”等美誉；这里也是太史公司马迁的故里，千载文脉传续，滋养着耕读于渭北高原上的芸芸众生。

腊月的一天日暮时分，我独自行走在韩城泌水河谷，但见黄土高原沟壑连绵不绝，气势磅礴。走近高数十米的土塬边缘向谷底眺望，一处呈葫芦形状，人称“党圪崂”的村落映入眼帘，只见

相机：佳能 Canon Eos-1DX，镜头：24-70mm f/2.8，光圈：f/11，快门：1/1250秒，感光度：ISO640，曝光补偿：0EV **党家村街巷**

房舍鳞次栉比，街巷阡陌井然，炊烟袅袅，紫烟升腾，整个村落都沐浴在夕阳的余晖之中，令人茫然不知所处。

天幕渐渐转暗，我刚好顺着下坡道走入村口，昏暗的街灯，将我的身形拉成长长的影子，投射在泛着幽光的石板路上，踢踏的脚步声，回荡在幽静的街巷上空。此时饥肠辘辘，寒意袭人，急需找家食宿之处落脚。我随意叩响街边一户农家大门上的铁环，大门应声而开。

主人一家三口热情地将我这位不速之客请进上房休息，男主人麻利地打扫火坑，并用煤将一旁的火炉引燃，屋内顿生暖意。不一会儿，西厢的厨房也飘来女主人现做的葱油烙饼和鸡蛋炒大蒜的香味。我与主人一家围坐在火炉边，边吃边聊，话题总绕不开党家村的奇闻轶事。

“元末志顺二年（1331年），先人移居至此，农耕为本，商业为副，到我这辈儿，已是党氏二门第二十四代传人了。”今年54岁的党敬儒，如数家珍地讲述起党家村的渊源。党姓始祖党恕轩，由陕西朝邑县逃荒至此，见村北土崖巍峨，村南泌水潺潺，于是便在此落脚开荒种田，繁衍生息。党恕轩所生四个儿子，除种田之外，开始兼营商业。历经三十余年的艰苦创业，至长孙党真于明永乐十年（1414年）中举，“党家湾”始定名“党家村”。

一百多年后，贾姓始祖贾伯通，从山西洪洞县迁居韩城经商，第五代和党姓联姻，其子在明嘉靖四年（1525年）定居党家村，成为党家村的第二大姓。至今党家村依然由党贾两大姓氏组成，外姓极少。党姓家族原以务农为本，而贾姓却有经商的传统。乾隆年间（1711—1799年），贾姓创立了“合兴发”商号，经营日用杂货、木材、瓷器、茶叶、药材等，在河南与湖北交界地带发迹，成为巨贾。在贾姓影响下，党姓也加入了经商的行列。道光至咸丰年间（1821—1861年），为党家村经商活动的黄金期。据说当年各地运往老家银两的骡马络绎不绝，号称“日进白银千两”。与此同时，

相机：佳能 Canon Eos-1DX，镜头：24-70mm f/2.8，光圈：f/10，快门：1/800秒，感光度：ISO640，曝光补偿：0EV **党氏祖祠**

党家村开始大兴土木，进入了持续百年的建房高潮期。全盛时，党家村建四合院数百座，还有泌阳堡和几十座哨门、祠堂与庙宇。清末民初，因战乱不断，应对有方的村人就不再经商，收缩营生，回归故里，泰然守护着祖辈的财富且耕且读。时至今日，在这1.2平方公里的土地上，仍完好保存着一百三十多套明清四合院和祖祠、文星阁等建筑，因古村寨集中完整，且活态传承至今，而被中外学者誉为世界的“民居瑰宝”。

躺卧在温暖舒适的火坑之上，脑际回味着党家村的传奇故事，不一会儿，我便进入甜美的梦乡。

I

The zigzagging Yellow River has been torrentially running eastward, until it reaches Longmen at the bordering area of Shanxi and Shaanxi Provinces, which is actually one of the birthplaces of the Chinese nation. It was the capital of China during 13 dynasties, including the West Zhou, Qin, Han, Sui, Tang, etc. it was the region that bred and nurtured numerous people that lived an agricultural life on the Weibei Plateau.

At dusk on one December day, I was walking alone along the valley of the river near Hancheng. I saw the ever-stretching and imposing loess plateau. When I came to the edge of the cliff dozens of meters deep, I looked into the distance and noticed an arc-shaped place, where was located a village, none other than Dangjia Village. Rows upon rows of houses were well-arranged, and the streets and lanes were laid out orderly. Smoke swirled from the kitchen chimneys up into the skies. The whole village was submerged in the twilight of the setting sun. I could not help feeling at a loss as to where I was.

As the night approached, I found myself coming down the slope and stepping into the main entrance of the village. The dim street lamps cast a long silhouette of my figure onto the stone-paved road. My footsteps made echoes floating in the quiet of the empty streets. Suddenly, feeling cold and hungry, I was in a hurry to look for board and lodging for the night. Therefore, I randomly knocked on the door of a house. Almost instantly, the door opened.

The three members of this family warmly welcomed me, a self-invited guest, into their house. With utmost hospitality, they offered me food and warmth. They and I sat around the stove, enjoying delicious pancakes and fried eggs. While eating, we had a hearty chitchat. The main topic of our conversation naturally focused on the anecdotes of the village.

Dang Jingru, aged 54, began to narrate the origin and history of the village. According to him, his ancestors came to this place as early as the second year of Emperor Zhishun at the end of the Yuan Dynasty. He belongs to the 24th generation of the Dang family. Dang Shuxuan, the first-generation forefather of the Dangs, came as a refuge from Shaanxi Province. When he saw the towering mountains and flowing river, he immediately decided to settle down. He had four sons. Besides farming, he was involved in commerce. After over thirty years of hard work, this place was named Dangjia Village in the 10th year (1414) of Emperor Yongle of the Ming Dyansty, when Dang Zhen, the eldest grandson of Dang Shuxuan, gained much status after passing the provincial civil service examination.

More than one hundred years later, Jia Botong, the first generation forefather of the Jia's family, moved from Hongtong County to Hancheng to do

相机：佳能 Canon Eos-1DX，镜头：24-70mm f/2.8，光圈：f/11，
快门：1/250秒，感光度：ISO640，曝光补偿：0EV **党家村贞节坊**

相机：佳能 Canon Eos-1DX，镜头：24-70mm f/2.8，光圈：f/11，
快门：1/1000秒，感光度：ISO640，曝光补偿：0EV **党家村文星塔**

相机：佳能 Canon Eos-1DX，镜头：24-70mm f/2.8，光圈：f/11，快门：1/640秒，感光度：ISO640，曝光补偿：0EV **党家村看家楼**

华山冬景

business. A member of the fifth generation of the Jias married into the Dang family. His son settled down in Dangjia Village in the 4th year of Emperor Jiajing of the Ming Dynasty, and gradually the Jias became the second largest family in the village. Even today, the village consists of the Dangs and the Jias. Almost no other name can be found. The Dangs family mainly lived by farming while the Jias had long been involved in doing business. In the Qing Dynasty, the Jias did business in various fields: household supplies, timber, porcelain, tea, medicinal herbs, and so on. They made a big fortune. Under the influence of the Jias, the Dangs also started to do business. Meanwhile, however, the Dangs began their construction of houses. At the peak time, several hundred courtyards were erected in the Dangjia Village, in addition to some castles, arches, and temples. At the end of the Qing Dynasty and the beginning of the Republic of China, the smart villagers gave up their business, probably because of constant wars. They returned to their home village, thus living a life of reading and farming while having the wealth accumulated by their forefathers well protected. Even up to now, more than 130 buildings are still kept intact. Therefore, this village is referred to by domestic and foreign scholars as "A jewel of a civil residence".

Lying on the Kang, warm and comfortable, I relived the legendary stories of the Dangjia Village. Before long, however, I fell asleep, beginning to be intoxicated by sweet dreams.

二

翌日一早，风和日丽，碧空如洗，窗外喜鹊唱枝头。盥洗简餐之后，老党今年25岁的儿子党少笃

相机：佳能 Canon Eos-1DX，镜头：24-70mm f/2.8，光圈：f/10，快门：1/1000秒，感光度：ISO640，曝光补偿：0EV **党家村四合院**

已在门外等候多时，为我当起了义务导游。

先祖的智慧，至今仍然庇荫着党家村的后人。“村址规划在东西走向的泌水河畔，依水傍塬，冬暖夏凉，杜绝灾患，这在咱关中地区的讲究中，这就是风水宝地。”站在土塬高处，我顺着少笃手指的方向远望，只见全村院落街巷布局紧凑、排列整齐、气势壮观，所有地面建筑设计精妙、用料考究、做工精良细腻。

少笃又进一步向我介绍党家村在中国民居中与众不同的三大特点：一是具有中国古代农村聚落生活、生产、防御三重架构的特点，防御的功能尤为明显；二是“村寨分离型”的聚落，这是迄今为止在中国民居村落类型中的孤例；三是以党家村为代表的韩城四合院中，上房（厅房）不是日常生活性空间，而是庄重、明快的礼仪空间和祭祀空间，北方民居中广泛采用的“一明两暗”式空间分隔，在此绝少采用。

我在村中走街串巷，进院入宅，从村东到村西来回寻访数遍，细细品味党家村建筑文化的无穷魅力。与其他地区的古代村落不同，党家村的四合院不是官邸，也不是商宅，而是以村寨合一的形式，整体设计而成的经典民居村落。村子中央，耸立着一座傲视群芳的砖砌方形四层雕花阁楼，站在楼顶能够瞭望全村四周的状况，这是当年护村人员站岗放哨的看家楼。村子东北部高处的泌阳堡，修建于清朝咸丰初年，是一座一夫当关、万夫莫开的坚固堡垒，两者合一组成了独特的村中、寨上两处宅院。

党家村四合院的外形是清一色的青瓦顶，“五脊六兽”。起墙是一砖到顶，各院虽有高低大小之分，却少有形态装饰之异。每家每户的宅院皆分为两层，上面的仓库高为七尺，用来储放粮食农具，下面的住房高度八尺，所谓“七上八下”。这种形制是其他地方，尤其是北京的民居不敢采用的。因有“僭越”之嫌，即超越封建社会对不同等级身份者建房的礼制规定。党家村的四合院，无论富裕、清贫、做官、为民，其形制规格颇为

相机：佳能 Canon Eos-1DX，镜头：24-70mm f/2.8，光圈：f/10，快门：1/1250秒，感光度：ISO640，曝光补偿：0EV **党家村四合院**

一致，绝无“僭越”之说。门额门楣的题字是每户建院时不可或缺之事，这是体现宅主身份和地位的象征，也是韩城民居的一种传统风俗。数百年来，代代延续。甫进院门，门额题字有：“耕读第”“诗书第”“登科”“文魁”“忠厚”“庆有余”等内容，多方位、多角度地诠释了中国古代儒家文化的内涵。若写着“进士”“世进士”“太史第”等内容的，这是宅主人在炫耀自己的政治地位或官爵。“忠恕”、“富德居”、“和为贵”，则是宅主人对门第不凡、富有道德修养的显示，且有警醒家人、训诫后人之意。还有祝颂幸福、平安吉祥，抑或揭示自己文化修养和情趣追求等内容的，如“居之安”“诗礼传家”等等。难能可贵的是，这些题字大多由当时当地有书法功力者书就，章法讲究，制作精细。

院门也别有情趣。大多开在门房偏右或偏左的一隅，或背墙上，少有开在中间的。开在背墙上的门，窄小朴素，略作装饰。有钱人家则大多占用门房一间的面积专建个“走马门”，高大、气派。有户人家，大概是虽有资财却未能做官，主人便将门上阁楼建成官轿模样，进出门必从轿下经过，以示坐了官轿，每日里都可过过当官的瘾。凡“走马门”，门旁总有上马石、拴马桩或铁环等设置。门前若设有旗杆斗子，那必定是官宦人家。门前有双斗旗杆者为进士，单杆者便是举人。

党家村全村一百多处院落，最大的共同点，莫过于随处可见的“三雕”（砖、木、石）了。砖雕大多见于脊砖、檐下带座的楣头、巷道门道及宅院里外的照壁等处。有两处巷道砖墙上雕刻着一米见方的“福”“寿”两字，尤为精美、古朴。木雕多用于门窗、门帘架、门楼、家具等处。凡牌坊、柱石、柱础、上马石、旗杆座、拴马桩等石质物料，大多被精雕细琢过。目不暇接的精美砖、木、石雕刻品，把一座座民居打扮成艺术殿堂。其中最具代表性的一座砖雕照壁：左下刻有梅花鹿，寓意求取俸禄钱财；鹿嘴衔着一支灵芝，象征长生不老；鹿

相机：佳能 Canon Eos-1DX，镜头：24-70mm f/2.8，光圈：f/10，快门：1/1250秒，感光度：ISO640，曝光补偿：0EV **泌阳堡党家寨**

的身后刻有山峦，意为寿比南山；山上松树趴着猴子、树枝挂着蜂窝，取“封侯”的谐音；另有一对喜鹊，代表双喜临门。“福禄寿喜”的美好愿望就在一幅砖雕作品中展现得淋漓尽致。

为什么党家村这处古代村落中耕读为本、积仁行善的纯净基因，历经数百载风风雨雨而不衰？面对我的疑惑，党少笃带我来到村中一处处宅院的照壁旁、山墙侧，一行行警世的文字，使我顿有省悟，这就是党家村民居最大的亮点“门庭家训”，其训词之多、内容之丰、保存之全，令人叹为观止：“动莫若敬，居莫若俭，德莫若让，事莫若咨”“言有教，动有法，昼有为，宵有得，息有养，瞬有存”“富时不俭贫时悔，见时不学用时悔”“薄味养气，去怒养性，处抑养德，守清养道”“傲不可长，欲不可纵，志不可满，乐不可极”“无益之事勿为，无益之人勿见，无益之书勿读，无益之话勿说”。这些饱经风霜洗礼的门庭家训，或道德教化，或劝学进取，或修身齐家，或治世济民，种种箴言训诫为后代提供着远超物质财富之外的精神养分。

中华民族数千年物质和文明的发展沉淀，形成了中国本土丰富多彩的村落群体，党家村就是其中的佼佼者。它们是中国传统文化的宝藏之一，蕴涵着宗法时代乡土文化和乡土生活的全部印迹，凝聚着中华民族的智慧和心血。

我在村东南六层砖塔的文星阁下，与党家父子依依惜别。见证了党家村六百余年风风雨雨的文星塔犹如玉树临风，塔上六角飞檐悠扬的风铃声，伴随着黄土高原的疾风，传得很远很远。

II

The next morning it was warm and bright, and the sky was blue. Outside the window, the magpies were twittering on the twigs of trees. After breakfast, I went outdoors. The 25-year-old Dang Shaodu, son of Dang Jingru, was already waiting for me to offer to be my tour guide.

相机：佳能 Canon Eos-1DX，镜头：24-70mm f/2.8，光圈：f/10，快门：1/1250秒，感光度：ISO640，曝光补偿：0EV **党家村过家楼**

相机：佳能 Canon Eos-1DX，镜头：24-70mm f/2.8，光圈：f/13，快门：1/1600秒，感光度：ISO640，曝光补偿：0EV **黄河龙门峡谷**

The wisdom of their ancestors was still shedding light on the descendants of the Dang family. Standing on the height of the plateau, I looked into the distance under Shaodu's direction and saw the well laid out and arranged streets and houses of the village. All the architecture was well designed, worked out with elaborately chosen materials, and built with high-quality craftsmanship.

Mr. Dang Shaodu further introduced the special characteristics of the civil residences in his village, which are uniquely different from those in other parts of China. Afterwards, I strolled in the streets and stepped into several houses, savoring the architectural charms.

All built with bricks and covered with black tiles, the courtyard houses here looked more or less the same in outer appearance, even though they might be different in height and size. To a certain extent, the similarity indicates a kind of social equality. Besides, all the houses bear inscriptions above or on the front gate. The inscriptions express the ideas of good wishes, sagacious exhortations, or eulogies of happiness and gratefulness. Most of them were written by those locals very good at penmanship.

Interestingly, the gates of the courtyard houses are more often than not on either the right or the left side of the front wall, or on the back wall; in any case, it is next to impossible to find a gate in the middle of the front wall. A common feature in all the over 100 courtyard houses is that carvings on bricks, wooden plates, and stones are almost everywhere.

As I was wondering how the Dangjia Village managed to survive the vicissitudes of time, I was taken to see the screen walls, on which were writ-

相机：佳能 Canon Eos-1DX，镜头：24-70mm f/2.8，光圈：f/13，快门：1/2000秒，感光度：ISO640，曝光补偿：0EV **韩城孔庙尊经阁**

ten sagacious epigrams that served as a way of moral education from generation to generation.

Of all the villages rich in local culture in China, the Dangjia Village ranks at the top. It is a treasure house of traditional Chinese culture. So far all the traces of local culture and local life have remained intact, fully displaying the wisdom and glory of the Chinese people.

At the foot of the six-story pagoda in the southeast corner, I reluctantly said goodbye to Mr. Dang and his son. The imposing pagoda is over 600 years old, and the ringing of the pagoda bells spreads far and wide on the loess plateau.

Tips 寻访者须知

佳境指数 Scenery Index：★★★★★

备选序列：山陕古民居（党家村古建筑群）——中国世界文化遗产预备名单第6号（国家文物局2012年11月版）

List Number: Ancient Civil Residences in Shanxi and Shaanxi Provinces (the Ancient Group Buildings of the Dangjia Village) — No. 6 in the preparatory list for Chinese World Heritage (November 2012 Edition by the State Cultural Relics Bureau)

寻访提示：韩城素有“东方建筑文化在中国，中国民居建筑文化看韩城”之誉，自然和人文景观高端大气上档次。除了党家村外，韩城古城，尤其是建于元代的文庙、关帝庙和城隍庙文物古迹精彩纷呈，规模宏大；芝川的司马迁祠墓筑于四大高台的陡坡之上，令人肃然起敬，魏长城、夏侯瀵、处女泉、龙门峡，也是黄河之滨著名的奇观。

Location Notes: Hancheng has long enjoyed the reputation of “It is in China that oriental architecture is located, and it is in Hancheng that the architecture of civil residences will be seen.” Both natural scenic spots and cultural sites are of high quality. In addition to the Dangjia Village, many places are worth visiting.

摄影提示：党家村摄影创作的题材丰富多彩，古老悠长的石砌巷道、千姿百态的高大门楼、雕刻考究的上马石、庄严的祠堂、挺拔的文星阁、华美的节孝碑、布局合理的四合院、坚固的城墙、耸立的看家楼、森严的泌阳堡，以及关中百姓的日常农作和生活场景，令人百看不厌、回味无穷。泌阳堡城墙边及塬上高处，是拍摄党家村全景和日出日落美景的最佳位置。

Tips for Photography: The Dangjia Village offers a rich variety of photographic themes: long

相机：佳能 Canon Eos-1DX，镜头：24-70mm f/2.8，光圈：f/11，快门：1/100秒，感光度：ISO640，曝光补偿：0EV **党家村民居**

ancient stone-paved streets, diversified tall gateway arches, stones with exquisite carvings, grand temples, towering scholar pavilions, gorgeous filial monuments, well-designed courtyard houses, thick and solid city walls, imposing towers and castles, and the scenes of local people's daily life and farming.

民俗提示：司马迁庙会始创于北宋，初为民间祭祀，明万历六年（1578年），韩城县令刘从吉，极力上报称“史臣烈士，万世之风教攸关，享祀以酬公德，礼制所不废也……”。获准后，司马迁庙会的祭仪便升格到差不多如正祀（祭孔）的程度。至清康熙初，韩城县令翟世琪将庙会时间定于司马迁的诞辰二月初八日，从此相沿为俗。司马迁庙会是韩城当地最大的民俗活动。是日，四方人士会集芝川，上庙朝礼者络绎不绝，而商贸活动更是盛大，从祠外到芝川镇都是熙熙攘攘的人群。

Brief Introduction to the Local Culture: Hancheng is famous for its temple fair, which can be traced back to the North Song Dynasty. It is held on the 8th day of the 2nd lunar month every year, when multitudes of people gather here, worshipping the gods and doing business.

美食提示：羊肉糊卜是韩城的特色饮食之一。用上等的农家自磨面手擀成圆形的面片，放到油光的铁烙饼锅上烙到六七分熟的时候取下，切成面条，放入油锅，加上熟羊肉片等即可。羊肉饸饹的主料为荞麦，经压制成饸饹，用鲜羊肉、熟羊油、香醋、葱花、油泼辣子、咸面酱、精盐、五香粉、咸韭菜段等制臊子汤，浇与其上。饸饹细长绵软，臊子酥烂浓醇，入口麻辣宜人，回味芬芳隽永，香中透鲜味美，油香爽口不腻。过桥馄饨用白萝卜做馅，馄饨汤讲究五味、五色、五形俱全。五味是调料齐备，五色是所用蔬菜有五种颜色，如木耳的黑色、胡萝卜的红色、豆腐的白色、黄花菜或鸡蛋皮的黄色、新鲜蔬菜的绿色等，而五形则是讲究刀工，要切出条块丝末片等形状来。韩城十三花，就是十三道菜，是将猪身不同部位的肉，经煮、炸、蒸、烧等工艺分别做成不同的菜肴。

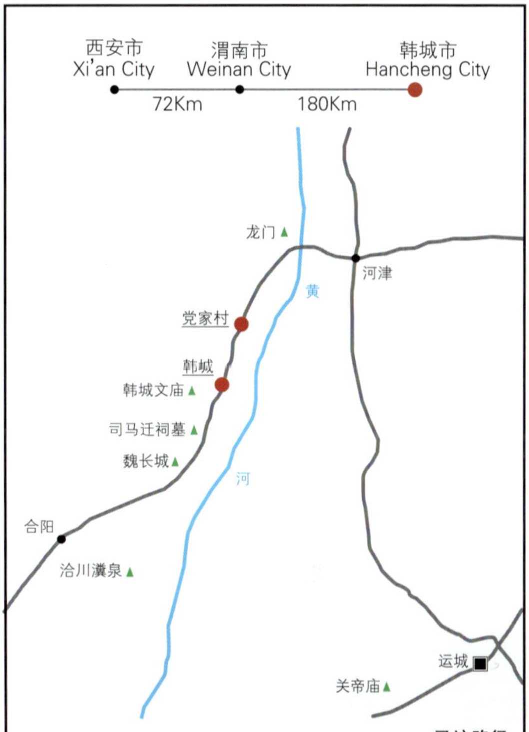

寻访路径
Geographical location

Food Tips: The popular local food is mutton pastry, which is widely enjoyed for its delicious taste and fragrant smell.

寻觅备选世遗佳境 1
新疆阿尔泰市布尔津县喀纳斯禾木村
Kanas Hemu Village, Burqin County, Altai, Xinjiang

04 秋醉山乡 Mountain Village in Autumn

中国最自然、最美丽山乡之典范
游牧民族图瓦人最大之聚居地

Most Natural and Most Beautiful Mountain Village in China
Largest Habitation of Nomadic Tuwa People

中国人都应该记住“禾木”这个名字，它是中国最自然、最美丽山村的代名词。

九月寒风起，当北方西伯利亚第一波寒流侵袭南下时，横亘在新疆北部雄伟壮观的阿尔泰山，落下了今年的第一场冬雪，连绵的群山银装素裹，一派北国风光。在阿尔泰山中部喀纳斯湖畔，我国最大的图瓦人集居村落、素有“天下第一村”之誉的禾木村，转眼间漫山遍野换上了金色的盛装，呈现一派令人陶醉的秋色。

Chinese people should all remember the name Hemu, which is a word standing for the most natural and most beautiful village in China.

Along with the cold wind of September, when the first cold current from Siberia invades southward, the first snow begins to fall along the grand and towering Altai Mountain, that stands in the north of Xinjiang. Ranges after ranges of mountains are covered with snow. By the side of Kanas Lake in the middle of the Altai Mountain is Tuwa Village, supposed to be the largest in China. It has the epithet "No. 1 village on earth", and is also known as Hemu Village. Within a second, the whole mountain is clothed with golden attire, presenting an intoxicating hue of autumn.

晨之幻

Miracle of Morning

禾木晨之醉，醉出一种难觅的温柔和神秘。

凌晨时分，禾木村万籁俱寂，好梦正酣。清澈蜿蜒的禾木河，在皎洁的月色下泛着幽光，从村中川流而过，尔后在村西的白桦林中，依依不舍地划出一道美丽的弧形，继续向西奔流，最后汇入滔滔的布尔津河。

闲云潭影日悠悠，物转星移几度秋。奔腾不息

相机：佳能 Canon Eos-1DX，镜头：24-70mm f/2.8，光圈：f/9.9，快门：1/160秒，感光度：ISO100，曝光补偿：0EV **喀纳斯禾木村村桥**

相机：佳能 Canon Eos-1DX，镜头：24-70mm f/2.8，光圈：f/10，快门：1/25秒，感光度：ISO100，曝光补偿：0EV **喀纳斯禾木村晨曦**

相机：佳能 Canon Eos-1DX，镜头：24-70mm f/2.8，光圈：f/10，快门：1/50秒，感光度：ISO100，曝光补偿：0EV **喀纳斯禾木村炊烟**

的雪山融水，以其巨大的能量，将宽厚博大的山体，切割冲积为宽阔无比的河谷盆地，形成水草丰美的大草原，禾木村就静静地躺卧在这群山环抱的肥沃草原之中。

深秋时节，尽管禾木周围群山耸立，白雪皑皑，寒风萧瑟，可镶嵌于盆地凹陷处的禾木村，依然风淡云清，波澜不惊，从容淡定。透过层层浓密的白桦林树梢，依稀可见村中密集的图瓦人木屋那三角形的尖顶。

拂晓时分，东方微白，禾木慢慢从沉寂中苏醒。三五座木屋的窗口，率先透出些许微弱的灯光，渐渐地在村中蔓延开来，星星点点，闪闪烁烁，恰似宇宙间深邃无际的星空。不一会儿，起早的牧民开始生火做饭，一缕缕淡淡的炊烟，从木屋顶部的烟囱中袅袅上升。

此刻，雾霭渐渐地稠密起来，弥漫缥缈，捉摸不定。村中木屋、围栏、毡房、草垛、树木、河流、道路……都在浮动的雾色中若隐若现。缘于禾木村独特的地理环境，白色的雾气始终在村庄、树林上方飘荡，逐渐形成一条绵长柔软、富有质感的白色帛带，在山腰之间缠绵悱恻，不离不弃。此境此景，宛如仙境。

彤红的太阳，终于从东方高耸的山顶上慢慢探出笑脸，整个禾木村顿时注入了活力，开始灵动起来。

第一缕阳光，首先照射在村庄周围耸峙的群山之巅，将青黛色的山体，染成耀眼的金色。尔后，阳光慢慢地铺撒开来，把村子四周浓密的白桦林晕染成夺目的金黄色，好似“满村尽带黄金甲”。接着，阳光又透过村庄上空浮动的白色雾带，慵懒地倾泻下来，似乎非常不情愿地打扰这座刚从睡梦中睁开惺忪双眼的静谧村庄。在柔和的晨曦照耀下，木屋、毡房、围栏、草垛、树木，在草地上拉出颀长无比的光影，恰如谱写在大地上跳动的音符。

此时，整个禾木村进入了晨曲的高潮。狗儿在空旷的草地上撒欢，偶尔惊起的乌鸦群，在木屋上

相机：佳能 Canon Eos-1DX，镜头：24-70mm f/2.8，光圈：f/10，快门：1/100秒，感光度：ISO100，曝光补偿：0EV **喀纳斯禾木村马队**

方迅疾掠过，即刻消失在远处的密林中。家家户户的牛、羊、马开始走出牲口棚，或在围栏中悠闲的踱步，或低头啃食还沾满晨露的新鲜嫩草。从木屋窗户中不时飘散出包尔萨克、酥油奶茶的扑鼻香气，沁人心脾。阡陌之上，随处可见成群结队的牧民骑着马，驱赶着牛羊群，争先恐后地漫过村西的禾木桥，最终隐没在远处满目橙黄的草场之中。

The morning in Hemu produces a kind of intoxication that leads to unfathomable softness and mystery.

In the small hours, the whole village of Hemu is nothing but quiet and all people are sound asleep. The transparent and meandering Hemu River flows through the village under the bright twilight of the moon. When it reaches the white birch forest, it keeps on flowing westward, leaving behind a beautiful arc, and finally merges into the Burqin River.

The torrential water from the melting snow cuts the broad mountain with its colossal momentum into several vast basin valleys, thus forming large prairies rich in water and grass. Hemu Village reclines quietly among the fertile grasslands surrounded by mountains.

At dawn, the east turns white and Hemu Village begins to awake gradually. In the windows of a few wooden houses first appear dim lamp lights. Window after window shows light. Dots of light twinkle like the stars in the depth of outer space. Soon the herdsmen that get up early begin to prepare breakfast. Streaks of gray smoke slowly swirl upward from kitchen chimneys at the top of the wooden houses.

The first beam of sunlight touches the top of the towering mountains that surround the village, making the dark green mountain turn into a daz-

相机：佳能 Canon Eos-1DX，镜头：24-70mm f/2.8，光圈：f/11，快门：1/125秒，感光度：ISO100，曝光补偿：0EV，**喀纳斯禾木村秋色**

相机：佳能 Canon Eos-1DX，镜头：24-70mm f/2.8，光圈：f/10，快门：1/125秒，感光度：ISO100，曝光补偿：0EV **图瓦木屋**

zling gold. Next, the sunlight slowly spreads out, rendering the dense white birch trees around the village into an eye-catching gold as well. And then, penetrating through the white mist floating above the village, the sun lazily sheds light on the village, as if it were unwilling to disturb the tranquility of the village that has just awaken from sleep. In the soft morning sun, wooden houses, yurts, fences, haystacks, and trees are attached by long, long shadows to the grassland. The shadows look like gamboling musical notes on the earth.

At this moment the whole Hemu Village reaches the peak of its morning melody. Dogs run wildly on the broad grassland, and groups of crows are occasionally stirred up, soaring high above the wooden houses and vanishing in no time into the distant forest. The cattle, sheep, goats, and horses start walking out of the stables, ambling in the rails, or grazing the tender grass still covered with morning dew. From the windows float out the aroma of bread and milk tea. On the crisscrossing footpaths between village fields can be seen teams of herdsmen on horseback driving the cattle and sheep vying to cross the Hemu Bridge in the west of the village. Finally they all disappear in the brownish yellow prairie in the distance.

村之魅

Village Charm

禾木日之醉，醉出一种久违的奔放和豪迈。

天高云淡，红日当空；蓝天如洗，白云飘浮；雪峰傲立，万山红遍。

从贾登峪至禾木四十余公里曲折迂回的山间小道，就是一条风光绮丽的景观道。连绵不绝的阿

相机：佳能 Canon Eos-1DX，镜头：24-70mm f/2.8，光圈：f/13，快门：1/20秒，感光度：ISO100，曝光补偿：0EV **喀纳斯禾木村余晖**

尔泰山脉，环绕着美丽富饶的冲乎尔山谷平原。这里水源充裕，牧草丰美，如茵的大地上散布着一座又一座优美的牧场。满山满坡的桦树林，一棵棵，一簇簇，一片片，如焰似火，肆意豪放，将大地装扮成金色的海洋，追风逐浪，汹涌澎湃。无论从哪一个角度放眼远眺，映入眼帘的都是灿烂夺目的金黄色。

温暖的阳光柔和地撒落在山谷中，草原上金色的牧草随风波浪起伏，忙于打草堆垛的牧民随处可见。得益于禾木河的长年滋润，这里的草场得天独厚，这是禾木人能够在严酷冬季也能生活在大山深处的主要原因之一。从每年七月中旬进入初秋开始，村民就不断地进行打草作业，山下的牧民打草一般只花费十天时间，而禾木的牧民要连续劳作两个月，直到雪落草枯才作罢。村子的房前屋后，高耸的草垛在阳光的映照下金光灿烂。

在广袤的草原中，牛羊群旁若无人的四处觅食，在齐腰深的草丛中时隐时现，它们要赶在寒冬来临之前，尽可能储藏积累更多的脂肪，以度过严酷漫长的冬季。在奇妙的光影中，牛羊身上细细的绒毛，勾勒出一道的金色轮廓线。草原上，纵马驰骋的牧民，驱赶着牧群抓紧转场，赶在大雪封山之前，让牛羊多长膘。草原深处，偶尔可见二三顶白色的毡房飘着炊烟，那是牧民正在赶制过冬时节食用的奶制品。

秋日的阳光温暖和煦，禾木村中泛着微光的小木屋鳞次栉比，这是禾木最为靓丽的符号，也是带有游牧民族传统特征图瓦人独有的标志。木屋的构造和功能，显示了图瓦人的勤劳与智慧。牧民先将粗壮挺直的红松木两端开槽，然后相互嵌扣，再一根根向上叠加，直至垒建成木屋。屋顶采用人字形坡顶，房门大多朝东，以用来晒入更多的阳光，抵挡寒冬猛烈的风雪。木头之间的缝隙和连接处，都由一种叫“努克”的干草填充，这种草吸水后会

喀纳斯湖

迅速膨胀，最终将缝隙填满，墙壁就会变得密不透风。有些木屋的大半截埋于土中，这样做的目的，也是为了抵御这里将近半年大雪封山期间的酷寒。

每间小木屋方方正正，棱角分明，整个村庄古朴厚重，粗犷豪放，象征着图瓦人热情彪悍的性格。经历悠悠岁月，木屋充满了日月沧桑，善良纯朴的图瓦人就在这小木屋中繁衍生息、世代延续。木屋与牧群、雪峰、森林、草地、碧水，同在蓝天下，构成了一道喀纳斯湖畔独特的自然与人文景观。身处这如画似锦的迷人秋色中，访客常常忘记了自己……

Daytime in Hemu is a kind of intoxication that implies a long-time-no-see boldness and heroism.

The sky is high above and the bright sun is in the very center of the sky. The blue sky is as clear as if it had just been washed, and a few white clouds are floating by. The snow-covered peaks stand erect and towering and all the mountains are draped with red flowers.

The zigzag mountainous path from Jiadeng Valley to Hemu for about 40 kilometers is a sightseeing boulevard of enchanting beauty. The Altai Mountains roll on and on around the rich and fertile Chonghuer Valley Plain. This place is rich in water resources; therefore, the pasture is plentiful and beautiful, and the carpet-like land offers one exquisite prairie after another. All the slopes of the mountains are covered with birch trees, one tree after another, one group after another, and one stretch after another. They all look like flames, turning the whole land into a golden sea with waves surging forward. Looking in all directions, one cannot help catching sight of the dazzling color of gold.

On the vast prairie, cattle and sheep that forage amongst the tall grass loom from time to time. They

相机：佳能 Canon Eos-1DX，镜头：24-70mm f/2.8，光圈：f/10，快门：1/80秒，感光度：ISO100，曝光补偿：0EV **喀纳斯禾木村秋季牧场**

相机：佳能 Canon Eos-1DX，镜头：24-70mm f/2.8，光圈：f/11，快门：1/200秒，感光度：ISO100，曝光补偿：0EV **暮秋四骏图**

相机：佳能 Canon Eos-1DX，镜头：24-70mm f/2.8，光圈：f/14，快门：1/60秒，感光度：ISO100，曝光补偿：0EV **天边的白杨林**

must accumulate as much fat as possible before the advent of the severely cold winter so as to survive the long cold season. In the mysterious light, the hairs of the cattle and sheep form a beautiful golden contour. On the prairie, the herdsmen on horseback are galloping to hurriedly drive the cattle and sheep to other places. They must make their animals fatten up before the heavy snows seal the mountain passes. Deep in the prairie, smoke from kitchens floats out from the top of two or three yurts, which indicates that some herdsmen are busy making dairy products for the winter.

Every wooden house is square and angular in shape. The whole village looks simple and thick, bold and unconstrained, which typically symbolizes the characteristics of enthusiasm and valiance of the Tuwa people. Despite the vicissitudes of time, the simple and kind Tuwa people have been living in such wooden houses generation after generation. Wooden houses amidst the herds, snow-covered peaks, forests, prairies, and blue waters make a unique view of nature and humanity by the shore of the Kanas Lake under the same blue sky. Finding themselves in the picturesque scene of autumn, visitors tend to forget themselves.

暮之眩

Brilliance of Dusk

禾木暮之醉，醉出一种深沉的醇厚和浓烈。

在斜阳的映照下，朴实敦厚的禾木桥金光闪烁，这座带有大门的古木桥，是禾木村的标志，也是外界进入这片圣洁之地的必经之处。历经百年的风吹雨打，桥上饱经沧桑的粗壮圆木，已褪去了昔日华丽的外表，露出木材天然的本色，更显厚重与沧桑。

落日时分，桥下湍急的禾木河水，冲击着卵

相机：佳能 Canon Eos-1DX，镜头：24-70mm f/2.8，光圈：f/10，快门：1/200秒，感光度：ISO100，曝光补偿：0EV **喀纳斯禾木村禾木河**

石，引得浪花四溅。河水湛蓝碧透，好似一坛烈酒，透出一股浓烈与甘醇。

在禾木桥上凭栏远望，对岸重峦叠嶂，层林尽染。在夕阳的余晖下，成排的白桦林橙黄似金。疾风吹过，金色的树叶缤纷散落，将如茵的大地铺上一层绵厚的金色地毯，充满着诗情画意。

又到了牧归时分，清晨出村觅食的牛羊群，腆着滚圆的肚子，慢悠悠地重返禾木桥，轻车熟路回归自家的围栏畜棚中。

高悬的太阳，从西边高耸的雪山顶上渐渐低垂，原先刺眼的阳光，也变得柔和起来。白云渐渐发红，不久彩霞满天，金光四射，道道霞光肆意铺洒开来，将整个禾木村披上一层眩目的金红色。

待太阳落尽，村北山顶上一轮皓月，在白云的衬托下半遮半掩，羞羞答答，悄悄地从树梢上升将上来。此时，白天奔腾不息的禾木河，似乎也放慢了倾泻的节奏。在阵阵微风中，马儿早已回到圈内，偶尔可见几只调皮的小绵羊，还在围栏中徘徊驻足。

全村上方的炊烟，再一次悠悠飘浮。村民们都在各自家中张罗晚饭，刚才还在屋前草地上玩耍的孩子们，在父母的呼唤中也回到了餐桌。劳作了一天的图瓦人，斟满酒，端起杯，用甘醇浓烈的美酒来驱散疲惫。同时，他们也以美酒迎接四方宾客，放开歌喉，唱起了热情洋溢的《敬酒歌》：

刚煮熟的羊肉
给灶膛里的火已祭过
刚出锅的奶酒
给毡房外的天已敬过
双手举起这
图瓦人酿造的琼浆玉液
献给你
四方的朋友
远道的贵客
祝福你
吉祥幸福安康！

当银盘似的一轮明月，高悬于夜幕之上时，白

相机：佳能 Canon Eos-1DX，镜头：24-70mm f/2.8，光圈：f/9，快门：1/60秒，感光度：ISO100，曝光补偿：0EV　**奔流不息的禾木河**

相机：佳能 Canon Eos-1DX，镜头：24-70mm f/2.8，光圈：f/13，快门：1/125秒，感光度：ISO100，曝光补偿：0EV **哈巴河白沙湖秋色**

昼里喧闹的禾木村，慢慢归于沉寂，再次进入甜甜的梦乡之中。

Dusk in Hemu brings about a kind of intoxication that induces a deep mellowness and strength.

At sunset, the torrential water of the Hemu River under the bridge dashes the pebbles, producing splashes. The river water, blue and transparent, looks like a kind of strong liquor emitting strong smell and fragrant mellowness.

It is time for the herdsmen to return home. The cattle and sheep that went out foraging in the morning are now on their way back with their full bellies. Slowly crossing the Hemu Bridge, homeware bound, they know their way to their barns within the rails.

The sun high in the sky is now gradually setting at the top of the snow-covered mountains in the west. The dazzling light is now turning soft. The white clouds go red little by little and soon the colorful sunset covers the whole sky. With golden rays radiating, the beams of sunset go in all directions, blanketing the whole Hemu Village with a blinding dazzle of reddish golden light.

After the sunset, a bright moon appears high above the top of the mountain to the north of the village. The moon is silently going up, half hidden behind the white clouds. At this time, the dashing water of the Hemu River has also reduced its torrential rhythm. As the breeze gently blows, the horses have long returned to their stables, but some naughty lambs remain outside, frolicking in the paddock.

Once more, the smoke coming out from kitch-

en chimneys floats above the village. The villagers are busy preparing supper in their houses. The kids that were playing on the prairie in front of their houses a few minutes ago are now at the tables upon their parents' summon. After a long day's toil, the Tuwas have poured to the brim and raised the cups, intending to drive fatigue away with the strong liquor. At the same time, they welcome visitors with the mellow wine. They begin to sing *The Song of Toast* at the top of their voices.

When the full moon hangs high up in the night sky like a silver plate, Hemu Village, full of hustle and bustle during the day, gradually returns to tranquility and is about to fall asleep again.

Tips 寻访者须知

佳境指数 Scenery Index： ★★★★★

备选序列： 新疆维吾尔自治区喀纳斯风景名胜区——中国国家自然遗产预备名录（国家建设部2006年7月版）

List Number: The Kanas Scenery Park of the Xinjiang Uighur Autonomous Region — in the preparatory list for Chinese World Heritage (July 2006 Edition by the State Construction Ministry)

寻访提示： 禾木村处于喀纳斯风景区的核心区域，自然的生态和旖旎的风光，常使游客"窒息"。这里地处北纬38度，也是中国少数几处近似北欧自然风光的游览胜地。禾木最佳的出游时节，为每年秋高气爽、气温适中的中秋节后的第二周。在一般情况下，北疆禾木的白桦林，中秋节前后就开始泛黄，而禾木山下的桦林，要在中秋节一周以后才开始染黄。村子较大，环绕一周（外环）大约需要三四个小时。贾登峪至禾木有一条约四十公里的山道，风光极佳，建议体力健壮者不妨骑马或徒步穿越，会有意想不到的收获。禾木地处北疆，纬度较高，秋季早晚间温差较大，行前要备妥防风、防寒和防雨措施。游览途中要尊重各少数民族的生活和风俗习惯。

Location Notes: Hemu Village is located at the exact center of Kanas Scenery Park, which is excellent in natural ecology and exquisite in scenic beauty, thus often making visitors feel breathless. It is also one of the scenic spots in the minority people's areas, which reminds one, in its beauty, of Northern Europe. The best time to visit Hemu is autumn, the temperature is ideal in the second week after the Mid-autumn Festival.

相机：佳能 Canon Eos-1DX，镜头：24-70mm f/2.8，光圈：f/9.9，快门：1/30秒，感光度：ISO100，曝光补偿：0EV **布尔津五彩滩落日**

摄影提示：禾木为中国为数不多的最佳摄影创作基地之一，佳作大片不断涌现。一年四季均可创作，尤以秋季为佳。禾木村子较大，雪山、密林、草原、牧群、河流、木屋、毡房、围栏等创作元素众多，日出日落为最佳拍摄时间。村西侧的山坡观景台为拍摄日出的最佳位置，村北侧的山坡观景平台为拍摄日落的最佳位置。村子内外景色宜人，民俗民风浓郁，均为摄影创作的极好题材，建议摄影者多走多观察，一定会有更多的惊喜。

Tips for Photography: Hemu happens to be one of the few places in China, where a large number of top-ranking photos are taken. Photos can be taken here all the year round; yet, the best time for photography is autumn. As the village is relatively large, there is quite a large variety of photographic themes such as snow-covered mountains, forests, herds of cattle and sheep, rivers, wooden houses, yurts, fences, etc. The best time for picture taking is at sunrise and sunset.

民俗提示：图瓦人比较大的节庆有春节、敖包节和邹鲁节。春节是图瓦人比较隆重的节日，每当春节来临时，他们一个个身着节日盛装，欢聚在喀纳斯湖周围，举行赛马、射箭、摔跤、滑雪橇等比赛。狂欢之后，要举行全村人的酒会，并由喇嘛举行诵经仪式。敖包节又称“塔克恩”节，在每年的农历五月十三日。图瓦人的信仰虽以藏传佛教为主，但原始宗教对其也有较深的影响，他们仍保留了许多原始自发的自然崇拜，敖包节就是图瓦人祭祀天地日月和大自然的节日。邹鲁节即汉语的“点灯节”，又称入冬节，时间是每年的农历十月二十五日，这也是图瓦人的特有节日，在这一天所有在外放牧的牧民都要回到村庄。

Brief Introduction to the Local Culture: The major festivals for the Tuwa people are the Spring Festival, Aobao Festival, and Zoulu Festival. During the Spring Festival, they put on their best clothes

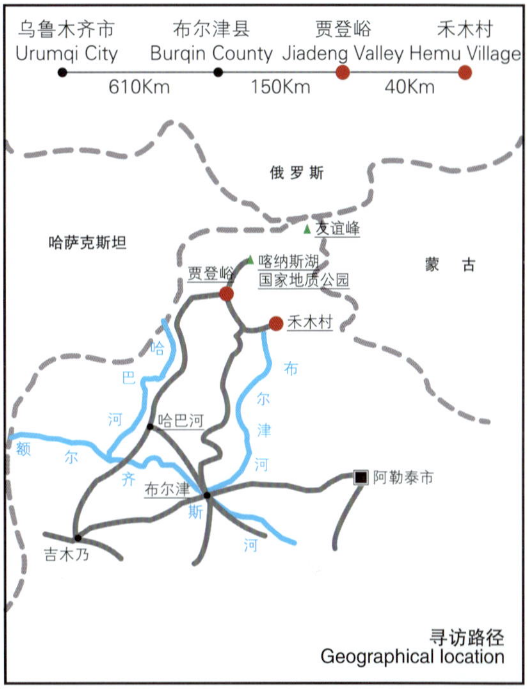

寻访路径
Geographical location

and hold galas around the Kanas Lake, holding-competitions in horse racing, archery, wrestling, skiing, etc.

美食提示：禾木的美食富有各民族特色。蒙古族美食主要以肉食为主，有烤全羊、烤牛排、烤马肉、烤鱼等，还有烩酸菜、蒸土豆片、大盘鸡、拔丝奶皮、野生桦树蘑菇等。另有一种叫“别克”的野菜，又叫鸡腿参，用奶煮着吃，美味无比。主食主要为莜面、大麦面、小麦面，奶制品更是丰富，有奶疙瘩、奶皮子和酥油等。哈萨克族美食主要是绵羊肉和山羊肉，做法主要有煮、熏、烤三种。熏肉时放些盐、葱，小块肉被做成马肠、香肠。用牛奶、羊奶、骆驼奶等制成的食品，有酸奶疙瘩、黄奶疙瘩、黑奶疙瘩、甜奶疙瘩等。

Tips on food: The food of Hemu Village is rich in ethnic flavour. The Mongolian people mainly eat meats, having such dishes as roast whole lamb, roast beef, roast horse meat, and roast fish.

寻觅备选世遗佳境 1
江苏省扬州市瘦西湖及盐商园林文化景观
Slender West Lake and Salt Merchants' Gardens, Yangzhou, Jiangsu

05 陨落的奢华
Fallen Extravagance

中国明清盐业制度的兴衰历史
中国园林文化南北并蓄的孤本范例

Historical Ups and Downs of the Salt Business during the Ming and Qing Dynasties;
Unique Model of Chinese Gardens of Northern and Southern Culture

清乾隆三十七年（1772年），扬州这座建于春秋战国，素有“淮左名都”之誉的江淮名城，走到了历史的巅峰。

这一年，处于鼎盛时期的扬州城，盐年销售量为一百八十万引。一引为三百六十余斤，一引盐在产盐区的售价是0.64两白银，运到扬州以后，加上运费、盐税，售价为1.82两白银。自扬州再将盐运至江苏、安徽、江西、湖北、湖南、浙江等东南六省销盐区，零售价上升至10两白银。就零售价而言，一斤盐在当地只售十文钱，加上税银七文，其成本不过十七文，而运到销盐区则涨至五六十文不等，售价翻了数倍。

也在这一年，扬州的经济规模跃居世界城市之首位。扬州盐商这一年赚银1,500万两以上，上交盐税700万两以上，占全国盐课总量的60%。而当年中央户部库存银为7,800万两，中央一年的财政收入约为4,000万两左右。扬州盐商成为我国封建社会晚期的最大财阀之一。当时，中国的经济总量为全世界的32%，扬州盐商提供的盐税，占了全世界经济总量的8%。

还是在这一年，扬州盐商为了迎驾清乾隆帝再次巡视江南，以期在业盐上获得更丰厚的利润，这个东方最富有的财团再次募集巨资，花费大量白银在瘦西湖上建造奢华的五亭桥。

而几乎在同一时期，英国的瓦特正致力于改进热效率较低的纽考曼蒸汽机，英国工业革命由此拉开序幕，旋即西方掀起了工业革命的狂飙。法国革命也势如破竹，攻占巴士底狱，推翻封建王朝，由人民组织起来的制宪会议掌握大权，并向全世界庄严宣布“人身自由，权利平等”的原则。

到了乾隆三十八年（1773年），堪称现代资本主义之父的英国人亚当·斯密完成了《国富论》的初稿，他在赞叹中国先贤的自由放任学说和经济的市场调节功效的同时，发出了这样的感叹：为什么这个东方帝国几百年来始终没有变化呢？

相机：佳能 Canon Eos-1DX，镜头：24-70mm f/2.8，光圈：f/11，快门：1/1250秒，感光度：ISO400，曝光补偿：0EV **扬州市瘦西湖钓鱼台**

相机：佳能 Canon Eos-1DX，镜头：24-70mm f/2.8，光圈：f/13，快门：1/160秒，感光度：ISO400，曝光补偿：0EV **扬州市瘦西湖五龙亭**

相机：佳能 Canon Eos-1DX，镜头：24-70mm f/2.8，光圈：f/10，快门：1/640秒，感光度：ISO400，曝光补偿：0EV **扬州市瘦西湖白塔**

相机：佳能 Canon Eos-1DX，镜头：24-70mm f/2.8，光圈：f/16，快门：1/80秒，感光度：ISO200，曝光补偿：0EV **扬州市瘦西湖凫庄**

In the 37th year (1772 A.D.) of the reign of Emperor Qianlong of the Qing Dynasty, Yangzhou, which was built up in the Spring and Autumn Period, reached its peak in history.

This was the year that Yangzhou, at its peak in history, made an enormous fortune in the salt business.

This was the year that Yangzhou jumped to the world No.1 city in terms of economic scope.

It was in that year that the salt merchants of Yangzhou made meticulous preparations for Emperor Qianlong's second trip to the south of the Yangtze River with the expectation of gaining more profits in their salt business. They spent a large amount of silver building up the magnificent Five-pavilion Bridge across the Slender West Lake. Almost at the same time, however, the invention of the steam engine by James Watt unveiled the Industrial Revolution in England, and the French Revolution overthrew the feudal dynasty and proclaimed to the world freedom and equality. In 1773, i.e. the 38th year of the reign of Emperor Qianlong, Adams Smith, founder of capitalism, put forward his manuscripts of *An Inquiry into the Nature and Causes of the Wealth of Nations*. He wondered, "Why has the oriental empire not made any change for hundreds of years?"

骤盛骤衰倏忽间

Ups and Downs in a Heartbeat

食盐是百姓最为日常的生活用品，在中国漫长的封建社会中，盐税一直是历代政府财政收入的主要来源之一，它的生产与运销关乎国计民生。

相机：佳能 Canon Eos-1DX，镜头：24-70mm f/2.8，光圈：f/13，快门：1/320秒，感光度：ISO400，曝光补偿：0EV **扬州瘦西湖五亭桥**

早在汉代，吴王刘濞即在扬州“煮海为盐”，“两淮盐，天下咸”。唐代将此作为海盐主要集散地之一，朝廷设盐转运院常驻扬州。白居易《盐商妇》诗中描绘：“官家利薄私家厚，盐铁尚书远不如。”历代王朝都从这项盐业专卖制度中获取了巨额的税收。至明孝宗弘治五年（1492年），明朝政府为减轻边疆驻军的财政压力，实行“开中折色制”，规定商人不用再到北部边疆用粮食换取盐票，在内地就可以到盐运司用银两换取盐票。这就造就了除晋商以外另一个著名商帮——徽商的崛起。自此以后，他们也拥有了介入业盐的入场券。

到了清代，清政府采取了官督商引制度，紧紧把控食盐的专卖权。盐商们要获得政府的特别许可从事盐业经营，就必须获得食盐专卖的凭证“盐引”，俗称“窝子”。在扬州，清政府专门设立了两淮巡盐御史、两淮盐运史，盐商在官府督办下才能经营盐业，即盐商每年必须先到专门机构购买盐引，凭盐引到指定盐场购买一定指标的盐，然后再运到指定的地区销售，在规定的范围内有专卖特权。在清康乾时期，全国各地经营淮盐的盐商巨贾纷纷涌入扬州，垄断两淮盐业的八大商会全部聚集于此。

垄断盐源的两淮盐商可以左右市场盐价。淮扬盐商的销盐区主要是安徽、河南、湖南、湖北、江西等省份，这里是清朝政府当时在全国划分十一个盐区中最大的一个销盐区域，利润高，销售范围广，使扬州盐商牟利甚厚。

扬州盐业的崛起和鼎盛，还得益于便捷的漕运。大运河是世界上开凿最早、里程最长、工程最大的运河。开凿始于春秋时期，吴王夫差十年(前486)在扬州开凿邗沟，连通长江与淮河，是大运河最早的一段河道，那时的扬州称为邗沟。京杭大运河北起北京(涿郡)，南达杭州(余杭)，跨河北、山东、江苏、浙江四省及数十座城市，贯通海河、黄河、淮河、长江、钱塘江五大水系，滋养沿河的世代华夏子孙，孕育了灿烂的运河文明。扬州因得水利之便，成为当时全国最大的食盐集散和贸易中心之一。每年有数亿斤的海盐，经过扬州转运到内地。

当时的业盐是一个暴利行业。两淮地区是当时中国食盐消费量最大的地区，还是以清乾隆三十七年为例，两淮地区每年核定的食盐运销总量为一百八十万引。以一引三百六十余斤计，一百八十万引就是六亿五千多万斤。盐商在两淮盐场的收购价格为每斤五文钱左右，而销售到消费者手中的价格为每斤二三十文钱，甚至更高，毛利高达数倍。扬州盐商正是从这悬殊极大的购销差价中获得了惊人的财富。盐商获得巨额利润的同时，清政府也获得了大量的税收。

当时的扬州盐商富可敌国。清著名学者汪中在《广陵对》记载："广陵一城之地，天下无事，则鬻海为盐，使万民食其业。上输少府，以宽农亩之力，及川渠所转，百货通焉，利尽四海。"当时还有人评价"天下第一等贸易为盐商"。故谚云"一品官，二品商""凡商贾贸易，贱买贵卖，无过盐斤"。扬州盐商通过业盐，瞬间聚集和积累了巨额的资本，"富者以千万计""百万以下者皆谓之小商"。

构建于封建社会腐朽没落政治和经济制度基础之上的业盐制度，其衰败和崩溃是必然的。扬州盐商集聚的财富，是利用清朝政府给予他们的特权——盐引制，通过垄断经营、贱买贵卖等手段获取的，凭借特权庇护，为不折不扣的官商。盐商们的大量财富，也成为清政府特殊用项的来源之一。两淮的盐税直接关涉到清政权的经济命脉，"损益盈虚，动关国计"。于是形成了上至皇帝、中至臣僚、下至扬州盐商在政治上、社会上和经济上的微妙关系。扬州盐商也在无形中承担了许多封建政府的义务。如遇大灾大难时，慷慨解囊是他们报效朝廷的最好时机。台湾林爽文起义时，扬州盐商江广达主动捐银200万两，"以备犒赏"。嘉庆年

相机：佳能 Canon Eos-1DX，镜头：24-70mm f/2.8，光圈：f/8，快门：1/100秒，感光度：ISO200，曝光补偿：0EV **扬州个园院落**

间（1796—1820年），川楚陕白莲教起义，清政府军饷匮乏，扬州盐商鲍漱芳积极向清政府“输饷”，清政府为此赏其“盐运使”头衔。清政府治河患经费不足，扬州盐商“集众输银三百万两以佐工需”。取宠皇帝也是他们维持特权的手段之一。乾隆于十八年（1753）南巡时，扬州盐商捐银20万两修建行宫。为此乾隆特允许纲盐、食盐每引增加十斤以示奖励。乾隆的数次南巡，盐商们都是绞尽脑汁，广筑园林，“一路楼台直到山”，以换取更大的业盐利益。无怪乎乾隆也惊叹说：“扬州盐商，拥有厚资，其居室园囿，无不华丽崇焕。”

著名学者韦明铧先生在《两淮盐商》中一针见血地指出：“在扬州盐商的身上，根本找不到同一时期西方资产阶级那种锐意进取的朝气蓬勃。”盐商那种寄生性、依附性和消费性的本质，决定了他们不可能把财富用于扩大再生产。真是应了好景不长这句话，到乾隆中叶，扬州盐业已出现衰败迹象。嘉庆道光年间（1796—1850年），清政府频繁无度的查收勒索，使扬州盐商已无利可图，一蹶不振，最后纷纷作鸟兽散。他们的衰亡，就像他们的兴起那样，骤起骤落，都在倏忽之间。当清政府盐业政策变化，盐商失去了对盐业贸易的垄断地位而一落千丈的时候，扬州这个随盐商而繁华一时的城市，也就如流星般陨落了。

Salt is the most common ingredient in ordinary people's daily life. In the long, long feudal society in China, the revenue from salt was always one of the chief governmental revenues from dynasty to dynasty. The production, transportation and sale of salt were closely tied with national plans and people's living.

In the Qing Dynasty, the government took a strict control over the salt trade. During the reigns of Emperor Kangxi and Emperor Qianlong, the salt trade all flocked to Yangzhou from all parts of China.

相机：佳能 Canon Eos-1DX，镜头：24-70mm f/2.8，光圈：f/8，快门：1/80秒，感光度：ISO200，曝光补偿：0EV **扬州市个园“壶天自春”**

暮秋瘦西湖

The lucrative profits and huge scales in buying and selling salt enabled the sale merchants in Yangzhou to amass an incredible amount of wealth.

The abrupt growth and peak prosperity of the salt business in Yangzhou resulted partly from the convenience of water transport to the capital. The Great Canal is the earliest, longest, and largest canal in the world.

The salt business at that time was an industry that could reap extravagant profits.

Therefore, the slat merchants in Yangzhou then were wealthier than the national treasury.

Nevertheless, the salt business, based on the corrupt political and economic system of the feudalistic society, was naturally doomed to decline and collapse.

The essence is that the salt merchants lived a parasitic, dependent and life of consumption meant that their lifestyle was unsustainable. Therefore, their life of luxury was really short-lived. In the middle of the reign of Emperor Qianlong, there appeared traces of decline in the salt business in Yangzhou. With almost no profit to make, the salt merchants in Yangzhou were finished for good. Just like its birth, the death of the salt business was within one twinkling of time. Yangzhou, a city of extreme prosperities, flashed out of sight like a comet in the sky.

扬州园林甲天下

Yangzhou Gardens: Best in the World

朱自清曾在《扬州的夏日》中说："特别是没去过扬州而念过些唐诗的人，在他心里，扬州真像蜃楼海市一般美丽；他如念过《扬州画舫录》一类书，那更了不得了。"

"何处估客豪，扬州估客豪!"在明清两代，扬州成为一座由财富堆积而成的城市，创造财富的人，就是以扬州盐商为代表的豪商巨贾们。在乾隆年间（1711—1799年），瘦西湖曾一度极盛。乾隆君临天下六十年，六下江南巡视，每次都到扬州，而瘦西湖又是必游之处，碧湖两岸园林连片，无一寸隙地，其奇思妙构，使"绿杨城廓是扬州"绝非虚名。

当时，全国各地豪商巨贾寄居扬州者不下数十万人，把扬州变成了一个举世惊羡的富人世界。而营造豪宅成为第一等要事。"园林多是宅，无园不安家。"对此，盐商们不约而同地找到了最好的住宅模式——私家园林。

扬州盐商对园林住宅的迷恋，带动了一方经久不息的造园热潮，形成了私家园林遍地开花、异彩纷呈的城市景观。在短短数百年间，扬州上规模的著名园林先后建起了两百多处。扬州盐商的巨大财力，与大江南北的艺匠大师们炉火纯青的造园技艺完美结合，开启了中国古典园林的"扬州时代"，"虽为人作，宛如天工"。在园林院落组合处理、园林建筑设计理念、园林水景独特处理、园林山石的布局等艺术表现方面独树一帜。

扬州地处江淮，大运河、长江在此交汇，独特的地域环境，造就扬州园林南北并蓄的特点。因此，扬州园林既有北方皇家园林大气磅礴、金碧辉煌、高大瑰丽的气势；又有苏州、杭州等江南私家园林的小家碧玉、精致秀丽、婉约含蓄的情调。南秀北雄，自成一格。保存至今的瘦西湖、个园、何园、小盘谷等，风格各异，造诣精湛，成为我国园林营造史上的孤本范例。清乾隆年间江苏仪征才子李斗花费三十年时间，详细记载和描述了清康雍乾年间扬州上百座盐商住宅园林的各自特色，汇集而成《扬州画舫录》，这本专辑被后人视为了解明清扬州社会的百科全书。

扬州繁华以盐盛。在广筑私家园林的同时，为攀附官府，争取更大的社会地位和利益空间，寻

相机：佳能 Canon Eos-1DX，镜头：24-70mm f/2.8，光圈：f/14，快门：1/400秒，感光度：ISO200，曝光补偿：0EV　**扬州何园蝴蝶厅**

相机：佳能 Canon Eos-1DX，镜头：24-70mm f/2.8，光圈：f/14，快门：1/400秒，感光度：ISO200，曝光补偿：0EV　**扬州何园水心亭**

相机：佳能 Canon Eos-1DX，镜头：24-70mm f/2.8，光圈：f/11，快门：1/400秒，感光度：ISO200，曝光补偿：0EV，**扬州卢氏盐商住宅**

求“贾而儒”做派也是暴富起来的扬州盐商附庸风雅的外在表现之一。于是，“扬州八怪”“昆曲七大内班”“淮扬菜系”等风生水起，把扬州造就成一座商业繁荣、文化发达、人文荟萃的园林城市。“十年一觉扬州梦，赢得青楼薄幸名”“二十四桥明月夜，玉人何处教吹箫”，则从另一个侧面，记录了当时扬州的富庶和繁荣。

扬州园林的命运和他们主人的命运息息相关。据统计，扬州城内私家园林最鼎盛时达两百多处。后经晚清盐制改革、鸦片战争、太平天国战争等，大量扬州园林或荒废，或焚毁，或拆卖，开始由盛及衰。太平天国起义衰亡后，两淮盐业曾死而复生，官僚和盐商又开始纷纷造园，但已力不从心，造园水平远不能与盛极时期相比。而此时，中国园林的建造中心已经转向苏州。至民国时期，扬州园林仅存残破的六十余处。新中国成立以后的“大跃进”和“文革时期”，扬州园林又一次面临摧残，仅剩下三十处左右。

改革开放以后，扬州园林枯木逢春，熠熠生辉。其品位极高的文化、艺术和审美价值，令世界瞩目。盐商园林是扬州文化的“灵魂”。那些保存至今的盐商深宅大院，以其高雅脱俗的气质，向人们娓娓诉说当年盐商巨贾的不俗业绩；用其富丽堂皇的外在形态，向世人讲述曾“精彩一座城市”的委婉故事。

昔日扬州盐商在有意无意间，客观上对继承中国优秀传统文化遗产起到了积极的促进作用，但因受时代局限，他们的主观动因，是仅以追求个人的喜好、享乐和功利为目的。站在更高的历史起点，更好地保护、传承和弘扬这些中华民族优秀文化遗产，增强民族自信心和凝聚力，是落在我们当代人肩上义不容辞的责任。

相机：佳能 Canon Eos-1DX，镜头：24-70mm f/2.8，光圈：f/8，快门：1/800秒，感光度：ISO200，曝光补偿：0EV **扬州小盘谷**

Zhu Ziqing (1898–1948), famous Chinese man of letters, once said, "To those that have never been to Yangzhou but got to know it in the Tang poems, Yangzhou is as beautiful as a mirage in their mind; however, if they should read the book *Records of Yangzhou*, the city would be unbelievably more magnificent."

In the Ming and Qing Dynasties, Yangzhou was actually a city built on a pile of wealth. During the reign of Emperor Qianlong, the Slender West Lake took the lead in natural scenery all over China. The emperor, ruling the country for 60 years, toured to the south of the Yangtze River six times. He went to Yangzhou each time, and the Slender West Lake was always a must in his itinerary.

At that time, hundreds of thousands of wealthy merchants from every corner of the country settled down in Yangzhou, thus making the city a world of enviable riches. What's more, the construction of deluxe houses and mansions was of paramount importance to the rich people. To them, "Gardens are found in their abodes, and without gardens homes cannot be set up."

The propensity on the part of the salt merchants in Yangzhou to abodes with gardens gave rise to a permanent surge in garden construction; consequently, private gardens came into being all over Yangzhou, which presented a landscaping of colorful and magnificent scenery. With in only a few hundred years, there appeared over 200 well-known sizable gardens in Yangzhou.

Yangzhou is located on the lower reaches of the Yangtze River and the Huihe River, where the Great Canal and the Yangtze River merge. The unique geographical location made it possible for the gardens in Yangzhou to demonstrate the special characteristics of both southern and northern garden construction.

The destiny of the gardens in Yangzhou was always linked to that of their owners. It is said that Yangzhou, during the time of its peak prosperity, boasted more than 200 private gardens. However, because of the reform of the salt business in the late Qing Dynasty, the Opium War, and the war during the Taiping Kingdom of Heaven, a large number of the gardens ended up dilapidated, deserted, burned, or pulled down and sold. The gardens in Yangzhou went from thriving to declining. During the period of the Republic of China, only some 60 gardens, shabby and damaged, were left in Yangzhou. During the Great Leap Forward and the Cultural Revolution after 1949, the gardens experienced devastation once again, and only 30 or so survived.

Ever since the adoption of the opening and reform policy, the gardens in Yangzhou, which seem to be living a new life after hardships, have been shedding new light of brilliance. Their high cultural, artistic and aesthetic value has won worldwide attention. The mansions and gardens by the former salt merchants that have been preserved tell romantic stories that Yangzhou used to be a dazzling city.

The salt merchants in the former times made, consciously and unconsciously, active and positive contributions to the heritage of excellent traditional Chinese culture in an objective way. However, because of limitations in history, their subjective motive was to pursue personal pleasures and to indulge in material gains. Standing at the vantage

相机：佳能 Canon Eos-1DX，镜头：24-70mm f/2.8，光圈：f/9，快门：1/160秒，感光度：ISO400，曝光补偿：0EV **扬州市东关晨曦**

相机：佳能 Canon Eos-1DX，镜头：24-70mm f/2.8，光圈：f/9，快门：1/320秒，感光度：ISO400，曝光补偿：0EV **扬州市东关街商铺林立**

point in history, to better protect, inherit and uphold the excellent heritage of traditional Chinese culture so as to boost our national confidence and cohesion has become a compelling obligation of ours.

Tips 寻访者须知

佳境指数 Scenery Index： ★★★★

备选序列： 扬州瘦西湖及盐商园林文化景观——中国世界文化遗产预备名单第13号（国家文物局2012年11月版）

List Number: The Slender West Lake and the Cultural Sites of the Gardens by the Salt Merchants of Yangzhou — No.13 in the preparatory list for Chinese World Heritage (November, 2012 Edition by the State Cultural Relics Bureau)

寻访提示： 除了瘦西湖以外，扬州数十处精美的私家园林主要集中在东关街、南河下和丁家湾等街巷之中，自南至北主要有卢氏盐商住宅、平园、何园、小盘谷、贾氏庭园、二分明月楼、刘庄、尉园、琼花观、马氏故居、汪氏小苑、刘文淇故居、江园、壶园、华氏园、李长乐故居、逸园、个园、街南书屋、武当行宫、谢馥春等。游客行前要做好案头工作，按图索骥。扬州还有众多自然和人文景观值得观赏，如以鉴真和尚闻名于世、建于南北朝的大明寺，以及汉陵苑、瓜洲古渡、二十四桥、文昌阁、史可法纪念馆、朱自清故居等。东关街是寻访大运河文明和古商埠的最好去处。

Location Notes: In addition to the Slender West Lake, Yangzhou has scores of exquisite private gardens. It also offers many natural scenic spots and cultural sites for visitors to appreciate.

摄影提示： 瘦西湖、个园和何园为扬州园林的扛鼎之作，是摄影创作的主要对象，且一年四季景色各异，尤以春季桃红柳绿和夏季琼花盛开时节为最佳拍摄时机。运用不同时节、不同光线，可营造出扬州园林千变万化不同凡响的艺术魅力。在突出表现扬州园林中亭、台、楼、阁、桥、塔、叠石等主要元素的同时，也要处理好这些元素在画面中的的比例关系。扬州园林极富特色的门楼、漏窗、厅堂、亭阁、假山

相机：尼康 NIKON D700，镜头：尼康 70-200mm f/2.8，光圈：f/7.1，快门：1/200秒，感光度：ISO200 曝光补偿：-1.3EV **苏北垛田春色**

等，都是创作园林摄影小品的上好元素。

Tips for Photography: The Slender West Lake and many of the gardens of Yangzhou are, of course, the best scenes for photography. They are excellent all the year round, but they look best in spring when the peach flowers are red and willow leaves are green and in summer when the snow-ball bushes burst into blossom.

民俗提示：一年一度的维扬灯会，农历正月十三上灯，十八落灯，十五是高潮。《望江南百词》中说："扬州好，灯节庆元宵。绛蜡满堂家宴集，金龙逐队市声嚣，花鼓又高跷。"扬州扎彩灯，集彩扎、裱糊、书画、诗文、剪纸、刺绣、编结等技艺于一体。灯的式样很多，有简易的兔子灯、西瓜灯、元宝灯、荷花灯、蛤蟆灯等，还有工艺复杂的龙灯、船灯、麒麟灯、寿星灯，更有扬州特有的琉璃灯。

百花生日也称花朝，为扬州时俗，每逢农历二月十二日，用红布条系在花枝上，谓之挂红，祈求良辰美景，百花繁盛。三月三为传统的踏青挑荠之日。

Brief Introduction to the Local Culture: A Lantern Fair is held once a year, with all the lanterns hoisted up on the 13th day of the first lunar month and pulled down on the 18th of the same month. The 15th is the very day for all kinds of activities. There are a wide variety of lanterns such as the rabbit lantern, the water-melon lantern, the shoe-shaped lantern, the lotus flower lantern, the toad lantern, etc. In addition, there are complicated lanterns like the dragon lantern, the boat lantern, the unicorn lantern, the longevity-god lantern,etc.

美食提示：淮扬菜自古与川、鲁、粤菜并称为四大菜系，注重本味、讲究火工、擅长炖焖，口味清淡鲜美、甜咸适中。淮扬菜又分为扬州菜、镇江菜、淮阴菜等流派，其中扬州师傅犹以刀工精细著称，特别精于食材雕刻，是著名的"扬州三把刀"之一。扬州菜尤以"三头"（拆烩鲢鱼头、扒烧整猪头、蟹粉狮子头）为代表，若想考验厨师的刀工，不妨点一道大煮干丝。而比这些大菜更为出名的则是各色扬州点心和小吃。扬州十大名点：三丁包子、千层油糕、双麻酥饼、翡翠烧卖、干菜包、野鸭菜包、糯米烧卖、蟹黄蒸饺、车螯烧卖、鸡丝卷。十佳风味小吃：笋肉锅贴、扬州饼、蟹壳黄、鸡蛋火烧、咸锅饼、萝卜酥饼、鸡丝卷、三鲜锅饼、桂花糖藕粥、三色油饺。十佳特色小吃：四喜汤团、生肉藕夹、豆腐卷、笋肉小烧卖、赤豆元宵、五仁糕、葱油酥饼、黄桥烧饼、虾籽饺面、笋肉馄饨。当然，别忘了著名的扬州炒饭！

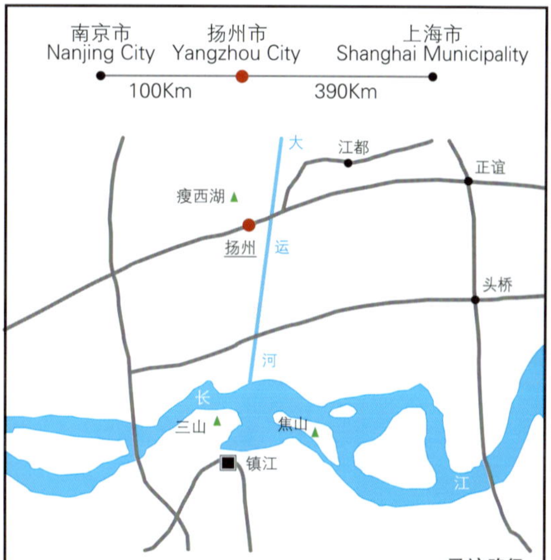

寻访路径
Geographical location

Food Tips: For a long time, Yangzhou Cuisine has belonged to the four major cuisines in China, along with Sichuan Cuisine, Shandong Cuisine, and Guangdong Cuisine. The Yangzhou Cuisine is famous for its originality in taste, particularity in cooking, and uniqueness in simmering. It is usually fresh and delicious, neither too sweet nor too salty.

寻觅备选世遗佳境 1
福建省福州市平潭县海坛风景名胜区
Pingtan County, Fuzhou, Fujian

06 青山共日月
Qingshan Mountain under the Sun and the Moon

海蚀地貌甲天下　海滨沙滩冠九州
Best Wave-eroded Landscape and Foremost Sea Beach

2010年末，福建省跨海特大桥——平潭海峡大桥正式建成通车，千年天堑变通途。一年之后，国务院正式批准《平潭综合实验区总体发展规划》，多项创新政策付诸实施，经济社会发展日新月异。曾一度蒙上神秘色彩的平潭岛，终于向世人撩开了其美丽迷人的面纱。

At the end of 2010, the Pingtan Strait Bridge, a gigantic cross-sea bridge in Fujian was officially opened to traffic. Therefore, a thousand-year-old chasm turned into a thoroughfare. Pingtan Island, which used to be quite mysterious, was finally unveiled, showing its exquisite beauty to the world.

海峡两岸共云雨

Rainfall for Both Sides of the Strait

从空中俯瞰，平潭岛像一只腹部朝向台湾的麒麟，这个“千礁岛县”共由126座岛屿和702个礁岩组成，主岛海坛岛面积为267平方公里，位列台湾岛、海南岛、上海崇明岛以及浙江舟山岛之后，为中国的第五大岛。平潭岛东临台湾海峡，与台湾新竹市相距仅68海里，是祖国大陆与台湾本岛距离最近的地方。因其地处福建沿海中心突出部，扼“海上走廊”台湾海峡与闽江口咽喉，为太平洋西岸航线连接东海与南海海上航线的中枢区位，战略位置尤为重要。

因远离内陆并孤悬于大海，平潭岛在民国元年（1912年）之前，一直未能独立建制，其漫长的历史似乎总与关卡、取税、屯兵、固防、动荡等词语联系在一起。由于特殊的地理位置，海岛历来是兵家必争之地，历代政府都在此屯兵固防。据《平潭县志》《福州府志》记载：唐为牧马地，宋初置牧监，不久撤销，允许岛民耕作，并增兵驻守。宋嘉祐四年（1059年），在钟门（今属苏澳镇）设巡检司，掌管海上巡防。此后，又曾数度“禁海”“迁界”。明洪武二十年（1387年），为防备倭寇袭扰，官府强迫岛民迁徙内陆，但在渡海时因“风涛

相机：佳能 Canon Eos-1DX，镜头：24-70mm f/2.8，光圈：f/11，快门：1/400秒，感光度：ISO200，曝光补偿：0EV **平潭岛坛南湾海蚀奇观**

大作，人力莫支，覆没之余，死亡过半”。岛上百业荒废，满目疮痍。至民国元年，平潭岛虽获准建县，但因时局动荡，匪患不断，加上瘟疫蔓延，民众生活陷入困境。抗日战争爆发后，日本侵略军多次窜犯平潭，抢掠劫杀，无恶不作，导致百业凋零，民不聊生。“平潭岛，平潭岛，男人多女人少，只长石头不长草”，便是昔日平潭岛的真实写照。

新中国成立以后，平潭岛百废待兴。但数十年来，缘于此地是“海防前哨，全岛皆兵”的地理环境，加上海峡两岸乍暖还寒的政治环境，平潭上空时晴时雨。台湾诗人余光中曾无奈地吟唱：“乡愁是一湾浅浅的海峡，我在这头，大陆在那头……”。台湾回归祖国，始终是平潭人民心中一道绕不开的情结。其间曾发生过两次“大动作”：第一次为1962年春夏时节，为反击台湾当局的骚扰和蠢动，我人民解放军驻岛三军部队强化战备，全力修筑公路和战壕，抢运和转移重要物资，有计划疏散人员，仅县城人口就疏散了三分之一；第二次为1996年台海风云突变之时，我人民解放军十万大军集结平潭岛，举行三军联合军事演习，规模空前，百位将军登临与台湾隔海相望的老虎山视察。平潭人民为了纪念这一重大事件，遂将这座临海而起、险峻陡峭、风景秀美的老虎山，更名为将军山。

虽然平潭岛坐拥两百多座优质港口，但因其特殊的地理环境，致使平潭岛社会经济的发展比较迟缓，全岛几乎没有像样的工业，为福州市下辖偏远和经济发展欠佳的地区之一。颇有意思的是，为构筑防空洞、修建地下粮库和大型军事设施，平潭人长期与岩石、流沙打交通，积累了修建岩石隧道的丰富经验。所以，在全国隧道工程中，经常可见平潭人的身影。

作为祖国大陆最早开展对台小额贸易的地区之一，平潭的澳前镇于1979年就被国务院批准为大陆第一批台轮停泊点，从而成为两岸经贸文化交流的

相机：佳能 Canon Eos-1DX，镜头：24-70mm f/2.8，光圈：f/11，快门：1/800秒，感光度：ISO200，曝光补偿：0EV **平潭岛坛南湾沙滩**

桥头堡之一。三十多年来，两岸渔民在同一海域撒网捕鱼，在同一港湾避风补给，在同一市场易货贸易，结下了深厚情谊。2011年冬天，“海峡号”客货滚装船首次直航台中市，这对海峡两岸同胞而言，真是可喜可贺。如今，平潭作为与台湾经济合作的“自由贸易港”，成为我国东南海疆对台经贸和人文交往的重要窗口，将创造辉煌的未来。

平潭与台湾隔海相望，近在咫尺，两岸共日月、同云雨、一家亲。两岸人民携起手来，支持、维护、推动两岸关系和平发展，增进两岸同胞福祉，共同开创中华民族新的前程，实为两岸人民的共同心声。

Viewed from high above in the sky, Pingtan Island bears a strong resemblance to a unicorn with its belly towards Taiwan. This thousand-island county consists of 126 islands and 702 reef rocks. With an area of 267 square km, its major island is the fifth largest island in China, next only to Taiwan, Hainan, Chongming and Zhoushan.

As it is isolated in the sea, far away from the mainland, Pingtan Island, for various reasons, was not administratively authorized. And because of turbulent social situations, constant lootings by gangsters, as well as the occurrence of plagues, the people on the islands lived a very miserable life. As a local saying goes, on Pingtan Island, there are more men than women and there is more stone than grass.

After the founding of the People's Republic of China, all neglected aspects on the islands came under reconstruction. With its closeness to Taiwan, the return of Taiwan to the motherland has always been haunting the minds of the people on Pingtan Island.

In spite of more than 200 excellent ports around Pingtan Island, economic development on

相机：佳能 Canon Eos-1DX，镜头：24-70mm f/2.8，光圈：f/11，快门：1/320秒，感光度：ISO200，曝光补偿：0EV **平潭岛海边神龛**

the islands has been quite slow because of their unique geographical location and environments. Almost no industry exists on the islands; therefore, the county is one of the faraway and economically underdeveloped places subordinate to Fuzhou. Interestingly, however, in order to build air-raid shelters, underground warehouses for grains and large-scale military installations, the Pingtan people have long been dealing with rocks and quick sand, thus accumulating rich experience in tunnel construction. It is no wonder that the people of Pingtan can be seen wherever tunnels are under construction all over the country.

As one of the first areas where the mainland government allowed small-sum trades with Taiwan, Aoqian Town, Pingtan County, was approved by the State Council in 1979 to be one of the ports for boats and ships from Taiwan to anchor. Therefore, it has been one of the bridgeheads for trade and culture between the two sides of the Taiwan Strait. Nowadays, Pingtan, a free trade port for economic cooperation with Taiwan, is an important window for economic trade and culture with Taiwan on the southeast coast of mainland China. It will create a brilliant future.

From a relatively short distance, Pingtan and Taiwan look at each other across the sea. The people on both sides of the strait are under the same sun and moon and share the rainfall from the same clouds. Holding their hands together, they are determined to support, maintain and promote peaceful development between the two sides, to enhance their happiness and benefit, to jointly create a bright tomorrow for the Chinese people, and to realize their heartfelt wishes.

相机：佳能 Canon Eos-1DX，镜头：24-70mm f/2.8，光圈：f/11，快门：1/200秒，感光度：ISO200，曝光补偿：0EV **平潭岛海蚀地貌**

海蚀奇观

海蚀奇观世罕有

Rare wave-eroded landscape

海坛岛本名平潭岛，因主岛远望如坛，所以又名“海坛”。岛上多云气，时常“东来岚气弥漫”，故又有别称“东岚”。天风海涛，造就了岛上景观的神秘、雄奇和绚丽多姿。因为拥有优质的海滨沙滩与奇特的海蚀地貌，海坛又被誉为海蚀地貌博物馆。

海蚀地貌的学术定义，是指海水运动时，沿岸陆地经海潮长期冲刷、海风及烈日的长期剥蚀，而形成的奇特地质景观，多发生在基岩海岸。海蚀的程度与当地波浪的强度、海岸原始地形和地质构造特征有关。

海蚀地貌在我国东南沿海较为常见，尤以福建省平潭岛独树一帜。沧海桑田，千万年的风吹浪打，千万年的潮至汐退，使得基岩海岸形成极其独特的海蚀奇观。海蚀地貌以大、奇、肖、特著称，海蚀崖、海蚀洞、海蚀穴、泊蚀桥、海蚀平台、海蚀阶地星罗棋布，蔚为奇观，有“奇甲天下”之誉。

“半洋石帆”和“海坛天神”被誉为平潭“海蚀奇观双绝”。

高耸于苏澳镇看澳村碧海之中的“半洋石帆”，为一对世界上最大的花岗岩球状风化天然海蚀柱。据《福州府志》记载，宋朝末代皇帝端宗在被元军追逼时，其母杨太妃携其海上逃亡途中曾驻足浏览，故又名“王母礁”。明朝有“南方徐霞客”之称的陈第将军曾誉之为“天下奇观”。远望礁石岛，只见两块花岗岩巨石，一高一低巍然屹立于万顷碧涛之中，东望如碑，南看似瓜，西视像帆，北见则似小巫见大巫，卓立中流，风雕雨塑，巧夺天工。

“海坛天神”位于碧海金沙的塘屿岛南中湾，为一具世上罕有的天然巨型象形男性裸状石人，体长三百三十余米，光头凸腹，双臂平伸，耳喉俱全，头枕金沙，脚踏碧海，仰面平卧，神态安详，比例匀称，栩栩如生。石人下身部残存一块海蚀柱状风化岩体，微斜上翘，高四米余，酷似男根。周边海蚀奇景洋洋大观，风动石、锣鼓石、香炉石、折柱石、帆石、围棋石等象形海蚀景观令人目不暇接。

最令人惊心动魄的海蚀奇观，是位于岛东流水镇东海村临海岬角处的“东海仙境”，海岸沿线悬崖峭壁犹如刀劈斧砍，这是远古火山岩受东海海浪强烈侵蚀而形成的自然杰作，陡峭断崖间营造出众多海蚀奇观。蚀井、蚀洞、蚀谷、蚀柱、蚀峰比比皆是。“仙人井”是一处天然海蚀洞，形如巨井，呈圆筒形，井壁近于垂直，口径和深度约为五十米，涨潮时海浪汹涌而至，井底浊浪翻腾，声若洪钟，蔚为壮观。岸边山峦起伏，奇峰林立，怪石峥嵘，雄奇壮丽，神秘诱人。

平潭岛海岸线蜿蜒曲折，长达408公里，其中一百余公里为优质沙滩。尤其是岛北、东、南面的长江澳、海坛湾、坛南湾三大海滨沙滩，沙质细白，海水清澈湛蓝，面积广大，相互连接，背靠葱郁的防护林带，并有海上岛屿岩礁作屏障，为目前国内最大的海滨浴场之一。尤其是坛南湾海滨，全长十二公里曲折绵延的海岸线共镶嵌有十三座金黄色海滨沙滩，呈新月牙型铺展，湾口朝向东南，每处沙滩三面环山，一面临海，均有岬角相隔，具有很好的封闭性和独立性。湾内地势开阔，沙粒均匀，晶莹洁白，恬静幽美。每当清风徐来，海不扬波，海滨环境自然天成，素有“华夏第一滩”之誉。

每天清晨，当一轮彤红的旭日从台湾海峡东边冉冉升起之时，第一缕阳光总是最先照射在海峡西岸的平潭岛上。崭新的一天又开始了，欢快、喜悦、活力、奔放，始终充盈着这片海天一色的神奇土地上。

By in the winds and splashed by the sea waves, Haitan Island presents a mysterious, grand and brilliant landscape. As it boasts excellent

相机：佳能 Canon Eos-1DX，镜头：24-70mm f/2.8，光圈：f/11，快门：1/500秒，感光度：ISO200，曝光补偿：0EV **平潭岛礁岩**

相机：佳能 Canon Eos-1DX，镜头：24-70mm f/2.8，光圈：f/11，快门：1/1250秒，感光度：ISO200，曝光补偿：0EV **平潭岛海蚀地貌**

beaches and grotesque wave-eroded landforms, Haitan is also referred to as a museum of wave-eroded landforms.

Although quite common along the coast in southeast China, the wave-eroded landforms of Pingtan Island in Fujian are rather unique. With the passing of time, the lands have been exposed to winds and waves for thousands and thousands of years, and, moreover, the ebb and tide for so many years have rendered the rocky seashore into a unique landscape of wave-eroded miracle.

The Stone Sail and the Heavenly God of Haitan are honored as two wonders of the wave-eroded miracle. The Stone Sail, standing among the blue sea waves of Kanao Village, Suao Town, is actually a pair of the largest naturally eroded granite pillars in the world. The Heavenly God of Haitan is located in the blue sea and golden sands of Tangyu Island's Nanzhong Bay. It looks like a gigantic nude man, unparalleled in all the world. Its body is about 330 meters long, and looks very lifelike.

This most breath-taking wave-eroded scenery is the Wonderland of the East China Sea, located at the seaside of Donghai Village of Liushui Town in the east of the island. The cliff along the seashore is as precipitous as if it had been chopped by a huge axe. It is truly an artwork of nature, the volcanic rock of ancient times having long been splashed and eroded by the powerful waves of the East China Sea. Among the steep cliffs are a series of miraculous wonders produced by wave erosion.

The coastline meanders around Pingtan Island for 408 km, and over 100 km of it offers very good beaches. In Changjiang Bay, Haitan Bay and Tannan Bay in the north, east and south of the

相机：佳能 Canon Eos-1DX，镜头：24-70mm f/2.8，光圈：f/13，快门：1/400秒，感光度：ISO2000，曝光补偿：0EV **平潭岛半洋石帆**

island are three wonderfully vast beaches where the white sands border the transparent blue sea waters. With the verdant protective trees in the background and sheltered by the islands and rocks on the sea, they are, to date, among the largest bathing beaches in China.

Every morning, when the red sun gradually rises over the Taiwan Strait in the east, the first ray of sunlight always sheds light first on Pingtan Island on the west side of the strait. With the beginning of a brand new day, this piece of miraculous land between the sea and sky is full of life, merry, joyful, vigorous, and energetic.

相机：佳能 Canon Eos-1DX，镜头：24-70mm f/2.8，光圈：f/11，快门：1/125秒，感光度：ISO200，曝光补偿：0EV **湄州岛妈祖的后代**

Tips 寻访者须知

佳境指数 **Scenery Index**：★★★★

备选序列：福建省海坛风景名胜区——中国国家自然遗产预备名录（国家建设部2006年7月版）

List Number: Haitan Scenery — in the preparatory list for Chinese World Heritage (November 2012 Edition by the State Cultural Relics Bureau)

寻访提示：平潭岛旅游资源十分丰富，海蚀地貌景观主要有半洋石帆、海坛天神、东海仙境、君山、南寨山、山岐澳六大景区。天然优质海滨沙滩主要有龙凤头、坛南湾、日岐澳等。因景观分布于全岛各处，相距甚远，游览时最好自驾或租车前往。事先做好案头寻访计划，以求事半功倍。另游览半洋石帆、海坛天神景区要乘船前往，行前做好安全和防晕船措施。海岸岬角多为悬崖峭壁，风疾浪高，游览时要注意安全。夏日出行要做好防晒防暑措施。

Location Notes: Pingtan Island is rich in tourism resources. The wave-eroded scenery consists of such views as the Stone Sail, the Heavenly God of Haitan, Wonderland of the East China Sea, Junshan Mountain, Nanzhai Mountain, and Shanqi Bay. As they are almost all located in the sea, tourists had better go there by boat. Before departure, they are advised to take measures for safety and against seasickness. In summer, they are also advised to be cautious against too much exposure to sunshine and heat stroke.

摄影提示：日出东方与日落夕照时分，为平潭拍摄海蚀景观的最佳时机，扫地光柔和且色彩丰满，以顺光和侧光为佳，更能突出奇岩怪礁的质感和风采。拍摄碧海金沙以侧光和逆光为佳，可利用海平面的反射，达到波光粼粼和天光云影的奇妙效果。岛上的石头民居为难得的拍摄元素，古朴厚重，层次分明，与

相机：佳能 Canon Eos-1DX，镜头：24-70mm f/2.8，光圈：f/6.3，快门：1/250秒，感光度：ISO400，曝光补偿：0EV **泉州市惠安县崇武古城**

蓝天白云、碧海金沙、奇岩怪礁相组合，构成一幅绝佳的海岛风情画。岛上渔民的养殖、捕捞等海上劳作场景，也不失为很好的人文创作元素。

Tips for Photography: At both sunrise and sunset, there are always golden opportunities to take photos of the wave-eroded sites on Pingtan Island. The stone residences on the island are excellent for photography. These houses, simple and thick, of varying heights, with the blue sea, white clouds, golden sands and grotesque rocks in the foreground and background, form excellent pictures of the island on the sea. What's more, the fishermen that are busy cultivating and harvesting sea fish are all worthy of appearing in your photos.

民俗提示：平潭藤牌舞又称藤牌阵、藤牌操，源自于戚继光当年所创的鸳鸯阵，经戚继光的部将晏继芳等改造而成，突出表现盾牌在阵中的作用。明嘉靖四十三年（1564年）戚家军追倭至平潭时，藤牌操传入民间。明末清初，郑成功部属驻军平潭，常操练藤牌军，也传教乡勇，由此逐渐演变成民间的健身活动，继而又在民间节庆和祭祀中表演，逐步演变为文娱活动中的藤牌舞。平潭岛的藤牌舞注重阵式演练，舞路程序共有六阵：一字长蛇阵、双龙戏水阵、三才定穴阵、四门兜底阵、五虎靠山阵、九宫八卦阵和十面埋伏阵。六阵之后即为单打、双打、三打，最后以藤牌手舞狮祝捷结束。

Brief Introduction to the Local Culture: The Rattan-shield Dance can be traced back to the military Yuanyang array created by Qi Jiguang in the Ming Dynasty. In the array, the rattan shields played a very important role in the offensive and defensive actions in battles.

寻访路径
Geographical location

美食提示：平潭岛盛产海鲜，品种繁多，有鱼、虾、蟹、贝、藻等海产品近七百种，其中金鲟、龙虾、对虾、螃蟹、紫菜、原始贻贝等享誉海内外。平潭岛特色美食主要有：一是“时来运转”：形似汤团，皮用地瓜和着地瓜粉糅合而成，薄而柔韧；内包馅料多为包菜、紫菜、猪精肉、鲜虾仁、鱿鱼、蟹肉等，蒸煮皆有。二是“天长地久”：用地瓜和地瓜粉做皮，内包豆沙或砂糖八果馅，状如水饺，入锅油炸，外呈金黄色，香甜可口。三是海蛎煎：大米混合黄豆磨浆，涂于油勺，以韭菜、紫菜或卷心菜、牡蛎、肉丁等为馅油炸成扁圆状，外酥内嫩，鲜香可口。四是鱼面鱼片：以黄鱼或马鲛鱼为主料，将鱼肉捣成糊状，粘少量薯粉，碾成薄片，切成细丝即为鱼面；切为块状即为鱼片，色香味俱佳，烹炒皆宜。五是九重粿：用米浆、薯粉加入适量五香末、蒜叶、食盐等，调成糊状浆，然后入蒸笼，蒸熟一层加一层，故称九重。待冷却后切成菱形扁块，入油锅炸熟即食，咸香可口，香而不腻。

Food Tips: Pingtan Island is very rich in a large variety of sea foods like fish, shrimp and prawns, crabs, shellfish, and aquatic plants.

07 百祠寻芳
Searching for Roots

塑千年文明中华魂 聚血脉传承民族心
续百姓人家吴地根

Ancient Souls, National Heritage, Ordinary Living

在运河畔、二泉旁、惠山麓、古寺边、名园中和民宅间不足0.3平方公里的弹丸之地上，自公元8世纪唐代华孝子祠始，至1949年民国秦周氏贞节祠止，在一千二百余年的时间跨度上，鳞次栉比林林总总建有118座祠堂，虽历经风雨沧桑、水火之灾和兵燹战乱，仍顽强地生存至今，且规模和数量堪称中国之最。这种独特的江南历史文化形态，到底隐藏着多少鲜为人知的秘密呢?

Beside the Great Canal, near Erquan Spring, at the foot of Huishan Hill, and by the old temple, within the tiny 0.3 square km area scattered with well-known gardens and civilian residences, there are altogether 118 temples built up over a time span of more than 1,200 years from the eighth-century Tang Dynasty to 1949. In spite of the vicissitudes of time, disasters such as fire and flood, and turmoil caused by wars, most of the temples remain intact. The scale and number of the temples rank at the top in China. However, how many little-known secrets are hidden in them?

百祠祀主领风骚

Worshipping Masters in Temples Leading Literary Excellence

祠堂萌于夏商周，雏形于汉，盛于明清，是中华农耕经济和耕读文化的产物，是中华宗族、纲常文化的表现形式，更是中华传统文化的重要组成部分。为何山南海北各色人等的祠堂，会如此不约而同地聚集在这片惠山东麓呢? 也许从这些祠堂祀主中，可以找到端倪和答案。

惠山现存最古老的祠堂当数“大王庙”。据《越绝书》记载：“汉时建春申君祠于此，每年祭之以酒，鼓乐喧天。”唐著名诗人张继也作诗为证，“春申祠宇空山里，古柏阴阴石泉水。”

春申祠是祭祀战国时期楚国宰相春申君黄歇疏浚古芙蓉湖的功劳而建，初建于惠山春申涧旁的春

相机：佳能 Canon Eos-1DX，镜头：24-70mm f/2.8，光圈：f/10，快门：1/400秒，感光度：ISO640，曝光补偿：0EV **惠山古镇牌楼**

申里，后唐人将之迁建至锡山西北麓。

位于观泉坊街的华孝子祠也属较早的惠山祠堂之一。原为东晋南北朝时期著名孝子华宝的故居，他因思念出征战死沙场的父亲，终身未行加冠礼，其孝行广为传颂，南朝齐高帝萧道成赐“孝子”匾额。华宝死后，家人以其故居为祠。后屡经修缮扩建，现存华孝子祠颇具规模，堪称惠山祠堂的典范。这一时期的祠堂还包括位于锡山北麓的东岳报功祠（又称东岳庙），祭祀兴周灭纣的功臣黄飞虎，以及该庙右侧的张中丞祠，由后人为祭祀唐靖忠殉难的御史中丞张巡及睢阳太守许远而募资修建。

寄畅园是惠山最为著名的园林祠。本为明代兵部尚书秦金衣锦还乡后修建的私人园林，其死后别墅曾被子孙分占。后秦氏家族出于宗族利益，将这倚山环水的园林改立为家祠。此处景色清雅宜人，周围密布大大小小几十座祠堂，现今完整保存有陆羽祠、尤袤祠、顾宪成祠和邵文庄祠等。

最为有名的神祠当属祭祀“茶神”陆羽的陆子祠。陆羽精于茶道，以著《茶经》闻名于世，后人奉之为“茶圣”。安史之乱后，陆羽来到无锡一带避乱，隐居惠山寺，品评惠山泉水，列其为天下第二，“天下第二泉”的美名从此享誉海内，陆羽也被祀为“茶神”。

群祠中等级最高的莫过于周濂溪夫子祠。“予独爱莲之出淤泥而不染，濯清涟而不妖，中通外直，不蔓不枝，香远益清，亭亭净植……”。该祠祭祀的对象是《爱莲说》的作者、明朝理学大家周敦颐。此祠属皇帝御赐，还享受当时明朝政府的财政补贴。据《周敦颐传》记载：有狱久不决，敦颐至，一讯立辨。邑人惊曰：“老吏不如也。”部使者荐之，调南安军司理参军。有囚法不当死，王逵欲深治之。逵，酷悍吏也，众莫敢争，敦颐独与之辨，不听，乃委手版归，将弃官去，曰：“如此尚可仕乎！杀人以媚人，吾不为也。”逵悟，囚得免。周敦颐因“上承孔孟、下启程朱”而备受后人

相机：佳能 Canon Eos-1DX，镜头：24-70mm f/2.8，光圈：f/11，快门：1/500秒，感光度：ISO640，曝光补偿：0EV，**华孝子祠**

相机：佳能 Canon Eos-1DX，镜头：24-70mm f/2.8，光圈：f/13，快门：1/1000秒，感光度：ISO640，曝光补偿：0EV **陆宣公祠**

推崇，其《爱莲说》更是流芳百世。

惠山最为典雅洁净的当属倪高士祠，也是祭祀人物中最有特点的。倪瓒为无锡云林人，元代绘画、书法大家。但使倪瓒声名远播的不是他的书画作品，而是他的洁癖。据载，倪瓒家中一尘不染，连厕所都是特制的，下置木格，内充鹅毛，出恭坠落，鹅毛便轻轻飘起将其覆盖，全无异味。倪家庭院中的梧桐树也因主人爱干净而死去，其每天都让下人挑水清洗梧桐，最后将梧桐树洗得枝枯叶黄枯萎至死。

“虫祠”刘猛将庙是惠山最有趣的神祠。祀主刘琦原是南宋抗金名将，曾大破金兀术的“拐子马”，后遭秦桧诬陷，被贬谪地方。在任期间治理水患，尤其因驱蝗有功，被后世尊为“虫神”。走进庙中，只见他右手执笏板，左手捏腰带，背后木匾上写着东、西、南、北、中的驱蝗咒语：“一洒东方甲乙木，东方蝗虫不入屋；二洒西方庚辛金，西方蝗虫都死尽；三洒南方丙丁火，南方蝗虫不敢过；四洒北方壬癸水，北方蝗虫不张嘴；五洒中央戊己土，中央蝗虫快飞走。急急如律令敕。”据说，只要无锡某方出现虫灾，当地百姓就会到虫神祠祭祀，然后抬起虫神像，敲锣打鼓到农田中驱蝗。有趣的是，在惠山祠群中，这间祠堂最小，连道光帝所赐的“福佑康年”匾额都容纳不下，正应了“庙小神仙大”的俗语。

忠节祠是群祠中最令人动容的祠堂，以纪念在晚清太平天国劫难中罹难的无锡人士，总共供奉有6,619个牌位。

惠山最为独特的景致为垒石而成的诗冢。主人名叫顾光旭，是无锡名人顾可久的八世孙。其少时从师饱学儒家经典，21岁中进士走入仕途，在从政25年期间，为官清廉正直，深受百姓爱戴。45岁时，顾因病辞官回乡著书立说，选辑了一本无锡地方诗歌总集《梁溪诗抄》，上自东汉，下至清代，共收录1,024位作者的两万余首诗作。对未入选的诗稿，顾光旭不舍得随意丢弃，而是做出了一个奇

相机：佳能 Canon Eos-1DX，镜头：24-70mm f/2.8，光圈：f/13，快门：1/800秒，感光度：ISO640，曝光补偿：0EV **范文正公祠**

妙的举动，他将这些诗稿收集在一起，采用设冢的形式将其埋于冢中，后人称之为诗冢。

惠山百祠中的每一位祀主，都是一位活灵活鲜、引领一方风骚的人物，其身后都有一则引人入胜的动人故事。特别是一些人数不算很多的小姓氏，在惠山祠堂群中也占有一席之地，充分体现了“姓氏有大小，地位相平等”的惠山独特祠堂文化。据统计，惠山祠堂群的一百十八座祠堂，涉及姓氏七十二个，所涉祀主多达一百八十位。其中有春秋时期开辟吴地的先贤秦伯，有各朝各代宰相级人物，如战国时期的黄歇（春申君），五代十国吴越王钱镠，唐代宰相李绅、陆贽、王旦，宋代宰相司马光、范仲淹和李纲，清代的嵇曾筠、嵇璜和李鸿章等；著名文人、理学家有周敦颐、张载、朱熹、顾宪成、高攀龙、苏东坡和陆羽等；著名书画家有倪云林和王绂等。这些祀主大多为备受世人敬仰的先贤廉官，也有造福一方的忠臣义士、乡贤俊杰，或是名声远扬的文化名流，还有创立近代民族工商业的时代先驱，以及各姓氏宗族的始祖和代表人物。

惠山群祠，清晰折射了吴地历代先民的精神崇尚、道德取向、宗教信仰和宗族制度的发展脉络，以及与之相对应的生活方式和民俗风情。其以一种难能可贵的“活的文化化石”，记录着中华五千年延续不断的血脉传承，凝聚着吴地先民千年积累的生活智慧。

Temples came into being in the Xia, Shang, and Zhou Dynasties, matured in the Han Dynasty, and prospered in the Ming and Qing Dynasties. The temple is the outcome of the Chinese agricultural economy and cultivation culture, the expression of patriarchal clans and cultwe of ethics and, what's more, is an important component of traditional Chinese culture. Why are the temples of different kinds of people clustered at the east side of Huis-han Hill? Perhaps clues and answers can be found

大运河临水人家

in the worshipping masters in these temples.

Of the existing temples, the Dawang Temple, meaning the Great King Temple, is the oldest. It is said to have been built in the Han Dynasty.

The best-known temple is the Luzi Temple, in honor of Lu Yu, the God of Tea. He enjoyed tea made with water taken from a nearby spring, which is world's second-best spring.

The temple of the highest rank is definitely the Confucian Temple at Zhoulian Stream.

Every worshipping master in each temple at Huishan Hill was an energetic and clever leader who is likely to have had a fascinating story. Even for those families that had only a small number of members, each temple of theirs was given its own space, which fully demonstrates the principle of equality.

In the temples can be seen the development of the spiritual status, moral orientation, religious belief, and religious systems of the ancestors of former generations. Meanwhile, the related life-styles and folk emotions of the people can be detected here. A kind of cultural fossil of praiseworthy living is recorded with the 5000-year-old Chinese heritage and is a condensation of the life wisdom accumulated over almost one thousand years by the ancestors in this part of China.

百祠聚集探成因

Reasons for the Gathering of Temples

惠山古镇祠堂群的集聚和形成，无不打上了中国社会、经济和文化发展的深深烙印。

京杭大运河从无锡惠山东麓蜿蜒而过，至黄埠墩延伸出一条小河汊——惠山浜，逶迤直抵惠山脚下。河道虽窄，却是当年历代帝王下江南、游惠山的必经之浜。“江南第一山”惠山在南北朝时即

相机：佳能 Canon Eos-1DX，镜头：24-70mm f/2.8，光圈：f/10，快门：1/640秒，感光度：ISO640，曝光补偿：0EV **惠山浜群祠林立**

建惠山寺，名列江南四百八十寺；唐代“茶圣”陆羽来此评泉，“天下第二泉”便驰名天下。惠山山麓“枕山面水”，自古就为历朝历代高官达贵乃至平民百姓争相追逐的风水宝地。两千多年前，楚考烈王以黄歇为相，封于吴邑，吴人立春申君祠于惠山脚下。自唐宋起，一些名门望族便先后在此地兴建祠堂。至明末清初，历代官府敕封或恩准一批官吏名士在此立祠。到了清末民初，随着无锡近代工商业的崛起，又为祠堂文化添上了城市商业文明的精彩一笔，大批外姓高官、达贵和商贾，以及一部分姓氏的支系也纷纷在此择地建祠。每年清明前后，各色人等在此祭祀列祖列宗，扫墓踏青，游山玩水、饮泉品茗，盛况空前。

惠山祠堂群落的集聚，缘于吴地较早萌芽并迅速发展的工商经济。京杭大运河穿城而过，水陆交通十分便利，加上当地民风务实，且极富经商之精髓，至清代，无锡已成为闻名全国的“米码头”“布码头”“丝码头”和“钱码头”。当时无锡紧邻京杭大运河的惠山一带，形成了大米、丝绸、布匹的交易市场及其与之配套的众多钱庄、货栈，四方商贾云集，物资交汇。以徽商为代表的一批外地客商，开始在惠山寺门前的秦园街、香塍街、绣嶂街等搭铺经商，其中一批精明的商人慧眼相中惠山的好风水，决定卜宅而居，沿惠山脚下的惠山浜修筑祠堂。清代惠山古镇所建祠堂达七十余座，堪称惠山祠堂修建的鼎盛期。

到了20世纪初叶，无锡迎来了民族工商业发展的第一个黄金期，惠山古镇也随之形成了大兴祠堂的又一轮热潮。据史料记载，19世纪末至20世纪20年代，无锡已形成了一个以薛、杨、荣、周、唐程、唐蔡六大资本集团为代表的庞大工商实业家群体，开办的工厂数及产值接近甚至超过上海、天津、广州、武汉等大城市。从事纺织、建筑、面粉等行业的杨氏、荣氏、钱氏等工商名家，为方便聚集四方商贾，开始在惠山增建行业会馆性质的祠堂，俗称行业祠、会馆祠，其中以杨藕芳祠最具代

相机：佳能 Canon Eos-1DX，镜头：24-70mm f/2.8，光圈：f/10，快门：1/1000秒，感光度：ISO640，曝光补偿：0EV **惠山古镇寄畅园园中祠**

表性。1896年，参与过洋务运动的官僚杨宗濂、杨宗翰兄弟创办业勤纱厂，这是中国历史上第一家民营大型机器化生产的工厂，生产经营模式已初具现代企业性质。杨家在惠山下本已建有“留耕草堂”，在留耕草堂对面又建了杨藕芳祠。该祠外观为西式小楼，建筑内部中西合璧，折射出民国时期西洋文化与中国传统文化的相互融合。

除了具有吴地祠堂的一般功能和文化元素外，惠山古祠堂群还有一些与众不同的特殊之处。群祠可分为“神祠”“墓祠”“祠”“专祠”“先贤祠”“忠烈祠”“寺院祠”“书院祠”“园林祠”“行会祠”和“会馆祠”等11个大类共27种，其中很多具有江南私家宅邸的格局，形成特有的祠堂园林群，集祭祀、教育、休闲娱乐等诸多功能于一体。其中最有名的为邵文庄公祠，就是邵宝讲学之处。据记载，当时的二泉书院清泉涧溪，茂林修竹，厅堂学舍错落，景观清雅优美。书院建成后，邵宝在此讲学多年，开东林之先声，也使后来的顾宪成在这里写出了“风声雨声读书声声声入耳，家事国事天下事事事关心”这副脍炙人口的楹联。不少祠堂中还建有戏台，供族人在祭祀外休闲娱乐，展现出当时江南地区经济发达、一片繁荣闲适的景象。

“胜地有佳山水，善人多贤子孙。”过郡子祠中的这副楹联，恰如其分地反映了惠山祠堂群的发展轨迹，完整和系统地体现了中国祠堂文化发展的历史年轮。其不愧为一座露天的祠堂文化博物馆，更是一部凝固的吴地史书。当我们穿行于这些历经千年沧桑几近湮没的祠堂之中时，思绪也随之穿越千年，经历着一场中国传统与现代文化之间的心灵碰撞和对话，其传递给我们几乎消失的文化符号、文化内涵和文化价值等信息，可以唤醒我们更好地传承和延续中华人文脉络，弥补不该出现的历史断层。

相机：佳能 Canon Eos-1DX，镜头：24-70mm f/2.8，光圈：f/13，快门：1/500秒，感光度：ISO640，曝光补偿：0EV **运河人家**

The gathering and formation of many temples in the old Huishan town are inextricably linked to social, economic and cultural development in China.

The Great Canal from Beijing to Hangzhou meanders along the east side of Huishan Hill in Wuxi. And on its way, a tributary, called Huishan Creek, flows zigzag to the foot of Huishan Hill. Narrow as it is, it was the only way for the emperors of various dynasties to pay visits to the south of the Yangtze River and Huishan Hill.

The clustering of temples also resulted from the birth and rapid growth of industrial and commercial economy. The Great Canal flows through the city and makes transportation by land and by water very convenient. Moreover, the people here are very matter-of-fact in life and quite adept at business. Therefore, in the Qing Dynasty, Wuxi already enjoyed the national reputation of rice pier, cloth pier, silk pier, and money pier.

In the first years of the 20th century, Wuxi witnessed a golden surge in the development of national industry and commerce. Thereupon, a new wave of temple building occurred in the old Huishan town. At the end of the 19th century and the beginning of the 20th century, Wuxi began to boast six corporations, run by the industrial and commercial tycoons Xue, Yang, Rong, Zhou, Tangcheng, and Tangcai. In order to muster and cater to merchants far and near, temples in the name of businesses began to be built in Huishan.

Besides the general functions and cultural elements of the temples in this vicinity, the cluster of old temples in Huishan seems to be quite usual. The cluster can be categorized into 27 kinds and 11 classes, such as God Temple, Tomb Temple, Clan Temple, Special Temple, Ex-scholar Temple, Martyr Temple, Monastic Temple, Academic Temple, Garden Temple, Gild Temple, and Assembly Temple. Many of them belonged to private owners and were often used for worshipping, education, relaxing and recreational activities.

The couplet "The scenic spots have mountains and rivers / The gentries bear virtuous sons and grandsons" in a temple accurately reflects the development of the temple cluster in Huishan and completely and systematically represents the history of the temple culture development in China. It is actually both an open-air museum of temple culture and a thick history book of temple culture in China. When we walk among the temples that might have fallen into oblivion due to the vicissitudes of time, our thoughts traverse through hundreds of years, hearing a dialogue and witnessing a confrontation between Chinese tradition and modern culture. The information we derive might be the cultural symbols, connotations and values that had nearly disappeared. We might be incited to better inherit and continue the Chinese thread of thoughts and even repair the historical gaps that have happened.

Tips 寻访者须知

佳境指数 Scenery Index：★★★

备选序列：无锡惠山祠堂群——中国世界文化遗产预备名单第14号（国家文物局2012年11月版）

List Number: Temple Cluster at Huishan of Wuxi — No.14 in the preparatory list for Chinese World Heritage (November 2012 Edition by the State Cultural Relics Bureau)

寻访提示：苏南名城无锡历史悠久，人文荟萃，自古有“太湖熟，天下足”之说。因此，鼋头渚、蠡园等太湖名胜不可错过。同时，东林书院、锡惠园林、大运河遗存等自然和人文景观可使人领略吴越文化的精髓。阳春三月，至无锡赏梅也为人生一大乐事。

Location Notes: Wuxi, a well-known city in south Jiangsu, has a long history and has been hometown to many talented people. As the saying goes, a bumper harvest near Taihu Lake can feed all the people under the sun. The scenic spots near Taihu Lake like Tortoise Head Garden and Liyuan Garden should not be missed. Meanwhile, other scenic spots and historic sites such as Donglin Academy and Xihui Park enable people to better understand the essence of Wuyue Culture. Last but not least, in March, appreciating plum blossoms in Wuxi is one of life's great pleasures!

摄影提示：惠山祠堂群具有寺中有祠、祠中有寺；园中有祠、祠中有园等特点，其运河、祠堂、园林、牌坊、碑刻、古桥、民俗、宗教和饮食文化极富吴地特色，摄影创作元素和题材众多，且一年四季都可拍摄。构图上宜以祠堂等为基准点，拍摄位置可多种变化，拍摄景别宜以近景和特写为主，用光上以自

相机：佳能 Canon Eos-1DX，镜头：24-70mm f/2.8，光圈：f/4.5，快门：1/40秒，感光度：ISO500，曝光补偿：0EV **梅园春色**

然顺光和侧光为主，但祠堂等众多拍摄对象位于惠山东麓，下午三时太阳便从惠山山顶西落，光线欠佳，因此创作活动最好在此之前完成。

Tips for Photography: The obvious characteristic in the cluster temples at Huishan is that there are ancestral halls in temples, temples in ancestral halls, ancestral halls in gardens and gardens in ancestral halls. The canal, temples, honorific arches, tablet inscriptions, old bridges, folk customs, religions and local cuisine all bear the special characteristics of Wuyue Culture. They can all serve as themes for photographic creations all the year round.

民俗提示：在惠山祠堂群中，各具地方特色的民俗活动十分丰富。如农历正月十三的“猛将巡会”；二月十二百花生日的“赏红花会”；“二月半，采茶看”的“二月茶会”；三月三的节场庙会；三月十四日的“清明祭会”；三月十五日王母生日的“王母香会”；三月十八日“东狱大帝”黄飞虎生日的“迎神赛会”；五月初五的“端午集会”；七月三十纪念张士诚生日的“寿诞集会”；九月九日的“重阳山会”；十二月初八的“腊八粥会”等。

Brief Introduction to the Local Culture: In the cluster temples at Huishan, a variety of colorful and meaningful local folk activities are held, such as the Generals' Tour on the 13th day of the first lunar month, the Appreciation of Red Flowers on the 12th day of the second lunar month, the February Tea Party, the Market Fair on the 3rd day of the third lunar month, Qingming Festival on the 14th day of the third lunar month, the Birthday of the Heavenly Queen on the 15th day of the third lunar month, the reception of the gods on the 18th day of the third lunar month, the Dragon Boat Festival on the 5th day of the fifth lunar month, the birthday party in memory of Zhang Shicheng (a peasant uprising leader), the Chongyang Festival on the 9th day of the ninth lunar month, the Special Porridge Gathering on the 8th day of the twelfth lunar month, etc.

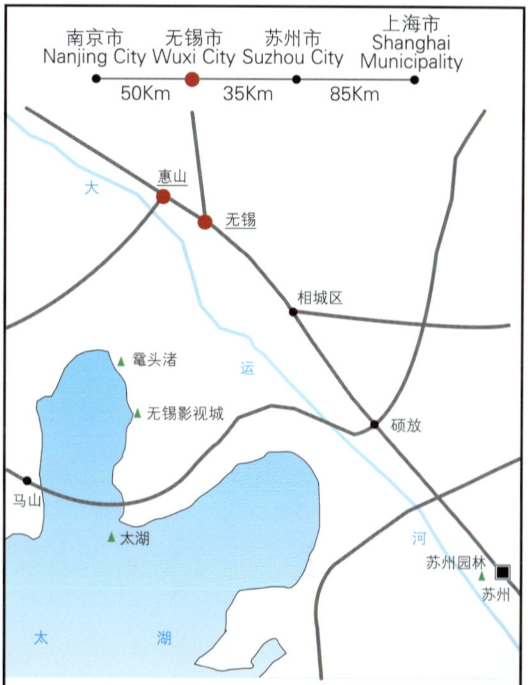

寻访路径
Geographical location

美食提示：无锡饮食属“四大菜系八大帮”的苏菜系苏锡帮，口味偏甜。著名小吃有王星记小笼包、三凤桥酱排骨、清水油面筋等。无锡太湖“三白”银鱼、白虾、白缌鱼为水中上品。秋季湖蟹体壮黄肥。市内主要美食街有：公园路皇亭美食街、崇安市场夜排档等。千百年来，惠山祠堂饮食文化也形成一大特色。主要美食有惠山油酥、清水油面筋、观墩蚕豆茅蓬菌、五里街香粳米、娲皇庙大栗（板栗），胡园的果品惠泉酒、山门口烧饼。

Food Tips: Wuxi food is characteristic of Suxi cuisine, one of the eight major types of the four cuisines of China. The food served there is somewhat sweet. Visitors can enjoy a variety of nice dish and snacks, especially fresh-water fish, shrimp, and crab.

寻觅备选世遗佳境 1
新疆阿尔泰市布尔津县喀纳斯白哈巴村
Kanas Baihaba Village, Burqin County, Altai, Xinjiang

08 净之土 Pure and Clean Land

西北边陲第一村　图瓦人风情园

No.1 Village at the Northwestern Border;
The Tuvan Lifestyle

一条两百余公里的沥青路，从新疆布尔津出发，穿过喀纳斯湖一路向西北延伸，抵达我国西北边陲第一村——白哈巴。

十月的阿尔泰地区，已飘落今年第一场雪，白茫茫的残雪将阿尔泰山脉连绵成蜿蜒起伏的一条线，山上密密麻麻的白桦树，也被这深秋的冰雪染成了金黄色。群山谷底被密林环抱的白哈巴村，从这一刻起跳起了秋天的舞蹈。

The over-200-km-long asphalt road, starting from Burqin in Xinjiang passing via Lake Kanas and stretching northwestward, ultimately leads to the first village at the northwestern border of China: Baihaba.

October in the Altai region witnessed the first snow of the year. The remaining white snow renders the Altai Mountains into a meandering up-and-down line. The dense birch trees on the mountains are also made golden yellow by the icy late-autumn snow. Baihaba Village, located in the deep mountain valley and encircled by dense forests, began its autumn dance from that very moment.

秘之净土

Mysterious Pure Land

白哈巴村位于阿尔泰山脉腹地。一进村，映入眼帘的就是村西那条涓涓流淌的碧河，哈巴在蒙语里是“落差大，迭水高”的意思，白哈巴村的名字，结合了汉语和蒙语，寓意为“落差大的白色河水流过的村子”。阿尔泰山上层林尽染的白桦林，像一排排军容肃立的卫兵，此刻，它们早已换上金黄的铠甲，排列整齐地延伸至白哈巴村里。图瓦人世代居住的木屋、圈养牲畜的栅栏和草垛，就这样错落有致地点缀在蓝天白云，以及金黄、橙红的松

相机：佳能 Canon Eos-1DX，镜头：24-70mm f/2.8，光圈：f/9，快门：1/160秒，感光度：ISO100，曝光补偿：0EV **白哈巴村两山夹峙**

相机：佳能 Canon Eos-1DX，镜头：24-70mm f/2.8，光圈：f/11，快门：1/100秒，感光度：ISO100，曝光补偿：0EV **白哈巴村晨曦**

相机：佳能 Canon Eos-1DX，镜头：24-70mm f/2.8，光圈：f/11，快门：1/100秒，感光度：ISO100，曝光补偿：0EV **白哈巴村秋色**

林和桦林之中。

爬上村东头的山坡，找一个有树阴的地方躺下，碧空万里，天空蓝得惊人，白云仿佛擦着头顶滚滚而过，从远处山脉吹来的微风，带着些许清凉寒意，深吸一口气，满是青草的香味。四周静谧无声，只听得林中河水淙淙，河水来自高山雪峰，此刻正在这空灵的山谷中，自顾自地缓缓流淌，一个温柔的拐弯，推动着另一个温柔的拐弯，仿佛无穷无尽，从远古一直流淌到当下，就这么顺流而去，不知所终。

白桦林边的草原是天然的牧场，虽已不复盛夏的碧绿，却仍铺着一层浅黄一层草绿，星星点点的牛羊，悠闲地低头吃草、饮水，它们似乎看不到远处的雪山已悄悄白了头，仍自顾自地享受着深秋温暖的阳光。渐渐地，牛羊的影子被拉得更长些了，本就不多的游人也陆续地搭车离去，而此刻的白哈巴，却仿佛一场盛大而无声的演出，在万籁俱静中拉开了它神秘的帷幔。

秋日的夕阳从山与山、林与林的间隙中斜射进来，远处的群山、白桦林、村口堆放的草垛、小木屋，仿佛披上了一层薄薄的金纱，大自然用金色的画笔，将原本寻常可见的景物一一勾勒出慑人的光影轮廓。图瓦汉子策马扬鞭，赶着之前还闲庭信步的牛羊群有条不紊地往回走，女人们坐在院子里挑水、择菜准备晚餐，第一缕炊烟从木屋的烟囱里升起，不一会儿便融入了远处的雪山中。紧接着，家家户户的木屋都升起了炊烟，仿佛是提醒出门在外的丈夫，家里已准备好可口的晚餐，就等忙碌了一天的男主人回家。而此时，也是村里的孩子们最快乐的时光，他们在放学的路上互相嬉戏、玩耍、在草垛里捉迷藏，采不知名的野花编成好看的手环。

沐浴在夕阳余晖中的白哈巴，让人想起陶渊明笔下《桃花源记》里那个远离世俗纷扰，“黄发垂髫，怡然自得，良田美池，鸡犬相闻”的世外桃源，从踏入白哈巴的那刻起，你会发现自己已远离熟悉的现代文明的尘嚣，这里的一切是那么自然、

相机：佳能 Canon Eos-1DX，镜头：24-70mm f/2.8，光圈：f/10，快门：1/250秒，感光度：ISO100，曝光补偿：0EV **哈巴河秋水**

原始，就仿佛人类最后的净土。

Baihaba Village is located in the hinterland of the Altai Mountains. Upon entering the village, the first sight that meets people's eyes is the ever-flowing Bihe River. Haba in Mongolian means "the big drop of the river waters" ; therefore, the name Baihaba is a combination of Chinese and Mongolian, referring to the village through which runs the white river , which has gone over a big drop. The deeply-dyed birch trees on top of the Altai Mountains look like arrays of armed soldiers. At this time of the year, they have already put on their golden yellow armors. Neatly arrayed, they stretch into Baihaba Village. The log cabins that the Tuvans have been living in from generation to generation, as well as the cattle sheds and haystacks, are scattered among the brown pine trees and golden yellow birch trees below the white clouds floating in the blue skies.

After reaching the slope of the hill at the eastern end of the village, you might lie down under the shelter of some tree. Looking at the amazingly blue sky with white clouds floating just above your head and intoxicated in the cool, moist breeze from the far-away mountains, you take a deep breath and enjoy the fragrance of the green grass. It is so tranquil that you could even hear the bubbling of the river water that comes down from the snow-covered peaks of high mountains. At this sacred moment in the valleys, the water is simply meandering slowly down the slopes, gently making one turn after another forever and ever. The water has been flowing down from ancient times to the present, on and on endlessly.

The natural pasture beside the white birch forest, though no longer verdant in the summer, is

相机：佳能 Canon Eos-1DX，镜头：24-70mm f/2.8，光圈：f/10，快门：1/320秒，感光度：ISO100，曝光补偿：0EV **额尔齐斯河秋色**

still covered with layers of yellowish and greenish grass, where herds of cattle and sheep are leisurely grazing and drinking water. As if not realizing that the mountains in the distance are already white with snow at the tops, they are still contentedly indulging in the warm sunshine of the late autumn. Little by little, the shadows of the animals are lengthening, and the few tourists are also leaving by bus. However, Baihaba Village at this very moment is just about to raise its mysterious curtain in the quietness as though a grand silent performance is to be staged.

The rays of the setting sun in autumn penetrate through the mountains and the forests, as if draping the distant mountain ranges, white birch forests, haystacks outside the villages, wooden huts, and so on with a golden veil. The Tuvan men on horseback drive the herds of cattle and sheep home. And the women in their respective yards are busy preparing the dinner. The first smoke comes out from the chimney, rising and then soon vanishing into the distant snowy mountains. Shortly after, smoke comes out of log cabin chimneys one after another, seemingly reminding the husbands outdoors that a delicious dinner is waiting for them at home. It is the happiest moment for the youngsters of the village. On their way back home, they are having a wonderful time, either gamboling and playing or enjoying a hide-and-seek game in the haystacks or making beautiful bracelets out of some nameless flowers.

Baihaba Village, submerged in the setting sun, is a land of idyllic beauty. From the very beginning of the time that you step onto the soil of Baihaba, you will find that you are already far, far away from the hustle and bustle of familiar modern civilization.

相机：佳能 Canon Eos-1DX，镜头：24-70mm f/2.8，光圈：f/9，快门：1/320秒，感光度：ISO100，曝光补偿：0EV **白哈巴图瓦人家**

相机：佳能 Canon Eos-1DX，镜头：24-70mm f/2.8，光圈：f/8，快门：1/40秒，感光度：ISO100，曝光补偿：0EV **白哈巴图瓦人家晨雾**

相机：佳能 Canon Eos-1DX，镜头：24-70mm f/2.8，光圈：f/11，快门：1/40秒，感光度：ISO100，曝光补偿：0EV **白哈巴图瓦人家炊烟**

Here everything is so natural and primitive that it is probably the last pure and clean land of the human world.

人之传奇

Legendary People

白哈巴是一个自然生态与古老传统文明相融合的村落，一切都还保存着几百年来固有的原始风貌，到了白哈巴村，一定要入住图瓦人的木屋。图瓦人会用整根原木垒砌、拼接成房屋的外墙和顶棚，再将屋顶搭建成“人字形 ”，除了防雪防灾，这两头通风的三角形地带还是天然的 “储藏室”，用以保存图瓦人抵御漫漫严冬的风干肉制品和喂养牲口的饲料。

走进木屋，你会发现，小小的木屋被女主人打理得如同一间小型艺品馆，炕上铺着花毡，墙上挂着刺绣的帐幔壁毯，地中央是精制的火炉，正煮着甜甜的奶茶……在图瓦族人家里做客，不到半夜12点是没法吃好饭的，好客的图瓦汉子会端上香气四溢的羊肉接待远道而来的客人。新疆的大尾羊大概是全中国最好的羊，不需要过多的配料，撒点盐，不多时，已满屋飘香，咬上一大口，已炖得酥软的肉里满是鲜美的汁水，瞬间羊肉特有的香味便充斥着整个口腔，那种酣畅淋漓的口感一定会让你毕生难忘。吃完肉，再喝上一大碗图瓦人自酿的奶酒，一口口小酌在这里是行不通的，举起杯，就必须一干为敬，豪迈的图瓦人还会吹起民族特有的乐器“苏尔”，远古流传的音律仿佛把客人带回图瓦祖先第一次来到白哈巴的年代……

据传，当年被称为“上帝之鞭”的成吉思汗西征凯旋，途经阿尔泰山喀纳斯湖时，这位几乎征服了半个地球的蒙古帝国可汗当即感叹道：“这才是人间的天堂！是神的眼睛注视的地方，理应属于最有权威的大汗！”于是，他留下近卫军团中的图瓦人部队驻扎下来，为他看守这片人间的天堂。就这样，这群“林中之子”一代又一代地在白哈巴繁衍生息，在口口相

相机：佳能 Canon Eos-1DX，镜头：24-70mm f/2.8，光圈：f/8，快门：1/60秒，感光度：ISO100，曝光补偿：0EV **白哈巴暮归**

相机：佳能 Canon Eos-1DX，镜头：24-70mm f/2.8，光圈：f/11，快门：1/160秒，感光度：ISO100，曝光补偿：0EV **白哈巴牧场**

传中传承着这段迁徙的民族史。

Baihaba is a village that combines natural ecology and traditional ancient civilization; therefore, the original flavor of all things here is still kept intact as it was hundreds of years ago. Upon arriving at Baihaba Village, you must stay inside the log cabins of the Tuvan people, who first build the exterior walls and the ceilings of their huts with whole logs and then the roofs into an inverted V shape. In addition to protecting against snow and disasters, the triangular parts at both ends of the cabin are helpful for ventilation and can also serve as natural storerooms, where the dried meats used by the Tuvan people to survive the long and cold winter and the feed for domestic animals are kept.

As soon as you step inside, you will see that the little log cabin is so well taken care of by the hostess that it looks like a small showroom of art works. The kang, a heatable brick bed, is covered with woolen sheets with floral patterns, on the walls are hung the knitted tapestries, and at the center stands the delicately-made oven on which the sweet and aromatic milk tea is being brewed. A guest in the Tuvan people's home is not likely to finish dinner before midnight. The hospitable Tuvan men treat their guests from far away to aromatic mutton. The fat-tailed sheep in Xinjiang is the best breed of sheep in China. Served without too much seasoning except a little salt, people begin to enjoy the juicy fragrant mutton, which tends to leave an unforgettable impression on the guests. After eating the mutton, people drink a big bowl of self-brewed milk wine. It is not customary here for people to drink sip by sip; instead, they hold up the bowl and drink in one gulp, expressing respect for their guests. Then, the open-hearted and enthu-

西北第一村

siastic Tuvan people will start playing their national musical instrument, and the ancient melody seems to take the guests back to the time when the forefathers of the Tuvan first came to Baihaba.

As the legend goes, Genghis Khan, called the Scourge of God in his time, was returning home after the triumphant victory of his western expedition. When he got to Lake Kanas of the Altai Mountains, the Khan of the Mongolian Empire, who had conquered almost half of the world, could not help exclaiming, "This is, indeed, paradise on Earth. It is a place under the scrutiny of God. Only the most powerful Khan deserves it!" Consequently, the troop of the Tuvan people, the sentinel regiment of the Khan, was left to station here, guarding this paradise on Earth. As a result, the "sons of the forest" began to live and multiply here generation after generation. They have passed their national history of migration by mouth to future generations.

神之花园

Sacred Garden

入夜的白哈巴如亘古般宁静，没有一盏路灯的村庄静悄悄的，只有小木屋里昏黄的炉火，忽明忽暗地发出微弱的亮光，稍微离远一点就伸手不见五指了。抬起头，漫天星斗铺满苍穹，或大或小、或远或近，在人的头顶汇聚成一条天河，指引着远方旅人归家的路。

在图瓦木屋内，酒足饭饱的客人正做着酣甜的梦，在梦境里，一条泛着微光的道路蜿蜒着伸向远方，漆黑的夜空中，启明星发出耀眼的光芒，指引着未知的方向，一路上，四野无声，只有来自心脏坚实有力的脉动声掩饰着兴奋与激动。终于，在路

相机：佳能 Canon Eos-1DX，镜头：24-70mm f/2.8，光圈：f/11，快门：1/100秒，感光度：ISO100，曝光补偿：0EV **哈巴河源头**

的尽头，出现了一个伊甸园般的村庄，白桦林如同卫士般日夜守护这里，而神的眼睛，正温柔地注视着这里的每一棵树、每一个人。一千年的时光，仿佛就凝固在看到它的第一眼中。

黎明的白哈巴像贪睡的客人还没彻底醒来，一切都笼罩在淡蓝色的雾霭之中，村落显得格外清新、安静，尘世的喧嚣和污浊都被高山挡在了外面。鳞次栉比的小木屋经过长时间的风吹雨淋，虽已褪去了原木的新鲜，开始变得暗淡、发黑，但仍散发出松木的香味和厚实的气息。

随着时光的推移，天边渐渐泛白，雪山上升腾着雾气，缥缈朦胧，远处的白桦林突然传来鸟儿清脆的歌声，笼罩在淡淡雾霭中的村子开始明亮了起来。纵横的阡陌与栅栏边，不时传来“哞哞”之声，图瓦大娘走进厨房，不久便端出一道道热气腾腾的早点。勤劳的男人们又赶着牛羊出门放牧去了，不一会儿，成群的牛羊都从各家栅栏里姗姗走出……，突然间一道金光洒下，太阳从高山背后跃了出来，接着无数道光芒像千万条金线照进美丽的白哈巴，顷刻间洒满了整片白桦林和小木屋，晨雾被驱散，整个村庄完全苏醒了过来，和煦的晨光下，图瓦族的老人唱起了那首古老的图瓦歌谣：

我们属于远方

有自己的群山、木屋和炊烟

流水是长长的歌

驼鹿的眼睛就像我的爱人

这安宁，有时绊倒死神的脚步

当云彩擦亮天空

爱人啊，我们就搬到天上去住

图瓦人相信，白哈巴是被神庇佑的地方，而他们，是神选中的子民，世世代代守护着这片神的花园、最后的净土。

（郑罗娜/文）

相机：佳能 Canon Eos-1DX，镜头：24-70mm f/2.8，光圈：f/11，快门：1/100秒，感光度：ISO100，曝光补偿：0EV **喀纳斯湖湖口**

Baihaba Village at night is of absolute serenity. The whole village, without a single street lamp, is quiet and peaceful with only the dim stove fires in the log cabins, shedding shimmering light. A little away from the cabins, you could hardly detect your own fingers. However, looking upward, you will see the vast vault of the sky dotted with stars, both big and small, both distant and near. Over our heads, there appears the Milky Way, showing the way home for the travelers far away.

In the Tuvan log cabins the guests sleep after a hearty meal. They seem to be dreaming a sweet dream, in which a glistening way is meanderingly stretching into the distance. In the pitch dark sky, Venus, which is brilliantly eye-catching, is pointing in an unknown direction. All along the way, there is no sound at all. All one can feel is but the vigorous pulse of the heart. Finally, at the end of the way appears a fable-like village, which is loyally guarded by the birch trees day and night. God gently watches every tree and every person. A thosand years seem to be frozen under his gaze.

Like a very sleepy guest, Baihaba at dawn is not yet entirely awoken. Everything is cloaked in a light bluish mist. Therefore, the village looks especially fresh and tranquil, and the worldly noise and dirtiness are all kept away by the high mountains. Log cabins, row upon row, still emit the fragrance of pine trees and the smell of old times, even though they have lost the original freshness of the logs and begun to turn grayish after having been exposed to rain and wind for a long time.

With the passing of time, the sky turns white and bright and mists rise up at the top of the Snow Mountain, which looks distant and vague. All of a sudden, the clear chirping of birds assails our ears

相机：佳能 Canon Eos-1DX，镜头：24-70mm f/2.8，光圈：f/10，快门：1/80秒，感光度：ISO100，曝光补偿：0EV **白哈巴牧场**

相机：佳能 Canon Eos-1DX，镜头：24-70mm f/2.8，光圈：f/11，快门：1/100秒，感光度：ISO100，曝光补偿：0EV **白哈巴牧场**

from the far-away birch forests. The small village in the light mists also begins to turn bright. Along the criss-crossing paths and by the fences come, from time to time, the mooing of cows and neighing of horses. The Tuvan housewives go into the kitchen and soon reappear with a hot breakfast. Meanwhile, the hardworking men begin to drive the cattle and horses out onto the pastures. In no time, the herds of cattle and sheep will leisurely come out of their respective pens. Very abruptly a golden ray pours down, for the sun has leapfrogged from behind the high mountains. Thereafter, numerous golden rays, like thousands of gold threads, illuminate the beautiful Baihaba Village. Within a twinkling moment, the whole birch forest and small log cabins are all exposed to the sunlight. With mists dispersed, the village comes to itself. In the warm morning light, the Tuvan old men begin to sing that old folk song of theirs:

In the distance where we belong
Stand mountains, cabins and kitchen smoke.
The flowing water is a long song,
The elks' eyes are like my beloved.
God of Death often stumbles in the serenity.
When the clouds clean the sky bright,
My dear, let's move and settle down in Heaven.

The Tuvan people cherish the belief that Baihaba is a sacred place blessed by God. They themselves are the people chosen by Him. Thus, generation after generation, they safeguard this sacred garden, the last pure land of the world.

Tips 寻访者须知

佳境指数 Scenery Index： ★★★★★

备选序列：新疆维吾尔自治区喀纳斯风景名胜区——中国国家自然遗产预备名录（国家建设部2006年7月版）

List Number: The scenic spot of Lake Kanas of the Xinjiang Autonomous Region — in the preparatory list for Chinese World Heritage (July 2006 Edition by the State Ministry of Construction)

寻访提示：白哈巴村处于喀纳斯风景区的核心区域，是一个原始自然生态与古老传统文化共融的村落，一切都还保存着几百年来固有的原始风貌，以图瓦人为主，位于阿尔泰山山脉的山谷平地上，与哈萨克斯坦的大山遥遥相望，村民住的木屋和圈养牲畜的栅栏错落有致地散布在松林和桦林之中，安宁、祥和。村子坐落在一条沟谷之中，建在两条小溪之间的狭长台地上，依山傍水而立。该村的所有建筑均由原木筑成，具有欧式村寨的特色。在落日的傍晚和雾气的清晨，炊烟袅袅飘荡，牛羊满坡，整个村落构绘出了一幅人与自然和谐共处的山水画。秋季一到，山村层林尽染，犹如一块调色板，加之映衬阿尔泰山的皑皑雪峰，构成一幅完美的油画。

Location Notes: Baihaba Village, located at the center of the Kanas scenic spot, is a combination of primitive natural ecology and traditional ancient culture. Almost everything here is still intact and looks as it used to be hundreds of years ago. The people here are mainly the Tuvans. Their villages are located on the plains in the valleys of the Altai Mountains, from which one can get a distant view of the big mountains of Kazakhstan. The villagers' log cabins and their animal pens are scattered in the pine and birch forests, quiet and peaceful. Situated in a valley,

相机：佳能 Canon Eos-1DX，镜头：24-70mm f/2.8，光圈：f/9，快门：1/80秒，感光度：ISO100，曝光补偿：0EV **喀纳斯湖滨秋色**

the village is built on the narrow platform between two streams. All the buildings in the village are constructed with logs, bearing the characteristic of European-style villages. At sunrise and sunset, when the kitchen smoke gradually rises and herds of cattle and sheep are grazing on the slopes, the whole village represents a mountain-and-water painting in which man and nature co-exist harmoniously. With the advent of autumn, the village becomes a sea of colors: red, yellow, green, brown, and so on, almost like a palette. With the snow-covered Altai Mountains in the background, the village makes a perfect oil painting all the year round.

摄影提示：白哈巴是中国为数不多的最佳摄影创作基地之一。一年四季均可创作，尤以秋季为佳。雪峰、桦林、草原、牧群、河流、木屋、草垛、毡房、围栏、牧民、孩童等创作元素较多，尤其是逆光拍摄的秋色作品，张力质感十足。日出日落为最佳拍摄时间。村东侧的高坡观景台，为拍摄日落的最佳位置（应注意的是，村子两山夹峙，下午三时许太阳就落山，村中再无阳光），村西侧的山坡为拍摄日出的最佳位置（但此山较为陡峭，体力欠佳者慎行）。村子内外景色宜人，民俗民风浓郁，均为摄影创作的极好元素，建议摄影者多走多观察，一定会发现更多的惊喜。

Tips for Photography: Baihaba is one of the few places most appropriate for photographic creation in China. Photos can be taken in all four seasons; however, autumn is best. A large number of elements, such as snow peaks, birch forests, pastures and grasslands, herds of animals, rivers, log cabins, haystacks, yurts, fences, herdsmen and children, could all serve as the subjects of photography. Photos with backlight in autumn are supposed to be the best. The best time for taking pictures is at sunrise and sunset. The ob-

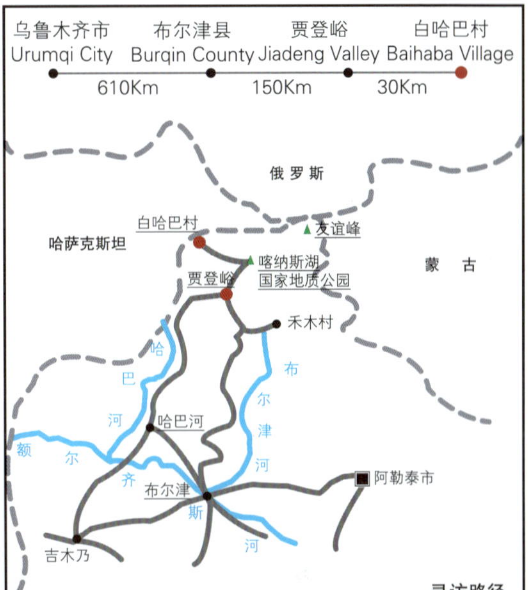

寻访路径
Geographical location

servation deck on the slope at the eastern side of the village may be chosen as the most appropriate position for taking pictures of the sunset. Attention should be paid to the fact that, as the village is flanked by mountains on both sides, the sun sets at 3 o'clock in the afternoon, after which there is no more sunlight in the village. The slope on the western side is most suitable for taking pictures of the sunrise. However, as the slopes here are rather steep, those who are not physically fit are advised not to go there. The views in and out of the village are very pleasant, and the folk customs are quite rich; therefore, they could all serve as nice elements for photographic production. Photographers are advised to walk around and keep their eyes wide open, for they are sure to chance upon many more surprising discoveries.

民俗提示和美食提示请参照第四章秋醉山乡。

As for the brief introduction of the local culture and the food tips, please see the description of Chapter 4, Mountain village in autumn.

09 舞之领者
At the Forefront of Dance

中国现代舞一代宗师吴晓邦之故里
江南水乡临水民居之典范

Hometown of Wu Xiaobang, Pioneer of Modern Dance in China;
Exemplary Waterside Residences in South China

与如今众多嘈杂喧嚣的江南名镇相比，江苏省太仓市沙溪镇似乎有些落寞，可这也正是它难能可贵和令人向往之处。

Compared with other noisy towns in the region south of the Yangtze River, Shaxi Town, Taicang City, Jiangsu Province, seems somewhat lonely and desolate. However, it's precisely because of this that makes it an attraction.

为民族复兴而舞

Dancing for National Revival

尽管这里的小桥流水，枕河人家景致极富韵味，令人陶醉，但是，沙溪镇悠久的历史和深厚的人文底蕴，更能使寻访者在此审视人生、涤荡灵魂。

在这里，我们重新认识了我国新舞蹈艺术的开拓者、播火人吴晓邦先生。这位将舞蹈事业作为终身追求、把自己的命运与民族的复兴大业紧紧联系在一起的艺术宗师，令人高山仰止。

1906年12月，吴晓邦生于沙溪镇一户殷实人家，原名吴锦荣，幼年时期饱受儒家文化熏陶。他自幼性格叛逆，青年时期受五四新文化运动和中国人民反帝反封建五卅运动的影响，积极投身爱国进步活动。1926年他考入武昌南湖武汉中央军事政治学校，曾参加由中央军事政治学校入伍生临时组编的中央独立师，担任叶挺团见习排排长，西征平定杨森、夏斗寅叛乱。后因时局动荡，家庭百般阻挠，他不得不选择东渡日本留学。

青年时期（1929—1936年），他曾三渡东瀛，早年留学日本并非研修舞蹈专业，而是专修小提琴。因仰慕波兰爱国主义音乐家肖邦的艺术才华和爱国情怀，他把自己的名字改为吴晓邦。一次偶然的机会，他在东京大隈会堂看到了由早稻田大学学生表演的舞蹈《群鬼》，舞蹈用极富张力的肢体语言，揭示了现实社会的黑暗与罪恶，深深震撼了他的心灵，浓烈的民族忧患意识，使他夜不能寐，立

相机：佳能 Canon Eos-1DX，镜头：24-70mm f/2.8，光圈：f/11，快门：1/200秒，感光度：ISO200（照片经后期处理） **太仓沙溪镇临水民居**

志献身中国的舞蹈事业。他的抉择和中国文坛巨匠鲁迅先生的弃医从文之举，有异曲同工之妙。

于是，吴晓邦转入日本高田雅夫舞蹈研究所，随高田苗子学习芭蕾，接着在江口隆哉、宫操子夫妇指导下学习现代舞，潜心研究现代舞先驱、美国女舞蹈家邓肯和欧洲现代舞创始人、德国女舞蹈家维格曼等的舞蹈理论，从中吸取养分。他的处女作《无静止的运动》和独舞《傀儡》，皆在东京公演。《傀儡》以模拟的手法，揭露和讽刺了一个摇尾乞怜“满洲国皇帝”的卖国贼丑恶嘴脸。

1932年，吴晓邦从日本归国，将现代舞蹈艺术引入中国，率先提倡新舞蹈艺术运动，主张为人生而舞，提倡用舞蹈反映现实人生的苦难与希望。他分别于1932年和1935年在上海开办中国第一所舞蹈学校和中国第一家舞蹈研究所，并于1935年和1937年举办了他自己、也为中国近代史上“第一、第二次个人舞蹈作品发表会”，创作演出了揭露社会黑暗、讽刺虚无主义、向往和憧憬光明的舞蹈《送葬》《傀儡》《黄浦江边》《小丑》《奇梦》《拜金主义》等十几个作品，开创了中国近现代舞蹈史上舞蹈艺术创作之先河。这些以反映现实生活为主题的“新舞蹈”，犹如清风拂面，对那些充斥于大都会灯红酒绿的色情、媚俗的颓废舞蹈，进行了有力的冲击与涤荡。

1937年，“七·七”事变爆发，国家和民族面临生死存亡的危急关头，吴晓邦血脉贲张，毅然离开上海，投身到抗日救亡的行列中。他这一时期的作品，在内容和形式上，都紧随时代脉搏。他参加了由文艺工作者组成的抗日救亡演剧四队，活跃在京沪线上。他用聂耳的音乐创作了同名舞蹈《义勇军进行曲》，以著名作曲家贺绿汀的同名歌曲创作群舞《游击队员之歌》，每场演出，观众群情激奋，同仇敌忾。他还排演了小舞剧《打杀汉奸》，根据《大刀进行曲》编排了《大刀舞》，排演了舞蹈《流亡三部曲》等充满爱国激情、具有强烈感染力的舞蹈作品，将“新舞蹈”汇入了民族救亡和复

相机：佳能 Canon Eos-1DX，镜头：24-70mm f/2.8，光圈：f/11，快门：1/125秒，感光度：ISO200（照片经后期处理） **太仓沙溪镇戚浦塘**

兴的主流。

1939年后，为实现自己的艺术追求，吴晓邦舍弃优裕的生活，积极奔走于上海、桂林、成都、重庆、广东等地，展开新舞蹈的教学和演出活动，创作了《丑表功》《思凡》《饥火》等十几出脍炙人口的舞蹈作品。《丑表功》分“献媚”“取宠”“得意忘形”“败落”四个段落，舞蹈采用戏谑式的乐曲和面具，尖锐地揭露和鞭挞了汉奸卖国贼的行径。《饥火》通过感情色彩的变幻和动作线条的流动，蕴含“朱门酒肉臭，路有冻死骨”的主题。同时，他还创作了舞剧《虎爷》《宝塔牌坊》和歌舞剧《罂粟花》《春的消息》等大量优秀作品。《宝塔牌坊》是用舞蹈艺术形象，揭露了封建制度对青年男女爱情的摧残，批判“忠孝节义”的虚伪性。

1945年，吴晓邦进入了艺术生涯的新阶段。在周恩来的安排下，吴晓邦夫妇到达革命圣地延安，执教于鲁迅艺术学院。后随“鲁艺”北上，先后在华北联大文艺部、内蒙古文工团、东北民主联军、沈阳鲁迅艺术学院从事舞蹈教学，并担任“四野”舞蹈团团长，其间创作了蒙古舞《希望》《内蒙人民三部曲》(《内蒙之路》)。伴随着解放军南下进军的嘹亮号角，他创作了由东北一直舞到海南岛的《进军舞》，为舞蹈现实主义的创作奠定了基础。

1950年，应欧阳予倩邀请，吴晓邦主持了中央戏剧学院“舞蹈运动干部训练班”，为新中国舞蹈事业培养了一大批骨干和中坚力量。1952年至1953年，吴晓邦担任中央民族歌舞团首任团长，主办“少数民族歌舞演出专场”，率领民族文工团赴云南、贵州、康定、甘孜等地大规模采风和演出。1957年，经周恩来总理批准，吴晓邦创立了“天马舞蹈艺术工作室”，开始着力于“古曲新舞”的创作研究，尝试结合古代音乐、诗歌、绘画等，探索一条戏曲舞蹈新路。短短三年时间，他在“天马”创作了《梅花三弄》《渔夫乐》《春江花月夜》《一枝春》《十面埋伏》等数十个优秀作品，并在全国巡演，观众好评如潮。

尽管他在十年浩劫中历经磨难，但丝毫没有动摇他为民族复兴而舞的坚强信念。改革开放以后，在连任“舞协主席”的十余年间，吴晓邦不顾年老体弱，不遗余力地著书立说，培育新人，出版了《我的舞蹈艺术生涯》《舞蹈新论》等数十部专著，形成了系统的舞蹈理论体系。

这位具有时代高度的中国当代舞蹈泰斗、新舞蹈艺术的一代宗师，走过了漫长的风雨历程，收获了丰富的舞者人生，于1995年7月8日，停下了他六十多年的辉煌舞步，病逝于北京。

Even simply the scenery of small bridges over streams, of houses along the water, is richly intoxicating. Nevertheless, the long history and profound cultural deposits of Shaxi Town are even more able to help visitors to scrutinize their own lives and cleanse their souls.

It is here that we are able to recognize, once more, Mr. Wu Xiaobang, the pioneer and promoter of the art of modern dance in China. This artist, for whom dancing was a lifelong pursuit and who associated his own destiny closely with the national revival, deserves admiration.

In December, 1906, Wu Xiaobang was born with a silver spoon in his mouth in Shaxi. He was first named Wu Jingrong and was strictly taught Confucian culture in childhood. However, he was rebellious in personality even as a child. In his youth, he was so strongly influenced by the May 4th Movement and the May 30th Movement that he plunged himself into patriotic, progressive movements.

In his youth (from 1929 to 1936), he went to Japan three times. At first, he went to Japan not to study dancing, but to major in violin. Because of his

相机：佳能 Canon Eos-1DX，镜头：24-70mm f/2.8，光圈：f/11，快门：1/160秒，感光度：ISO200（照片经后期处理） **太仓沙溪镇戚浦塘**

admiration for the Polish composer Chopin's artistic talent and patriotism, he changed his name to Wu Xiaobang. On one occasion, he chanced upon a dance of performance of *A Group of Ghosts* by the students of Waseda University in Tokyo. The dancers revealed the darkness and evil of the real society by means of such drastic body language that Mr. Wu was touched heart and soul. His strong sense of worry for his country and people kept him wide awake night after night. Finally, he decided to dedicate himself to a career of dance in China.

Therefore, he was transferred to an institute of dance in Japan. He began with ballet and then shifted to modern dance. He seriously studied the different schools of modern dance of the United States and Germany. His maiden work *Non-static Movement* and solo dance *Puppet* were staged in Tokyo. *Puppet* revealed and satirized, by means of simulation, the ugly traitor's face of the Emperor of Manchuria.

In 1932, he returned home from Japan. He introduced modern dance into China. He initiated the New Dance Art Movement, advocating the idea of dancing for life and promoting the use of dance to reflect the misery and hope of real life. In 1932 and 1935, respectively, he set up the first dance school and first dance research institute in Shanghai. And in 1935 and 1937, he held the press conferences on his own first and second dance works, which was also unprecedented in the history of modern China. During the conferences, he presented more than a dozen dances, such as *Funeral*, *Puppet*, *Beside the Huangpu River*, *Clown*, *Grotesque Dreams*, *Money Worship*, etc., that he had created

东南第一镇

相机：佳能 Canon Eos-1DX，镜头：24-70mm f/2.8，光圈：f/11，快门：1/160秒，感光度：ISO200，曝光补偿：0EV (照片经后期处理) **沙溪镇单孔石拱桥**

with the intention of disclosing the social darkness, satirize nihilism, and look forward to a bright future. His dances actually initiated creative artistic dance in modern.

In 1937, when the July Seventh Incident broke out and the country was at a critical moment of life and death, Mr. Wu Xiaobang, excited and indignant, decisively left Shanghai to participate in the Anti-Japanese National Salvation. The dances he created during this period were closely related to the pulse of the times both in content and in style. He joined the troupe of the Anti-Japanese National Salvation with other artists, and they were quite active along the Beijing-Shanghai Railway. He created a dance *March of the Volunteers* with the music composed by Nie E, and a group dance *Song of Guerrillas* based on the song of the same name composed by the famous musician He Luting. Every performance won the audiences' fervent responses and aroused their indignation against the Japanese invaders. In addition, he conducted and staged many other patriotic dances. He introduced the new dances into the mainstream of the national salvation and resurrection.

After 1939, in pursuit of his artistic dreams, Mr. Wu Xiaobang gave up his comfortable life and, instead, traveled to Shanghai, Guilin, Chengdu, Chongqing, Guangdong and other places, busily engaged in teaching and performing the new form of dance.

In 1945, Mr. Wu Xiaobang entered a new phase of his art career. With the help of Zhou Enlai, he and his wife arrived in Yan'an, where he taught at Lu Xun Art College. Later on, he went north with

相机：佳能 Canon Eos-1DX，镜头：24-70mm f/2.8，光圈：f/11，快门：1/200秒，感光度：ISO200，曝光补偿：0EV（照片经后期处理） **沙溪镇临水民居**

the college. Subsequently, he taught dancing in the Art Department of North China University, Inner Mongolia Song and Dance Ensemble, the Northeast Democratic Allied Army, and Shenyang Lu Xun Art College, and and at the same time worked as the Director of the Dance Troupe of the Fourth Field Army. During this period, he created the Mongolian dances *Hope and Road of Inner Mongolia*. Accompanied by the blaring bugle of the PLA soldiers marching southward, he created *Dance of Marches*, which was staged from Northeast China to Hainan Island, laying a solid foundation for the realistic creation of dances.

In 1950, at the invitation of Mr. Oyang Yuqian, Mr. Wu Xiaobang sponsored dancers' cadre training at the Central Academy of Drama, thus cultivating a large number of dancers who would be the backbone of dance in China. In 1952 and 1953, he served as the first Leader of the Central National Song and Dance Troupe. He organized special performances of *Minority Peoples' Songs and Dances*. He led the National Song and Dance Ensemble to Yunnan, Guizhou, Kangding, Ganzi, and other places to collect local songs and dances and to present performances as well. In 1957, approved by Zhou Enlai, Mr. Wu Xiaobang established Tian Ma Dancing Art Studio, beginning the creation and research of old music and new dance to explore the possibility of combining ancient music, poetry and painting for operatic dancing. Within three years, he put forward more than ten works, which received favorable responses during performances on tour all over the country.

After the adoption of the opening up and reform policy, he served as Chairman of the Dance Association for more than ten years. In defiance of advanced age and declining health, Mr. Wu Xiao-bang still dedicated himself to the writing of books and to the cultivation of new dancers. He had quite a large number of works published, such as *My Dancing Career, New Theory on Dancing*, etc., thus forming a systematic theory of dance.

This giant and master of modern Chinese dance passed away in Beijing on July 8, 1995, after making many glorious achievements over the course of his some 60 years.

东南古镇第一乡

No.1 Ancient Town in the Region South of the Yangtze River

沙溪，又名印溪、团溪，唐代已聚村落，佛教寺庙兴盛；元代自涂菘西迁，形成市集；明代商运通达，成为商贸重埠；清末民初近代工业起步，新式教育推行，开风气之先。历朝历代沙溪均为太仓大镇。志书记载：“镇地延袤可数里，多富家巨室，其缙绅学士几当一州之半，为士好文章，习仪观，济济相望，而民之耕于野者，亦勤稼穑谨财用，有蟋蟀代檀之风，人称乐土。”古有“戚浦听潮、虹桥夕照、长寿钟声、竹林晚翠、松墩鹤唳、北院荷香、通津渔火和天泉望月”八景，以其富庶与秀美，赢得“东南十八乡、沙溪第一乡”之誉。

除了具备江南水乡的基本特征外，别致的临水建筑、古宅密集的老街和古朴雄浑的石桥，是沙溪与众不同的三大亮点。

绵延数里的戚浦塘在古镇中穿行而过，两岸的

相机：佳能 Canon Eos-1DX，镜头：24-70mm f/2.8，光圈：f/11，快门：1/250秒，感光度：ISO200，曝光补偿：0EV（照片经后期处理） **沙溪镇单孔石拱桥**

临水民居错落有致、鳞次栉比。沙溪镇因水而兴，家家有水埠，户户有船棚。在典型的水巷风貌中，建有众多沿河吊脚楼。临水一面，木格漏窗，尽显精彩，既可从窗口眺望河景，又可汲水购物，形成了一道别有韵味的风景线。

依然如故的沙溪老街与戚浦塘平行延伸。沿街的古宅民居粉墙黛瓦，风格别致。民居多为二层砖木结构，前后多为三进，底楼店铺挑梁出檐、斗拱齐全。梁拱上装饰浮云、花卉等雕刻精美的吉祥图案。二进和三进是风格各异的客厅和起居室，“印溪书舍”“南野斋居”“莲蕊楼”等古宅名居充满人文气息。古园东荫园则为宋代隐士瞿孝祯所建的私家园林。

沙溪老街自东至西坐落着三座横跨老戚浦塘的明清古桥。分别为明代的新桥、宋代的庵桥，以及始建于明代的义兴桥。均为清一色古朴苍劲的单孔石拱桥。桥上人来人往，桥下舟楫鱼贯而行，天光水色交相辉映。

沙溪镇水乡风光古韵犹存、引人入胜，但更能激起访客感叹不已的，是中华民族漫漫复兴之路，正是因为涌现了许多像吴晓邦这样的领舞者，才使中华民族屹立于世界之林。

In addition to all the common features of the towns in the region south of the Yangtze River, Shaxi is unique in the special waterside architecture, the old streets amidst the old houses, and the simple but solid stone bridges.

Qipu Creek, meandering for several kilometers, goes through the ancient town. The civil residences by the waters, high and low and row by row, look quite attractive. Shaxi Town was formed and developed because of the waters. Every house has a quay and every family has a boat shelter. Among the typical water scenery are many suspended buildings above the creeks. Alongside the waters are wooden-framed open windows. People can either enjoy a wonderful view of the creek or get water and shop at the same time. What an unusual sight!

The old Shaxi Street is parallel with Qipu Creek. The old civil residences along the street are special with their white walls and black tiles. Most of them are of two stories and of three rows.

From east to west along the old street, there are three old bridges above Qipu Creek, the Xinqiao Bridge of the Ming Dynasty, the Yanqiao Bridge of the Song Dynasty, and the Yixing Bridge of the Ming Dynasty. They are all single span stone arch bridges. On the bridges people walk to and fro, and under them boats float one after another. The sky and the water make each other more radiant and beautiful.

With the old charm of an aquatic place, Shaxi Town is most attractive. What makes the visitors even more inspired is that among the Chinese people on the long road of renaissance emerge more and more leading dancers like Mr. Wu Xiaobang, thus enabling China to stand tall among all the nations of the world.

Tips 寻访者须知

佳境指数 Scenery Index： ★★★

备选序列： 江南水乡古镇・江苏省太仓市沙溪镇——中国世界文化遗产预备名单第15号（国家文物局2012年11月版）

List Number: Shaxi Town, Taicang City, Jiangsu Province, an Ancient Town South of the Yangtze River — No.15 in the preparatory list for Chinese World Heritage (November 2012 Edition by the State Cultural Relics Bureau)

寻访提示： 江南是一处让人充满回忆的地方，徜徉在水乡古镇之中，会令人感慨这片土地经久不衰的繁荣。周边分布风格各异的甪直、锦溪、周庄、千灯、同里、木渎、光福等江南名镇。若在桃红柳绿，烟雨蒙蒙的阳春三月前往踏青寻幽，更能领略江南水乡的别样韵致。

Location Notes: The region south of the Yangtze River is a place full of memories. A saunter in the old town will make people realize the ever-lasting prosperity and wealth here. In this vicinity are scattered such well-known towns as Luzhi, Jingxi, Zhouzhuang, Qiandeng, Tongli, Mudu, Guangfu, etc. A visit to these places in early spring when peach flowers are about to go pink, willow trees are about to turn verdant, and misty rains are about to drizzle will enable people to more thoroughly appreciate the uncommon local beauty.

摄影提示： 沙溪的摄影创作活动可紧紧围绕“古巷同户宽，古街三里长，古桥为单孔，古宅均挑梁，户户有雕花，家家有长窗，桥在前门进，船在门前荡”的民谣而展开，临水古居、千年老街和单孔古桥为主要创作元素，若能捕捉到展现江南水乡风情的人文活动，更能为作品增光添彩。

相机：佳能 Canon Eos-1DX，镜头：24-70mm f/2.8，光圈：f/11，快门：1/125秒，感光度：ISO200，曝光补偿：0EV（照片经后期处理） **太仓沙溪镇**

Tips for Photography: Photographers can focus on old lanes and streets, the single spans of the bridges, waterside residences with unusual windows, etc. Of course, the local activities can enhance the beauty of the photos.

民俗提示：要了解江南古镇的民俗民风，可至坐落在该镇橄榄岛陆京士故居内专题收集和展示江南民俗生活、生产用品和用具的沙溪江南民俗用品馆看看。该馆共收藏有生活用品、生产用具两大类四百余个品种近千件明、清、民国至改革开放前的传统物品。老屋里，摆满了各式各样的木器、铜器、竹器、陶器、瓷器及大型家具、老式服装等生产生活用品，其中有纺织用的手摇纺车、脚踏纺车、织布机，有农用机具风车（轧米机）、独轮车、罱泥网，有日常生活用品千工床、立桶、汤婆子和陶瓷品酒坛、钵头、馆箩、罩篮，等等，令人目不暇接。这些展品是江南民族风情、民族文化、民间传统技艺的直接载体和物化表现，直观地反映了社会历史、社会生产、社会生活的真实情况，留下了历史变迁的深深轨迹。

Brief Introduction to the Local Culture: If you want to have a better understanding of the local folk culture, you'd better go and have look at the former residence of Lu Jingshi, on Ganlan Island, where there is a collection and exhibition of implements from daily life, production tools and utensils from the region south of the Yangtze River.

美食提示：沙溪凤和楼的酱肉、鳝丝面、虾仁面、大排面等各式浇头面点远近闻名。陆家牛杂面是镇中当下人气最旺的美食，注重牛肉的烧制火候，在汤料上精益求精，力求口齿留香、回味悠长。杨嘉振卤菜坊以酥香鲜醇见长，“老法爊鸡”“严家老鸭”等招牌熟食吸引着来往食客。熏鱼、糖醋小排、猪头糕等名菜数十年来长盛不衰。

Food Tips: Shaxi is famous for pork and fresh-water fish dishes and noodles. It offers dozens of

寻访路径
Geographical location

dishes of local specialty, and anyone who tastes them will always have a long memory of these delicacies.

閩海蓬萊

寻觅备选世遗佳境 1
福建省泉州市清源山风景名胜区
Qingyuan Mountain, Quanzhou, Fujian

10 历史的脉动
Pulse of History

海上丝绸之路宋元时期之始发港
世界多元文化兼容并蓄之道教圣地

Starting Port for the Silk Road on the Sea in the Song and Yuan Dynasties;
Sacred Place for Taoism and Merging Place of Multiple Cultures

“山不在高，有仙则名。”在中国的名山大岳中，“儒、道、释”三教并存并不鲜见，但同时又能与伊斯兰教、摩尼教、印度教等世界多种宗教兼容并蓄的人文名山，唯素有“闽海蓬莱第一山”之誉的泉州清源山莫属。

胜景天成的清源山，坐落于台湾海峡西岸的闽南大地。千百年来，她吸纳日月之精华，宛若慈祥的大地之母，张开温暖的怀臂，呵护着美丽富饶的晋江平原，守望着古老而充满活力的鲤城泉州。

作为国家首批历史文化名城之一的泉州市，千年大美难于言表。早在唐代，泉州刺桐港就是我国四大外贸港口之一，至宋元时期，泉州成为海上丝绸之路的重要始发港，被誉为“东方第一大港”。多元文化在这里交流融会，造就了浩若繁星的历史名人、商界精英，以及南戏、南音、南少林等辉耀古今的人文遗产，而集大美者则是钟灵毓秀的清源山。

当你走进清源山，亲近清源山，对话清源山，才能领略这座“泉南佛国”大道清源的人文魅力。

感悟大道清源之一，是这里有我国现存最大、年代最久、艺术最美的道教老君石刻造像。据《泉州府志》载：“羽仙岩，在罗、武二山之下，今名老君岩。”“石像天成，有好事者略施雕琢。”明代著名史家何乔远《闽书》亦载：“今曰老君岩，盖石镌李老君宴坐像，高十余尺，不知何年？”这尊完全是由整座巨石构成的老君造像，高近六米，宽八米，厚约七米，席地面积达五十余平方米，其左手扶膝，右手凭几，垂耳飘髯，指能弹物，目光炯炯，独具超尘脱俗、仙风道骨的神韵。整座石刻造像神态浩然，豁达大度，和蔼近人，充满魅力，堪称我国石刻艺术的瑰宝。

比石刻造像更引领我们追寻大道源头的是老子充满穿透力的哲学思想。汉代著名史学家司马迁在《史记·老子韩非列传》中记述：“老子姓李氏，名耳，字伯阳，谥日聃。”老子留给后人的五千字《道德经》，阐释了致虚守静、立德修身的朴

相机：佳能 Canon Eos-1DX，镜头：24-70mm f/2.8，光圈：f/11，快门：1/500秒，感光度：ISO500，曝光补偿：0EV **清源山南岩胜境**

素哲理。他主张“善而下之”，不与外来文化思想与宗教论短长，致外来文化和宗教最终与中华优秀传统文化妥协，在道的基础上融入中华文化。这就是“有容乃大”“厚德载物”的文化胸襟，也是“上善若水，水善利万物而不争”的实力。体现了中国古代先哲深层次的精神追求和行为准则，渗透在中华民族的民族心理和民族性格中，成为滋养炎黄子孙精神家园的重要源泉。

如今，这尊举世罕见的道德天尊羽化造像，成为世人朝觐的千古灵圣，也为中华道家文化留下世代延续的精神香火……

感悟大道清源之二，是这里有我国现存年代最早、保存最完整、位于最东南的元代喇嘛教“三世佛”石雕造像。“三世佛”是13世纪以来藏传佛教（俗称喇嘛教）佛堂中所供奉的主要佛像。清源山碧霄岩“三世佛”为摩崖浮雕，作长方形石龛，高三米，宽五米。“三世佛”并排结跏坐在仰覆莲花座上，中尊为现在佛，左尊为过去佛，皆作触地印之降魔相，但过去佛左掌上托钵，右尊为未来佛，作施定印之禅定相，皆为吐蕃式样。整座造像布局匀称，雕工精湛，造型优美。

造像左侧的元代造像记事石刻碑文中记载，元代至正二十七年（1367年）十月丙年日，岩僧志聪题刻于摩崖记文云：“透碧霄北山第一胜概。至元壬二十九年（1292年）间，灵武唐吾氏广威将军阿沙公来临泉郡，登兹岩而奇之，刻石为三世佛像，饰以金碧，构殿崇奉，以为焚修祝圣之所……”。现殿堂为1991年重修，三层敞开式阁楼，成品字形布局，具有泉州古建筑特色。从崖下仰望，整座建筑物古朴典雅，气势雄伟，蔚为壮观。

此外，基督教、印度教、摩尼教等，以及闽南民间诸神位都在清源山留下了遗迹。清源山多元文化相容并蓄的文化生态，展示了泉州海纳百川的博大胸怀。

感悟大道清源之三，是这里有我国现存最古老、最完好的唐代伊斯兰教圣迹。据明代何乔远

相机：佳能 Canon Eos-1DX，镜头：24-70mm f/2.8，光圈：f/14，快门：1/60秒，感光度：ISO500，曝光补偿：0EV **清源山老君造像**

《闽书》记载：唐武德年间（618—626年），穆罕默德遣四贤徒来华，一贤传教广州；二贤传教扬州；三贤沙仕谒、四贤我高仕传教泉州，卒葬灵山。现存两墓并列，墓盖用花岗岩雕刻，墓后倚山建马蹄形回廊，高约三米，回廊中的几根石柱颇似织布的梭子，古建筑专家称之为梭形柱，具有典型的唐代建筑特色。廊内有历代石碑五方，正中为元至治二年（1322年）立的阿拉伯文辉绿岩碑刻，记述两位先贤在法厄福尔时代（系古代阿拉伯对唐朝皇帝的称呼）来到这个国度。右侧一方为明永乐十五年（1417年）郑和第五次下西洋途经泉州，来此祭告行香后属下为之所立的记事碑，上刻："钦差总兵太监郑和前往西洋忽鲁谟斯等国公干，永乐十五年五月十六日于此行香，望圣灵庇佑。镇扶蒲和日记立。"墓上的石亭系1962年重建，墓周围还有一些历代的伊斯兰教徒的石棺墓，上刻伊斯兰教常用的"云月"图案或《古兰经》片段。这些遗存成为证明泉州海外交通史，以及伊斯兰教传播史的重要史据。

感悟大道清源之四，是这里有我国现存最多的宋代祈风石刻群。九日山以"山中无石不刻字"饮誉宇内。历代摩崖石刻达七十余方，其中海交祈风及市舶司事石刻有十三方，记载了从南宋淳熙元年至咸淳二年（1174—1265年）冬季遣舶和夏季回舶的祈风情况，由太守亲临主持，仪式隆重，市舶提举及其他官员参加，向海神通远王祈祝"蕃舶"一帆风顺，来往平安。当时海潮涨满金溪，百舸云集，沿岸旌旗蔽空，鼓乐喧天，人马车轿，连绵数里。昔日祈风场面，十分壮观。

这些石刻是古泉州海外交通和海上丝绸之路的重要史迹，也是我国与亚非各国人民友好往来的见证。宋元时期，泉州与埃及的亚历山大港齐名为世界大港，与世界上一百多个国家和地区有着通商贸易，开放赋予了泉州包容的个性。泉州还是我国著名的侨乡，七百多万祖籍泉州的侨胞分布全世界百余座城市和地区，泉州在中国史和世界史上均有特

相机：佳能 Canon Eos-1DX，镜头：24-70mm f/2.8，光圈：f/10，快门：1/1250秒，感光度：ISO500，曝光补偿：0EV **清源山海神庙**

相机：佳能 Canon Eos-1DX，镜头：24-70mm f/2.8，光圈：f/10，快门：1/100秒，感光度：ISO500，曝光补偿：0EV **清源山弥陀岩**

大道清源

殊的地位。联合国教科文组织“海上丝绸之路”综合考察团曾对此胜迹赞叹不已，临返之前又留下考察记事石刻一方，为九日山增添了新的光彩。

千百年来，泉州的海外交往，推动了海洋文明、海上丝路文明与闽南文明的融合，构成了泉州独特的社会生态基因，为泉州社会、经济和文化发展注入了生生不息的活力。

在清源山，每一处文明遗存，都有一段历史的脉冲。在一草一木之间，自然和人文正穿越历史的时空相约而至，神秘的神，与神圣的道，可以与世俗社会相融相通。

当我们重新审视这一方青山碧水，感悟之情悄然而生。这是一处绝美山水与璀璨人文水乳交融的所在，也是一处心灵与圣灵跨时空对话的所在，更是一处当今国人心灵深处精神洗礼的所在。

On all the famous mountains in China, it is by no means uncommon to see Confucianism, Taoism and Buddhism co-exist; however, it is only on Qingyuan Mountain in Quanzhou that the above three religions also co-exist with Islam, Hinduism, and other religions of the world.

Boasting wonderful scenery, Qingyuan Mountain is located in south Fujian on the west side of the Taiwan Strait. For thousands of years, the mountain has looked like a benevolent mother, stretching out her arms to embrace the beautiful and prosperous Jinjiang Plain, and keeping an eye on the ancient and vigorous Quanzhou City.

Only when you approach, step into, and have a dialogue with Qingyuan Mountain, will you be able to appreciate its literary charm.

The first thing people will appreciate is the stone-carving statue of Laojun, meaning The Grand Supreme Elderly Lord, which is the largest, oldest and most beautiful in China today. This

相机：佳能 Canon Eos-1DX，镜头：24-70mm f/2.8，光圈：f/16，快门：1/640秒，感光度：ISO500，曝光补偿：0EV **九日山海神庙**

statue of Laojun, carved out of a single piece of huge rock, is approximately six meters tall, eight meters wide and about seven meters thick, covering an area of some fifty square meters. With his left hand on his knee and right hand on a side table, with long earlobes and a long beards, and a pair of sharp eyes, he obviously bears an unearthly verve. The whole stone-carved statue looks so lifelike, magnanimous, amiable, and inviting that it is a treasure of the stone-carving art of China.

However, it is the penetrating philosophical thoughts of Lao Zi, more than the stone-carving statue itself, that lead us to the exploration of the origin of Taoism. Lao Zi was a philosopher in the Spring and Autumn Period, and founder of Taoism. His 5,000-word book *Dao De Jing* advocates his simple philosophy of how to live a moral and simple life. It is his ideas that usually allowed foreign culture and religion to reconcile with the excellent traditional Chinese culture and even merge into Chinese culture. His preaching stood for the in-depth philosophical spiritual aspiration and behavioral standard, which infiltrated deep into on national psychology and character, becoming an important source for the cultivation of the Chinese people's spiritual morals.

The second thing for people to appreciate is the stone statues of the Three-Generation Buddha of Lamaism of the Yuan Dynasty, which are the earliest and most complete, and located in the southernmost part of China. The Three-Generation Buddha is supposed to be the main statue enshrined and worshipped in the main hall ever since Lamaism was introduced into the interior in the 13th century.

The third thing for people to appreciate is the

相机：佳能 Canon Eos-1DX，镜头：24-70mm f/2.8，光圈：f/16，快门：1/640秒，感光度：ISO500 曝光补偿：0EV **九日山娘娘庙**

相机：佳能 Canon Eos-1DX，镜头：24-70mm f/2.8，光圈：f/11，快门：1/80秒，感光度：ISO500，曝光补偿：0EV **九日山祈风石刻**

remains of Islam of the Tang Dynasty, which are the oldest and best preserved so far in China. It is recorded that in the years 618–626 of Emperor Wude of the Tang Dynasty, Mohammed dispatched four of his disciples to China to do missionary work, the first to Guangzhou, the second to Yangzhou, and the other two to Quanzhou, who passed away and were buried on Lingshan Mountain. These remains are the historical records to verify the history of international transportation of Quanzhou and the history of the spread of Islam in China.

The fourth thing for people to appreciate is the cluster of the largest number of stonecarvings of the Song Dynasty. It is said that there is no stone in Jiuri Mountain that bears no carving. There are over 70 carvings on the cliffs spanning from dynasty to dynasty.

These stonecarvings are not only important historical remains to verify the overseas transportation of ancient Quanzhou and the Silk Road on the sea, but also witness to the friendly exchanges between Chinese people and Asian–African peoples. In the Song and Yuan Dynasties, both Quanzhou and Alexandria of Egypt ranked the largest ports in the world. Quanzhou had trades with over one hundred countries and regions in the world, and its openness endowed it with inclusiveness. What's more, it is also the best–known hometown of overseas Chinese, for over seven million descendants of Quanzhou inhabitants are scattered in more than one hundred countries and regions; therefore, Quanzhou occupies a special position in both Chinese history and world history. The Silk Road Inspection Group of UNESCO marveled so much at the cultural site that they left behind a stone seal recording their inspection, thus adding more brilliance to Jiuri Mountain.

On Qingyuan Mountain, all remains of civilization are historical pulses. Among the trees and grass, nature and humanity meet here after traversing time and space, while the mysterious gods and sacred morals communicate with the earthly world.

When we scrutinize once more the green mountains and blue waters, we can't help feeling emotions welling up in our chest. This is a place where the exquisite beauty of mountains and waters and the splendor of humanity merge together. It is a place where human beings and holy beings hold dialogues across time and space. And it is also a place where the present–day people enjoy their spiritual baptism.

Tips 寻访者须知

佳境指数 Scenery Index：★★★★

备选序列：福建省清源山风景名胜区——中国国家自然与文化双遗产预备名录（国家建设部2006年7月版）、海上丝绸之路·福建省泉州市——中国世界文化遗产预备名单第16号（国家文物局2012年11月版）

List Number: Qingyuan Mountain Scenery of Fujian Province — No.16 in the preparatory list for Chinese World Heritage (November 2012 Edition by the State Cultural Relics Bureau)

寻访提示：鲤城泉州作为首批国家历史文化名城，曾是宋元时期海上丝绸之路的起点，极具审美价值的自然和人文遗存众多。如"三大禅林"之称的开元寺、承天寺和崇福寺，中国唯一海事博物馆"海外交通史博物馆"，中国古代"四大名桥"之一的洛阳桥，以古代抗倭而名闻天下的崇武古城，等，都会令到此的访客惊喜连连。

Location Notes: Quanzhou, on the list of first national historical cities, was once the starting point of the Silk Road on the sea in the Song and Yuan Dynasties. There are many natural scenes and cultural sites that are of high esthetic value. The three Buddhist temples, Kaiyuan Temple, Chengtian Temple and Chongfu Temple, China's only maritime museum, the Museum of Overseas Transportation History, Luoyang Bridge, one of the four famous ancient bridges in China, and the ancient town, Chongwu, well known for its resistance against Japanese invaders, will keep giving visitors surprises.

摄影提示：清源山遍布天湖流泉、奇岩异洞、峰峦叠翠、寺庙宫观、书院石室、石雕石刻等，均为摄影创作活动的极好元素，尤其是巧遇云蒸雾腾、彩霞映天之时，更能使作品展现清源山仙风道骨的迷人神韵。建议摄影爱好者在开展创作活动时，先坐车至山顶观景台和天湖，然后沿登山道逐级下行，边走边拍，捕捉沿途佳景。崇武古城的惠安女是闽南地区一道独特的人文风景线，为摄影创作的极好去处。

Tips for Photography: Lakes and springs, rocks and caves, tall mountains and green trees, temples and monasteries, academies and stone houses, stone sculptures and stone carvings all serve as good themes for photography. Pictures taken specially when clouds and mists go up and colorful twilight appears in the skies further reveal the bewitching atmosphere of Qingyuan Mountain.

民俗提示：泉州民俗文化积淀深厚，绚丽多彩。元宵节最为风光，届时城乡各地花灯展览，文艺踩街，万人空巷。五月节即端午节，"龙舟竞渡""采莲"习俗蔚为壮观。泉州过中秋节的热闹程度仅次于元宵节，明月当空，家人团聚赏月、吃饼或搏"状元"饼。入夜后江上泛舟赏月，鸣奏南曲，雅趣宜人。

泉州素为"戏曲之乡""戏窝子"，拥有一批风情万种、不可多得的传统艺术珍品。有优雅委婉的梨园戏，妙趣横生的木偶戏，端庄诙谐的高甲戏，武功高超的打城戏，以及韵味深长的南音艺术。如今，这些"中国不多，世界少有"的古稀艺术，仍以其旺盛的生命力，传诵于泉州城乡、海峡两岸、东南亚乃至欧美拉。除此，笼吹、北管、十音、茶歌、民谣、大鼓吹、拍胸舞、彩球舞、车鼓舞、火鼎公婆，以及泉州方言说书讲古等民族音乐、舞蹈、曲艺等也琳琅满目、美不胜收。

泉州是南派少林拳术的摇篮。其中，五祖拳、白鹤拳等南少林武术祖拳独树一帜，流传于福建、广东、台湾地区以及东南亚、日本等国家。

在传统工艺方面，彩扎、剪纸、刺绣、竹编等千姿百态、精彩纷呈。木雕、石雕、瓷雕蜚声中外，惠安青石雕更是引以为豪。

Brief Introduction to the Local Culture: The folk culture in Quanzhou is rich and colorful. On the 15th of the first lunar month, i.e. the Lantern Festival, all the towns and villages are decorated with lanterns and colorful streamers. As lanterns are exhibited and artistic performances are staged, almost all the people flock out of their houses and have a great time together. On the Dragon Boat Festival during the 5th lunar month, people hold dragon-boat races and lotus-picking rituals. The celebration of Mid-autumn Festival in Quanzhou is second only to the Lantern Festival in excitement. When night falls and the full moon shines brightly in the sky, family members gather together, appreciating the moon and enjoying moon cakes.

Quanzhou has long been known as the home of operas, with a large variety of priceless traditional operas in its possession. Some of the rare varieties, hard to come across in China and almost unheard of around the world, are still enjoying high vitality in Quanzhou, and have even spread to Taiwan, Southeast Asia, Europe, America and Latin America.

美食提示：泉州美食继承了闽菜的优点，又因海上丝绸之路的关系，从海外带来不少新奇的食材、调味品和调味技法，影响并丰富了泉州的饮食。像咖喱、辣椒、沙茶、芥末等香辣性调味品都是“舶来品”，小粒花生是明万历年间从东南亚引进的，番薯是从吕宋岛传入的，这些物产经过精巧制作，均成为独具风味的泉州名点名菜。

泉州烹调技艺多样，有蒸、炒、炸、焗、烤、卤、煨、炖、煎、淋、烧等，博采各路菜肴之精华，且以讲究佐料、擅用酱汁而著称，在使用沙茶、芥末、茄汁，以及药物、佳果等方面均有独到之处。名菜有“东譬龙珠”“芥末拌螺片”“炒

寻访路径
Geographical location

沙茶牛肉”“葱烧蹄筋”“肉末海参”“当归牛腩”“红烧黄花鱼”“永春白鸭汤”“红菇炖排骨”“糖醋菠萝排骨”等菜肴，突出反映了泉州浓郁的食趣。同时，泉州菜很重视汤的熬制，所制的汤羹必须达到质鲜、味纯、滋补的目的，熬制羹汤采用炖、煲、煨、旱蒸等，讲究慢火调制，确保汤汁的甘鲜清醇。

Food Tips: Quanzhou food mainly inherits the merits of Fujian food. However, because of the Silk Road on the sea, quite a number of new ingredients, seasonings and cooking methods introduced from abroad enriched Quanzhou food. Curry, chilli, satay, mustard and other spicy seasonings are all imported goods. The small-size peanuts that were introduced from Southeast Asia in the years of Emperor Wanli of the Ming Dynasty and the sweet potatoes that came from Luzon Island have turned out specialties of strong Quanzhou flavor after careful cooking.

月明园糕点房

寻觅备选世遗佳境 1
浙江省湖州市德清县新市古镇
Xinshi Ancient Town, Deqing County, Huzhou, Zhejiang

11 运河之子 Son of the Great Canal

大运河重要聚落　鲜活的江南水乡
Important Meeting Place along the Great Canal
and Lively Southern Water Town

因河成市

Birth of the City beside the Canal

新市古镇是京杭大运河上一处仍在流动、鲜活的运河聚落。

与万里长城一起，京杭大运河一直被世人视为中国古代最为杰出的两项工程，在两千多年的历史进程中，恩泽华夏子孙，并留下了众多灿烂的历史文化遗存。

京杭大运河全长一千七百余公里，跨越四省两市，是世界上开凿时间最早、流程最长的人工运河，其长度是苏伊士运河的16倍，巴拿马运河的33倍。作为古代丝绸之路的源头之一，古京杭运河始终发挥着重要作用。通过这条黄金水道的漕运，江南富庶之地盛产的土丝、羊毛、茶叶等资源源源不断地流向外地。自鸦片战争以后，列强在上海等地纷纷建立洋行，当地客商利用船运将土特产通过水路运到洋行，返程时再将当时畅销的洋肥皂、洋火、洋油等商品输回当地。在活跃经济的同时，也对周边地区形成了辐射力，使运河沿岸的一个个集镇，成为一处处商品贸易的集散地，对当地的经济文化生活发展起到了巨大的拉动作用。这条伟大的人工运河，不仅是我国重要的南北水上运输大动脉，撬动经济繁荣的大杠杆，同时也孕育和沉淀了深厚悠久的中华人文脉络。

“千年小上海，江南百老汇。”新市位于杭嘉湖平原腹地，处在德清、桐乡、余杭、湖州市区的交界处，秦汉聚村，三国两晋渐趋繁荣。自京杭大运河开通后，穿境而过，尽得舟楫之利，成为运河上的一个重要商贸集散地，并逐渐演变成为杭嘉湖地区的重镇。据明代嘉靖《德清县志》载，宋明时期新市素有“琳宫梵宇之壮，茧丝粟米之盛”之誉。明代起居民日益增多，商业日趋繁荣。至民国抗战爆发之初，沪、杭、嘉、湖等地市民来新市躲避战乱，经商者骤增，时有工商企业五百五十余家，员工三千余人。市场之繁荣，为当时杭嘉湖一带所罕见，素有“小上海”之誉。

相机：佳能 Canon Eos-1DX，镜头：24-70mm f/2.8，光圈：f/10，快门：1/120秒，感光度：ISO320，曝光补偿：0EV **新市古镇西河口**

相机：佳能 Canon Eos-1DX，镜头：24-70mm f/2.8，光圈：f/11，快门：1/40秒，感光度：ISO320，曝光补偿：0EV **新市古镇廊棚**

相机：佳能 Canon Eos-1DX，镜头：24-70mm f/2.8，光圈：f/9，快门：1/125秒，感光度：ISO320，曝光补偿：0EV **新市古镇廊棚**

因河成市的运河特色是新市最具魅力所在。河埠群和南圣堂是展现京杭大运河魅力的精华，主要以西河口至陈家潭的市河河道为主线，一条与京杭大运河直接相通的市河环镇而流，其中在一千五百余米的市河河段上，保留完好的明清河埠头、驳岸，花样繁多的拴缆石，堪称江南一绝。整个新市古街区，犹如一幅徐徐铺开的运河文化长卷。

曾几何时，随着公路、铁路、航空等现代交通方式兴起之后，京杭大运河黄金水道的作用逐渐淡出人们的视线，曾经滋润养育了江南众多城市文明的大运河也逐渐式微。进入新世纪以来，随着对京杭大运河价值的重新认识，在现代社会资源日益枯竭、环境不断恶化的情况下，大运河水运低碳、低成本的优势日益显现。投入巨资的新市镇东五龙桥畔的内河航运码头正抓紧建设，这必将给新市的运河文化注入新的活力。

The ancient town of Xinshi is still a gregarious meeting point along the Beijing-Hangzhou Canal.

Both the Great Wall and the Beijing-Hangzhou Canal have long been considered all over the world as ancient China's two most outstanding engineering projects.

The Beijing-Hangzhou Canal is over 1,700 km long, and travels through four provinces and two cities. As the first man-dug canal, earliest and longest in the world, it is sixteen times the length of the Suez Canal and thirty-three times the length of the Panama Canal. As the starting point of the ancient Silk Road, the Beijing-Hangzhou Canal played an important role. By means of this water way, the raw silk, wool, tea and other materials produced in the affluent region south of the Yangtze River continually flowed to other parts of the world. After the Opium War, the foreign powers set up their companies in Shanghai. The local merchants transported by ship the local products to

相机：佳能 Canon Eos-1DX，镜头：24-70mm f/2.8，光圈：f/9，快门：1/500秒，感光度：ISO320，曝光补偿：0EV **新市古镇大运河埠头**

the foreign companies and brought foreign soaps, matches and gasoline back home. While enlivening the local economy, the transportation had a radiating effect on the surrounding areas. Thus many trading towns came into being along the canal, which eventually became the reception and distribution places of various goods for trade, turning out to be a propelling force for the local economic and cultural life. Not only is this great man-made river an important artery for the north-south water transportation, giving rise to the economic prosperity, but it also served as a nest where Chinese culture was incubated.

Xinshi is located in the hinterland of the Hangjiahu Plain, bordering Deqing, Tongxiang, Yuhang, and Huzhou. It came into being as a village as early as the Qin and Han Dynasties, and the by the time of the Three Kingdoms and the Jin Dynasty it had grown quite prosperous. Ever since the Great Canal flowed through, Xinshi, taking advantage of the thousands of boats and ships, turned out to be an important gathering and distributing place, thus gradually transforming into a key town in this area. Starting from the Ming Dynasty, the local population grew and the commerce got more and more prosperous day by day. And shortly before the outbreak of the anti-Japanese War, refugees from Shanghai, Hangzhou, Jiaxing and Huzhou flocked to Xinshi, where the number of merchants abruptly went up. In those days, there were over 550 industrial and commercial enterprises with more than 3,000 employees. With unprecedented prosperity, Xinshi acquired the reputation of Little Shanghai.

The most prominent characteristic of Xinshi lies in the fact that it grew into a city because of the Great Canal. The encircling city river that flows

相机：佳能 Canon Eos-1DX，镜头：24-70mm f/2.8，光圈：f/13，快门：1/80秒，感光度：ISO320，曝光补偿：0EV **新市古镇河道**

运河明珠

相机：佳能 Canon Eos-1DX，镜头：24-70mm f/2.8，光圈：f/10，快门：1/80秒，感光度：ISO320，曝光补偿：0EV **新市古镇河道**

around the town directly joins the Great Canal. Along the over 1,500 meter section of the city river are the well-kept ports, revetments, and various tethered cable stones of the Ming and Qing Dynasties, which is unique in the regions south of the Yangtze River. The whole old area of Xinshi is almost like a scroll of the Great Canal Culture that is gradually unfolding.

Not long ago, however, the significant role played by the Great Canal started to fade with the advent of the modern transportation means such as highways, railways, and aviation. Consequently, the Great Canal that gave rise to the urban civilization of the various cities and towns in the areas south of the Yangtze River began to decline. Yet, the arrival of the 21st century brought about a renewed understanding of the value of the Great Canal. With the increasing depletion of resources in modern society and the worsening of the environment, the merits of low carbon and low cost in water transportation on the Great Canal have been recognized again.

因水成市

Growth of the City beside the Canal

江浙多水乡，唯此藏深闺。与江南其他古镇相比，建制一千七百余年，藏匿于长三角腹地的新市古镇，民俗依旧，民风淳厚，几乎延续了原生态的水乡韵味。

因水成市的运河形态是新市古镇最独特的亮点。2.5公里长的市河贯穿并环绕全镇，河道如网，水街相依。纵横的溪塘穿街傍市，溪上古桥飞架，塘畔绿树成荫，河中舟楫不绝，市上笑语声声。

水巷和街巷是支撑新市古镇整个空间系统的骨架。水巷既作为水上运输的要道，是城镇与四邻农

相机：佳能 Canon Eos-1DX，镜头：24-70mm f/2.8，光圈：f/9，快门：1/100秒，感光度：ISO320，曝光补偿：0EV **新市古镇太平桥**

村、城市联系的纽带，也是人们日常生活的主要场所。街市则是富庶和繁盛的表现，新市古镇的民居带有显著的商贸特色，店坊、民居临街而建、傍水而居，驳岸商铺林立，前店后坊（寝）、厅大院小，封火墙、骑楼、廊棚紧密相连。商店毗邻，货物满目，人流来往，繁华异常。

新市最令人难忘的是各具姿态的古石桥。清晨，桥边人家升起袅袅炊烟，粉墙、竹影入河中，再揉入三两声鸡鸣犬吠，如水墨淡染的拱桥被朝阳放倒，荡漾于水面中，落影似弓。小舟荡过，影像瞬间碎裂化去，沉入河底。夏日傍晚，新雨过后，桥净如洗。两岸桥头人家摆出竹制桌椅、一壶香茗、几碟闲食，聚在桥头纳凉闲聊，手持一把芭蕉扇斜倚美人靠，几多逍遥，几多满足。秋夜，月挂枝头，风送桂香，石桥像一位饱经风霜的老汉，失却了白日的硬朗，只剩下弱弱软软的剪影。千百年风风雨雨，古桥老矣，可那遍缀的苔藓、横展的藤蔓，便是石桥的掌纹和年轮。一座座石桥，似一道彩虹，悬挂于河道之上，古韵氤氲，宁静安逸。

虽然，现今的石桥失去了昔日彩虹卧波的风姿，以及行人纷至沓来的鲜活。然而，这些承载了千年文化记忆的珍贵文物，并未全部退出历史，除了千年风姿，还有不死的风骨。

Jiangsu and Zhejiang are rich in water villages and towns. The ancient town of Xinshi, officially set up about 1,700 years ago, still maintains its original ecological charms with traditional folk customs and ambience.

What deserves special attention in this old town is that it has been growing along with the Great Canal. The five-li city river runs through and around the whole town, making up a grid of water ways alongside the streets. The criss-cross streams cut the streets in the town; therefore, old bridges span above them. The green trees beside the streams provide good shelter, boats sail back

相机：佳能 Canon Eos-1DX，镜头：24-70mm f/2.8，光圈：f/20，快门：1/80秒，感光度：ISO400，曝光补偿：0EV **南浔嘉业堂**

and forth in the river, and the whole town is permeated with merry laughter.

The water ways and street lanes form the framework of the ancient town of Xinshi. The former are important passages for water transportation, the links between the town and the nearby cities and villages, and the major locations for the local people's daily activities. The street markets indicate the wealth and prosperity of the local area. Shops and stores, full of a large variety of goods, are arranged one by one, with customers coming and going, a pleasant picture of thriving businesses.

The most unforgettable thing in Xinshi are those old bridges that are respectively unique in form. At dawn, the smoke flows out from the chimneys of the households next to the bridges. The white walls and the bamboos make reflections in the river. And here and there can be heard cocks crowing and dogs barking. When boats float by, the reflections are smashed into fragments that sink to the river bottom. At dusk in summer, the rain that fell a few moments ago has washed the bridges clean and fresh. The families living at both ends of the bridges set up bamboo tables and chairs. Drinking tea and cracking melon seeds, the local people gather near the bridges, chatting and enjoying the coolness of the summer evening. A palm fan in hand and reclining on a deck chair, how relaxed and greatly contented these people look! At night in autumn, however, the moon is hanging high above the tree branches, and the wind is spreading the sweet fragrance of osmanthus in all directions. The stone bridge looks like an old man that has weathered a lot. No longer robust and vigorous, it is more or less but a weak and frag-

相机：佳能 Canon Eos-1DX，镜头：24-70mm f/2.8，光圈：f/9，
快门：1/500秒，感光度：ISO250，曝光补偿：0EV **南浔张氏故居**

相机：佳能 Canon Eos-1DX，镜头：24-70mm f/2.8，光圈：f/9，
快门：1/500秒，感光度：ISO250，曝光补偿：0EV **南浔张氏故居雕花楼**

ile silhouette. After the passing of several hundred years, the bridges are really old! The moss on them and the vines across them are actually the prints and rings of their age. The bridges, one by one, are rainbows, suspended above the river, which appear so tranquil, peaceful, and yet quite ancient-flavored.

Even though the bridges at present no longer look grand and colorful as they used to be and become less lively because of fewer people walking over them, they are still our treasured cultural relics that bear the memories of our history. They have not faded away from history. Besides their traditional beauty, the bridges bear the immortal soul of our nation.

Tips 寻访者须知

佳境指数 **Scenery Index**：★★★½

备选序列： 江南水乡古镇·浙江省湖州市德清县新市古镇、大运河·浙江省——中国世界文化遗产预备名单第15和第2号（国家文物局2012年11月版）

List Number: The Great Canal and Guzhen Town, Xinshi City, Deqing County, Huzhou City, Zhejiang Province — No.15 and No.2 in the preparatory list for Chinese World Heritage (November 2012 Edition by the State Cultural Relics Bureau)

（作者注：本篇在发稿付印前，欣闻中国大运河于2014年6月22日在卡塔尔多哈召开的联合国教科文组织第38届世界遗产委员会会议上正式入选《世界遗产名录》，成为我国第32项世界文化遗产。）

(Author' s Note: Before the present writing i went to print, the present writer was gladly informed that the Great Canal were officially selected and listed among the World Heritage at the 38th World Heritage Conference held in Doha, Qatar on June 22, 2014, thus becoming the 32th in the list of world heritage in China.)

寻访提示： 青藤、粉墙、黛瓦、石桥、流水、人家，是这座具有一千七百年历史古镇的看点。保存较为完整的古民居主要集中在觉海寺、西河口、南栅三个区域，风格独特的走马楼、工艺精湛的砖雕门楼、飞檐翘角的屋脊，无不折射出浓郁的水乡古镇韵味。新市的名门望族很多，粉墙黛瓦、风韵独特的老宅至今保存完好的有数十处之多，其中数俞吉祥、方伯第、爱敬堂、钱宅等较有特色。周边临近南浔、乌镇、西塘等古镇，可顺道游览。

Location Notes: Green vines, white walls, black tiles, stone bridges, flowing water and local households are what deserve attention in this historical 1,700-year-old town. Well-preserved old residences can be found in Juehaisi, Xihekou, and Nanzha. The buildings there are traditional local architecture with remarkable brick carvings. Xinshi boasts quite a number of noble families, whose houses, all having white walls and black-tiled roofs, are relatively well preserved, even up to now.

摄影提示： 古运河与传统街弄、古桥梁、古民居、古刹、驳岸、单孔石桥等，是新市摄影创作的主要元素，尤其是在日出日落时分，斜阳如金，光线柔和，可捕捉上述景观产生的神奇光影变化。要充分利用古运河水面的反光效果，使作品更具水乡韵味。如能捕捉到当地百姓的日常生活劳作场面，能更增添作品的张力。

Tips for Photography: By the side of the Great Canal, the traditional streets and lanes, old bridges, residences, temples, revetments, and single hole bridges make up the major elements for photography in Xinshi. At sunrise or sunset, the slanting sunlight is gentle and soft; therefore, the miraculous changes in the mysterious light and shade can be reproduced in our cameras. The reflective effect on the surface of the canal water ought to be made full use of so as to put out photos rich in the flavor of water villages.

民俗提示： 古镇的寺前弄，有一处江南蚕文化馆，楹联道："探丝路源头蚕俗蚕花，望仙潭陌上桑园桑梓"。道出了新市丰富多彩的蚕桑文化。最具代表性的是蚕花庙会，源于春秋时期，越国美女西施于越都会稽前往姑苏送蚕花，途经新市，遇到十二位美丽的采桑姑娘，围在西施轿前翩翩起舞，西施姑娘手托花篮，把绚丽多彩的绢花分赠给采桑姑娘，以祈佑蚕桑丰收。从此西施送蚕花这个美丽的传说，就在新市乡村广为流传。每年清明，当地民众自发相聚举办蚕花庙会，以追念西施。

Brief Introduction to the Local Culture: In Xinshi there is the Jiangnan Museum of Silkworm Culture, which fully exhibits the rich colorful silkworm culture in Xinshi. The most representative is the Silkworm Fair, which originated in the Spring and Autumn Period. As a story goes, Xishi, a beauty of the Yue Kingdom, on her way from Guiji, the capital of the Yue Kingdom, to Suzhou, was sending newly-hatched silkworms. When she reached Xinshi, twelve pretty girls that were picking the mulberry leaves encircled her and began to dance gracefully. Holding a flower basket in hand, Xishi presented silk flowers to the girls, wishing them a bumper harvest of the silkworms. Therefore, the charming legend that Xishi delivered silk flowers has long been spread far and wide around Xinshi. On the day of Qingming every year, the local people gather together and run a Silkworm Fair, with the intention of commemorating Xinshi.

美食提示：新市美食首推湖羊肉：用文火加酱油、红糖、饴糖等数十种调料焖煮一整夜而成，其特点是肥而不腻，酥而不烂。二是茶糕：采用糯米粉蒸制，中间嵌一团剁碎的猪肉，刚出锅的茶糕香气四溢，滋味悠长。三是烧卖：用剁碎的猪肉加冬笋制作而成，吃时蘸点香醋，回味无穷。四是烧饼加臭豆腐：将现烤的烧饼剪开一小口，放入一块现炸的臭豆腐，吃时凭个人喜好抹上甜（辣）酱，又香又脆。五是芽麦圆子：这是新市四乡八村农家的传统点心，大多为农家自制自食，也有为馈赠亲友而特制的，主要原料为糯米粉、小麦芽、棉线草、白糖、芝麻等，口感香甜糯软，冷食尤佳。

Food Tips: Of all the delicacies in Xinshi, stewed mutton ranks at the top. The second best are tea cakes, which can be thought of as Chinese sandwiches, layers of glutinous rice powder cakes with minced pork in between. The third best is shaomai, made from minced pork plus chopped winter bamboo shoots, which is so tasty that one cannot help being intoxicated by its flavor and taste afterward. Pancakes and fermented stinky bean curd could be counted as No.4. Putting a piece of newly fried stinky bean curd in freshly baked pancaks together with some paste, sweet, salty, or spicy as one likes, one would totally indulge in the specially flavored crispiness. And another that is worth mentioning is malted dough, which is made of glutinous rice powder, malt, herbs, sugar, and sesame. It tastes soft, tender and sweet, especially when eaten cold. The local people make such dough either for self consumption or as gifts for relatives and friends.

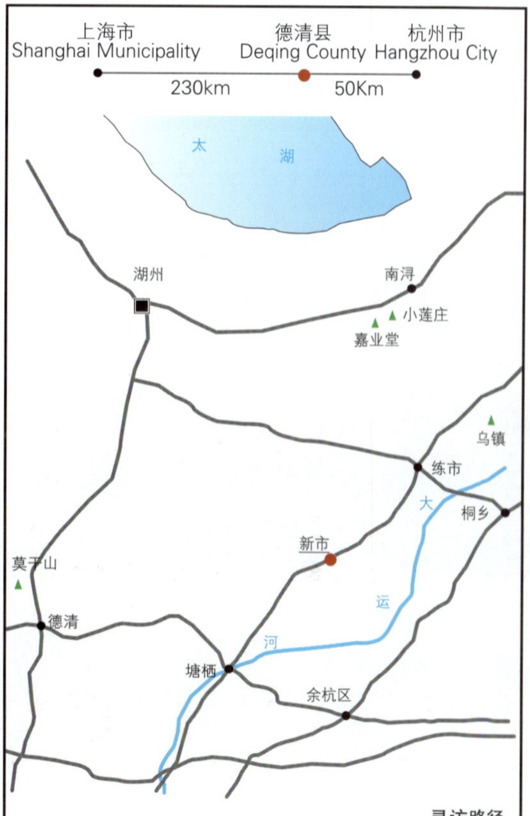

寻访路径
Geographical location

寻觅备选世遗佳境 1
甘肃省敦煌市玉门关
Yumen Pass, Dunhuang, Gansu

12 大漠丰碑 Glorious Desert Monument

古丝绸之路河西之险关要塞
中西方文化经济交往之见证

Defense Fortress on the Ancient Silk Road; Cultural and Economic Exchanges Between China and the West

千百年来，在中国所有的险关要隘中，没有哪座雄关，比它承载了中华民族如此众多的历史记忆和精神象征。

大漠、戈壁，长河、落日，长城、烽燧，驼队、牧群……构成了一幅大西北磅礴恢宏的历史长卷。恍惚间，蛰伏千年的战马蹄声，从沉寂的大漠深处蓦然响起，激荡人心。呼啸的荒漠疾风，吹唤起尘封千年的历史涟漪。

这座已在戈壁大漠中默默矗立了两千多年的险关要塞，作为中国西部边陲的咽喉要隘之一，见证了中国敞开胸襟、包容开放的胸襟和气度。

汉武帝建元二年（前139年），张骞应募曾两度经此关隘出使西域，历尽千辛万苦，开辟了中原通往西域的经济文化沟通之路。自此以后，中西方数不胜数的马帮商队、使节遣臣、僧侣游客，纷纷在此隘下留存印迹。

汉武帝太初元年至四年（前104—101年），因不堪边关对方多年滋事，汉大将李广利率数万精兵西出此关，血战四年，击败大宛，威震西域，换来双方难得的安宁。

汉明帝永平十六年（73年），班超从此城关出使西域三十一载，“宜荡佚简易，宽小过，总大纲而已”，实现了西汉与西域数十年间的和平与共赢。其在耄耋之年，挥泪写下“不敢望到酒泉郡，但愿生入玉门关”的不朽诗句。

唐太宗贞观三年（629—645年），汉传佛教史上最伟大的译经师之一，中国佛教法相唯识宗创始人玄奘法师，从京都长安出发，途经此关后，历经磨难，最终抵达天竺，取回真经，成就唐代第一高僧。同样通过这一关隘，公元2世纪，波斯王子安世曾经此东往洛阳。至三国时，我国第一位西去求法的僧人朱士行，也由此踏上漫漫西行之路。

此处不仅是著名的险关要塞，而且象征着西域通往中原腹地的门户，中原西行的征人、商客、官吏、僧侣，只要双脚一跨进此关，就视为回归中原故土，心中油然而生一种亲切和安定的归属感。

相机：索尼 Sony Nex-7，镜头：18-55mm，光圈：f/9，快门：1/80秒，感光度：ISO100，曝光补偿：0EV **嘉峪关城楼夕照**

唐朝的伟大诗人，更是赋予了这座城关深远绵长的意境。千百年来，因受这种汉唐风韵的浸润，不知在多少中国人的内心深处，打下了深深的文化烙印，更增添了国人对这座古老而又神奇关塞的向往。李白在《关山月》吟咏道："明月出天山，苍茫云海间。长风几万里，吹度玉门关。"王之涣的《凉州词》也是脍炙人口："黄河远上白云间，一片孤城万仞山。羌笛何须怨杨柳，春风不度玉门关。"而王昌龄的《从军行七首其四》，更是气度不凡："青海长云暗雪山，孤城遥望玉门关。黄沙百战穿金甲，不破楼兰终不还。"

这座令人魂牵梦绕的小小方城，就是位于甘肃河西走廊西端与古代西域交界处，中原通向西域的重要门户之一的玉门关。

秦时明月汉时关。自秦汉以来，匈奴对中原汉民族的侵扰不断。汉初，匈奴东败东胡，西逐大月氏，占据河西走廊，并以此为基地，屡犯中原汉境。汉王朝之初，曾对匈奴采取怀柔政策，希冀换取暂时的安宁，但始终未果。至汉武帝时，舍弃了和亲策略，对匈奴发动了大规模的军事反击。汉武帝元狩二年（前121年），汉骠骑将军霍去病率兵西征，沉重打击了匈奴右部。同年，西汉政权"列四郡，据两关"，分河西为武威、酒泉两郡。元鼎六年（前111年），又增设张掖、敦煌两郡。与此同时，分别构筑玉门关和阳关，成为西汉王朝设置于河西走廊西部的两处重要关隘。

自河西走廊归属大汉以后，开辟了中原大地通往西域及欧洲诸国的通衢大道。这条古代陆路商业贸易线，起始于古代中国政治、经济和文化中心的古都长安，连接亚洲、非洲和欧洲诸国。它跨越陇山山脉，穿过河西走廊，经过玉门关和阳关，抵达新疆，沿绿洲和帕米尔高原，再通过中亚、西亚和北非，最终抵达非洲和欧洲。它同时也成为一条东方与西方之间经济、政治和文化交往的主要通道。它最初的作用，只是输出中国特有的优质丝绸。因此，当德国地理学家最早在19世纪70年代将之命名

相机：索尼 Sony Nex-7，镜头：18-55mm，光圈：f/9，快门：1/100秒，感光度：ISO100，曝光补偿：0EV **嘉峪关晚霞**

相机：佳能 Canon Eos-1DX，镜头：24-70mm f/2.8，光圈：f/13，快门：1/800秒，感光度：ISO200，曝光补偿：-1EV **玉门关**

为“丝绸之路”后，即被世界广泛认同和接受。

这条大道自敦煌以西，又分成两路，一条出敦煌向西北经玉门关、鄯善北行，为天山北路；另一条出敦煌向西南经阳关、安南坝，沿塔克拉玛干大沙漠南行，为天山南路。玉门关是北道的出发点，到现今哈密后，沿天山南麓一直向西，经西域诸多城邦后，越过葱岭（帕米尔高原），再通向大秦（古罗马帝国）。

在这条绵延万余公里的大道上，丝绸与同样原产自中国的瓷器一起，成为当时一个东亚强盛大国的文明象征。丝绸不仅是丝路之上重要的奢侈消费品之一，也是中国历朝政府一种行之有效的政治工具，中国的友好使节出使西域乃至更远的国度时，往往将丝绸作为表示两国友好的有效手段。由于当时西传至君士坦丁堡的丝绸和瓷器价格奇高，使相当多的异国人认为中国乃至东亚，是一个物产丰盈的富裕地区。有些国家的元首及贵族，曾一度以穿着用腓尼基红染色的中国丝绸、家中拥有中国青花瓷餐具，为富有和荣耀的象征。

此外，阿富汗的青金石也随着商队的西进不断流入欧亚各地。这种远早于丝绸的贸易品在欧亚大陆的广泛传播，也为带动欧亚贸易交流做出了贡献。这种珍贵的商品曾是两河流域各国财富的象征。当青金石流传到印度后，被那里的佛教徒供奉为佛教七宝之一，为青金石增添了神秘的宗教色彩。而葡萄、核桃、胡萝卜、胡椒、胡豆、菠菜、黄瓜（汉称胡瓜）、石榴等的传播，为东亚人的日常生活增添了更多的饮食选择。西域特产的葡萄酒，也融入到中国的传统酒文化之中。商队还从中国西运铁器、金器、银器、镜子和其他豪华制品。西方运往中国的还有长颈鹿等稀有动物，和鸟类、植物、皮货、药材、香料、珠宝首饰等。

不难想象，当时的玉门关，作为中原通往西方的重要关卡和驿站之一，是何等繁荣。

相机：佳能 Canon Eos-1DX，镜头：24-70mm f/2.8，光圈：f/9，快门：1/400秒，感光度：ISO200，曝光补偿：-0.3EV **敦煌鸣沙山**

相机：佳能 Canon Eos-1DX，镜头：24-70mm f/2.8，光圈：f/8，快门：1/80秒，感光度：ISO100，曝光补偿：0EV **敦煌月牙泉**

雄关夕照

大漠雄关

相机：尼康 NIKON D700，镜头：尼康 70–200mm f/2.8，光圈：f/11，快门：1/400秒，感光度：ISO200，曝光补偿：0EV **敦煌魔鬼城雅丹地貌**

丝绸之路的辟通，有力地促进了东西方之间的经济文化交流，对促进汉朝的强盛产生了积极作用。直至近代工业革命到来之后，它才被东起连云港、西至荷兰鹿特丹的一万余公里长的新亚欧大陆桥取代，渐渐淡出了历史舞台。今天，它像一个被遗忘的戍卒，孤寂地驻守着中国西北的门户。

大漠孤烟直，长河落日圆。现在的玉门关遗迹，是一座四方形小城堡，耸立在茫茫戈壁和沙漠之中。南北夹峙有高耸的阿尔金山和马鬃山，中间为走廊式平原，敞向新疆东部，疏勒河流经其间，向西最终流入东疆的罗布泊盆地。

关城全用黄土夯筑而成，面积约六百多平方米。西、北两面各开一门，城垣东西南北各宽二十余米，残垣高近十米，上下宽约四米。城顶四周有宽一米多的走道，设有内外女墙。城内东南角有一条宽不足一米的马道，靠东墙向南转上可直达顶部。登上古关，举目远眺，四周沼泽遍布，沟壑纵横；长城蜿蜒，烽燧兀立；胡杨挺拔，泉水碧透。悠古之情，油然而生。

看大漠孤烟长河落日，秦燧汉关今犹在；听塞外羌笛胡角马嘶，张骞李广俱往矣。

玉门关是一种符号，是一种象征，更是一座丰碑。它凝结和昭示了千百年来中华民族既勤劳坚韧，又睿智果敢；既渴望和平，又不惧淫威；既自强不息，又包容开放的人文精神和价值取向。这是中华文化最本质、最集中的体现，也是中华民族生活方式、理想信仰、价值观念的文化浓缩，更是中华民族赖以生存和发展的精神纽带、精神支撑和精神动力。

虽然玉门关城墙的高度，可以用尺度来衡量，但是，它的灵魂高度和人文意义，是无法用任何仪器丈量的。

Over thousands of years, among all the passes in China, none bears so many memories and spiritual symbols in the history of China as Yumen Pass.

The Gobi Desert, long river, setting sun, Great Wall, beacon towers, caravans, and herds of cattle and sheep form a magnificent history of Northwest China. All of a sudden, the galloping hoofs that have hibernated for hundreds of years burst into a roar in the quiet from the depth of the desert. The strong wind that swept over the desert awoke the historical ripples that have been stagnant for over a thousand years.

One of the important passes on the western borders of China, this pass that has been quietly standing in the Gobi Desert for over 2,000 years, fully witnesses the broad-mindedness and inclusiveness of China.

In the second year (139BC) of Emperor Wudi of the Han Dynasty, Zhang Qian went out of this pass to the west twice. He overcame numerous difficulties and hardships, and succeeded in opening up the road for economic and cultural communications from the Interior Plains to the West. Ever after, many, many caravans and merchant groups, envoys and officials, monks and tourists left their footprints at the pass at one time or another.

In the 16th year (73AD) of Emperor Mingdi of the Han Dynasty, Ban Chao went out of this pass and worked as an envoy in the west for 31 years.

In the third year of Emperor Taizong (629-645AD) of the Tang Dynasty, the monk Xuanzhuang left Chang'an via this pass and reached India after a lot of hardships. He brought back the Buddhist scriptures and became the most important monk of the Tang Dynasty.

Quite a few poets of the Tang Dynasty endowed this pass with enduring prospects. For thousands of years, many a Chinese, under the cultural influence of the Han and Tang Dynasties, seems to bear such a cultural brand and strongly yearns for this old but glorious pass.

This small area that has made many people lost in a reverie is Yumen Pass, which is located at the cross-section of the west end of Gansu Corridor and the ancient Western Regions, one of the major passes through which the Central Plains lead to the Western Regions.

After Gansu Corridor was subordinated to the Han Dynasty, a thoroughfare was opened up from the Central Plains to the Western Regions and even to European countries. This ancient commercial route on land started from the ancient capital Chang'an, the political, economic, and cultural center of ancient China, and connected the countries of Asia, Africa, and Europe. It traversed Longshan Mountains, went through Gansu Corridor, passed by Yumen Pass and Yangguan Pass, and reached Xinjiang. And then it traveled along oases the Pamirs, and, via Middle Asia, West Asia, and North Africa, finally reached Africa and Europe. Meanwhile, it was also a major channel for the economic, political and cultural exchanges between east and west. In the early stage, its major, or only, function was to export the good-quality silk exclusive in China. Consequently, when the German geographer coined the name The Silk Road in the 1870s, it was unanimously agreed on and accepted all over the world.

From Dunhuang westward, this road branched into two. One is the north route along Tianshan Mountain, going northwestward through Yumen Pass and northward through Shanshan; and the other is the south route along Tianshan Mountain, going southwest from Dunhuang through Yangguan Pass and Annan Dyke and southward through the Taklimakan Desert. Yumen Pass was the starting point of the north route, which led, after reaching what is now Hami, straight westward along the south side of Tianshan Mountain. After going though many countries in the Western Regions, it climbed over the Pamirs and then pointed toward Daqin, which was the name for the Roman Empire at the time.

On this road that meanders over some ten thousand kilometers, silk and porcelain made in China were the symbols of civilization of a country that was powerful in East Asia then. Silk was not only one of the important luxury products but also a kind of effective political instrument used by the Chinese government of different dynasties. When Chinese good-will envoys went to the Western Regions or even farther countries, they usually used silk as an effective means to express good will between two countries. As the prices of silk and porcelain that went westward to Constantinople were exorbitantly high, many foreigners thought that China, even East Asia, was an area abundant in natural resources. Therefore, the state leaders and aristocrats of some countries felt proud that they were wearing Chinese silk that had been dyed the Phoenician red and had dinner services of Chinese blue and white porcelain.

In addition, the lasurite of Afghanistan began to trickle to various places of Asia and Europe along with the caravans going westward. This kind of commercial goods that spread far and wide in Asia and Europe, much earlier than silk, made contributions to the European and Asian trade. Such precious goods were once the token of wealth in all the countries in Mesopotamia. After lasurite entered India, it was worshipped by Buddhists as one of the seven Buddhist treasures, thus adding a mysterious religious color to such stone. The introduction of grapes, chestnuts, carrots, lima beans, spinach, cucumbers, pomegranates, etc. offered many choices in the daily diets for East Asians. The wines brewed in the Western Regions also blended in the traditional Chinese liquor culture. Caravans also carried ironware, gold and silver articles, mirrors and other luxury articles westward. Rare birds and animals like giraffes as well as plants, leather goods, medicinal materials, spices, jewels, etc. were brought into China from the West.

The remains of Yumen Pass today are only a small square castle standing in the vast Gobi Desert. On its north and south are the towering Altun Mountains and Mazong Mountains, and in between is a corridor-like plain open to the east of Xinjiang. The Shule River runs through the plain and finally ends up in the Lop Nor Basin in East Xinjiang.

Yumen Pass is a sign, a symbol, and a glorious monument. It has condensed and reflected the industriousness, tenacity, intelligence and courage that the Chinese people have demonstrated for thousands of years. The Chinese people yearn for peace, but fear no threat. Their living spirit and value orientation that they constantly strive to be powerful and are ready to include others is the essence of Chinese culture as well as the cultural condensation of the living style, ideal beliefs, and ideological values of the Chinese people.

相机：佳能 Canon Eos-1DX，镜头：24-70mm f/2.8，光圈：f/11，快门：1/1000秒，感光度：ISO200，曝光补偿：-1EV **敦煌魔鬼城孔雀开屏**

Tips 寻访者须知

佳境指数 Scenery Index： ★★★★

备选序列：丝绸之路·甘肃——中国世界文化遗产预备名单第16号（国家文物局2012年11月版）

List Number: The Silk Road · Gansu — No.16 in the preparatory list for Chinese World Heritage (November 2012 Edition by the State Cultural Relics Bureau)

（作者注：本篇在发稿付印前，欣闻丝绸之路于2014年6月22日在卡塔尔多哈召开的联合国教科文组织第38届世界遗产委员会会议上正式入选《世界遗产名录》，成为我国第33项世界文化遗产。）

(Author's Note: Before the present writing i went to print, the present writer was gladly informed that the Silk Road were officially selected and listed among the World Heritage at the 38th World Heritage Conference held in Doha, Qatar on June 22, 2014, thus becoming the 33th in the list of world heritage in China.)

寻访提示：河西走廊是一条承载着两千余年厚重历史的古丝绸之路。武威、张掖、酒泉、嘉峪关和敦煌等绿洲，似一串明珠镶嵌在漫长的古道之上，其间审美价值甚高的自然景观和人文景观众多，魅力无穷，令人神往。出行时尤其要注意，从敦煌市区去玉门关、雅丹地质公园游览，要请当地熟知戈壁路线的司机和向导引路，以防迷路。大漠中气候干燥，日照强烈，昼夜温差大，夏季出游前须备妥衣物。同时要做好防晒措施，注意补充水分。

Location Notes: Gansu Corridor is a 2,000-year-old Silk Road, along which there are the oases of Wuwei, Zhangye, Jiuquan, Jiayuguan and Dunhuang. They are bright pearls imbedded on the long ancient road. The numerous natural scenes

相机：索尼 Sony Nex-7，镜头：18-55mm，光圈：f/13，快门：1/160秒，感光度：ISO100，曝光补偿：0EV **嘉峪关内城**

and cultural sites of high esthetic value are very appealing to people.

摄影提示：在摄影创作活动中，作为拍摄主角的玉门关，现仅存一座孤小方城，构图和元素难免单一。因此，最好结合戈壁、荒漠、长河、落日、长城、烽燧、驼队等大西北特有的元素开展创作，以提升作品的人文内涵，增加作品的信息量和感染力。另外，玉门关以西百余公里处的敦煌雅丹地貌，为世间罕见的地质奇观，神秘而壮观，日落时分的景观尤为震撼，是摄影创作的极好题材。

Tips for Photography: Yumen Pass, obviously a major subject for photography, might be monotonous in pictures because it is only a small square structure. Therefore, it's better for the pass to be incorporated with the Gobi Desert, long river, setting sun, Great Wall, beacon tower, caravans and other stylistic elements of Northwest China so as to produce better-quality pictures.

民俗提示：农历四月初八是佛祖释迦牟尼生辰，莫高窟届时举行盛大的浴佛节庙会。从四月初一开始，善男信女陆续会聚于此，至初八达到人流高潮。香客游人来到大佛前敬香献供，叩头还愿，默念心中的祈求，求佑平安吉祥。林中席棚林立，各种当地风味小吃应有尽有。民间艺人聚在林荫下、小溪旁，弹奏着三弦，拉着二胡，演唱敦煌小曲，民俗感人。

农历六月六晒腰腿为敦煌民间的习俗之一。鸣沙山沙粒纯正，不含尘土，热沙浴具有治疗风湿性关节炎的奇效。传说此法在农历六月六这天最为灵验。所以，敦煌有六月六上鸣沙山晒腰腿的习俗。每年此日，凡有腰腿病患者，熬好乌鸡汤，备上老黄酒，正午以后，来到鸣沙山下的沙梁上，喝汤、饮酒，然后用热沙埋住腰腿部，头上打伞遮凉，让身体受损部分在烈日下暴晒数小时，以期消除腰腿疾病。

Brief Introduction to the Local Culture: The 8th of the 4th lunar month is the birthday of Sakyamuni, the founder of Buddhism. On that day,

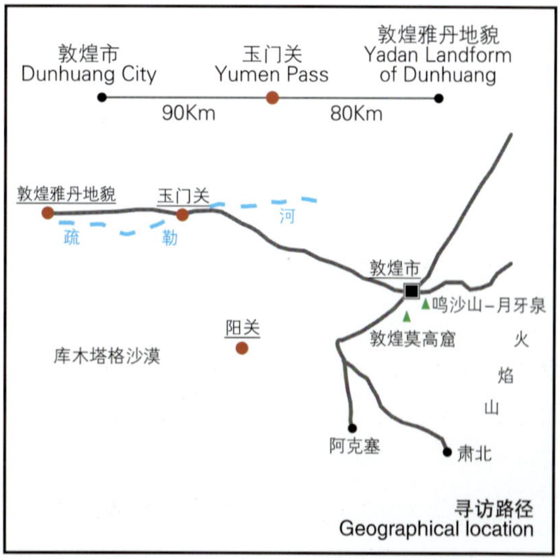

a grand fair is held at the Mogao Grottoes. Starting from the 1st of the 4th lunar month, men and women will begin to come and congregate here. On the 8th, the number of people will reach its peak.

美食提示：敦煌本地喜食羊、鸡、牛肉，但对面食制作尤其讲究。敦煌臊子面是一种传统手工麦面制品，做法是将面粉加水和匀，用面杖把面团擀薄，切成长条煮熟，加汤食之。

羊肉粉汤是敦煌传统小吃。选用敦煌本地饲养的膘肥体壮羯羊，宰好洗净切成大块，然后清水下锅。待快熟时，撇净血沫，放人少许精盐，肉熟后捞出，剔骨，后将剔骨回锅，温火熬煮成汤。

Food Tips: The local people of Dunhuang like mutton, beef and chicken. They are especially particular about flour-based foods. The Saozi Noodles are a traditional hand-made flour-based food in Dunhuang. The mutton soup is a traditional local snack.

寻觅备选世遗佳境 1
广西壮族自治区北海市
Beihai, Guangxi Zhuang Autonomous Region

13 蓝之源 The Origin of the Blue

孕育中华民族海洋文明的起始之地

Breeding Place for the Sea-and-Ocean Civilization of the Chinese People

中国大陆最南缘濒临北部湾蓝色大海之畔，有一座充满亚热带旖旎风光的浪漫海滨城市北海市。它是古代中国跨海路与欧亚诸国进行文化交流和商品贸易最早的通道之一，因其为汉时中国“海上丝绸之路”的始发港，从而成为孕育中华民族蓝色文明的起始地。

The southernmost part of Mainland China borders the vast blue waters of the Beibu Gulf, where Beihai, a fascinating and romantic subtropical city is located. As it used to be on the sea route that connected ancient China and the countries of Asia and Europe, by which cultural exchanges and commercial trades were carried out, it was referred to as the starting port of the Silk Road on the sea. Therefore, it became the original breeding place of the blue civilization of Chinese culture.

由珠兴城见沧桑

The Vicissitudes of Time in Beihai

初识北海是缘于“珠还合浦”的成语典故和南珠文明。

2010年上海世博会期间，广西馆的“镇馆之宝”——手托“南珠王”的“珍珠仙女”，成为世界各地游客关注的焦点。那“珍珠仙女”头上戴着的“海之皇冠”，镶嵌有228颗南珠。手上托举的“南珠王”，是目前中国最大的一颗天然海水珍珠，直径1.55厘米，重3.6克，可谓价值连城。

秦汉以来的古籍中，有大量记载百越先民开采和使用珍珠的史料，尤以合浦为最。《旧唐书·地理志》载：“廉州合浦县有珠母海，郡人采珠之所。”《粤西杂录》曰：“南珠出合浦白龙，历为贡品。”

《后汉书·循吏传·孟尝》记载：“（合浦）郡不产谷实，而海出珠宝，与交趾比境……尝到

相机：尼康 NIKON D70S，镜头：尼康 18-55mm，光圈：f/10，快门：1/200秒，曝光补偿：0EV **北海老街骑楼**

官，革易前敝，求民病利。曾未逾岁，去珠复还，百姓皆反其业。”这段记载说的是“珠还合浦”成语的典故：合浦这个地方历来“海出珠宝”，而“不产谷实”，当地民众靠入海采珠，然后与前来贩珠的中外商贾交易后，再易米为生。东汉汉安（142年）前后，合浦地方官吏“多贪秽”，一方面逼民滥采珍珠，一方面关闭交易市场，禁止珍珠外流。历来以珍珠贸易作为当地经济支柱的合浦，很快陷入“行旅无至，人物无资，贫者饿死于道”的绝境。海水中赋有灵性的珠蚌，纷纷迁徙至邻境的交趾（今越南）一带。合浦从此成为“夜海无光”的黑暗世界。

为改变合浦珠乡的昏暗状况，汉顺帝遴选“能吏”孟尝到合浦任太守。孟尝一到任，便深入民间“革易前敝”“求民病利”，鼓励民众有节制地开采珍珠，并恢复对外珍珠贸易市场。新政实施不到一年，原来“渐徙于交趾郡界”的珍珠，“复还”合浦。时人感慨：孟尝太守两袖清风拂得海晏河清，合浦方得“去珠复还，夜海重放珠光”！

成语典故不足为信，但合浦白龙城却真真切切地见证了“南珠”数千年来的兴衰史。

“南珠”的身价，在明末清初著名学者屈大均的《广东新语》中可见一斑：“合浦珠名曰南珠。其出西洋者曰西珠，出东洋者曰东珠。东珠豆青白色，其光润不如西珠。西珠又不如南珠，南珠自雷廉至交趾千里间六池（所出）。”合浦南珠自古美名远扬，身价不菲。当时合浦的“数万金（意为价值）珠，至五羊（现广州）之市，一夕而售”，十分抢手。

“南珠”价值如此之高，自然引起历代朝廷的极大关注，将其视为国库进项之一。明洪武七年（1374年），朝廷下令在合浦白龙村一带建造白龙城，城墙南北长三千多米，东西宽两百多米，高六米。城内设有采珠太监公馆、珠池大使官邸和珠场巡检司等官衙。起初，白龙城官员还兼有海防之职。后来，海防功能渐渐丧失，白龙城成了名

相机：尼康 NIKON D70S，镜头：尼康 18–55mm，光圈：f/3.5，快门：1/1250秒，曝光补偿：0EV **北海城市雕塑群**

相机：尼康 NIKON D70S，镜头：尼康 18–55mm，光圈：f/8，快门：1/80秒，曝光补偿：0EV **北海市银滩**

符其实的“南珠城”。在珠池太监的监督下，采珠人下海采珠完全是拿身家性命作赌注。明朝陆容的《菽园杂记》记述，采珠人以长绳缚腰，携竹篮深潜海底，拾取珠蚌置于篮中。待采珠人摇动绳子，船上人便收绳，将采珠人和篮子一起拽上水面。采珠时，时常遇上食人鲨及“大鱼蛟鳌诸海怪”，船上人只要看到海水中有一缕缕殷红的鲜血浮至水面，“则知（水下人）已葬鱼腹”。即使侥幸逃得性命，也必然是肢残臂断。有的恶吏为防止珠民“偷懒”，竟在珠民脚上缚绑大石块，不许“随意上浮”，结果“溺而死者相随”。在明代两广都御史林富向朝廷的奏疏中，就将采珠形容为“以人易珠”。看似简简单单的四个字，包含着采珠人多少血和泪啊！

由于历代封建统治者的竭泽而渔，至清代，合浦采珠业渐趋衰落。据统计，从顺治元年（1644年）到康熙三十四年（1659年）的五十多年间，每次下海采珠，所得皆“寥若晨星”。到乾隆年间，有时采珠常为一无所获。新中国成立前夕，当地珠民仅靠采珠已不能维持生计。陷入困苦境遇的民众，在合浦廉州建起一座“还珠亭”，以怀念孟尝。如今亭已不存，但亭上的一副对联却流传至今：“孟尝何处去了，珍珠几时飞回。”

“南珠”真正“飞回”合浦，是在新中国成立后。1957年，在周恩来总理的亲自关心下，将延续了几千年的自然采珠改变为人工养殖。1958年，我国第一个人工养殖海水珍珠基地在北海市合浦营盘建立。随后又突破了珍珠贝人工养殖育苗技术难关，南珠养殖从此步入一个全新的发展阶段。

The name of the city, Beihai, originates both from the Chinese idiom *zhu huan he pu*, implying a sense of the recovery of lost things or people, and from the South Pearl Culture.

During the 2010 Expo in Shanghai, China, the

相机：尼康 NIKON D70S，镜头：尼康 18-55mm，光圈：f/8，快门：1/60秒，曝光补偿：0EV **夏日银滩**

most treasured exhibit of Guangxi Pavilion was the Pearl Fairy Maiden holding up the South Pearl King, which attracted tourists from all over the world. The crown on top of the maiden's head was imbedded with 228 south pearls. The South Pearl King held high up in her hand is, so far, the largest natural sea pearl in China, 1.55 cm in diameter and 3.6 gram in weight. Therefore, it is priceless.

In the archives since the Qin and Han Dynasties, there are a large number of records about the ancient local people diving for and making use of pearls, especially the people of Hepu.

It was said that the place by the name of Hepu produced sea pearls, but not grains. The local people dove into the sea for pearls, with which they bartered with merchants, Chinese and foreign. And then they bought rice to live on. Around 142 A.D., during the East Han Dynasty, the magistrates were so corrupt that they compelled the local residents to endlessly pick pearls, on one hand, and closed down the trading markets with the intention to prevent the outflow of the pearls, on the other. As a result, the pearl trade, which had been the economic pillar in Hepu, went bankrupt. Thus, Hepu became a world of darkness.

To make a drastic change in the economy of the pearl town, the then emperor appointed a new magistrate, Mengchang. By taking various measures over the course of one year, Mengchang people picked pearls moderately and restored the pearl markets. Very soon, pearls returned to Hepu, which was brightly lit again!

Because of its high value, the south pearl naturally drew imperial attention from dynasty to

百年老街

dynasty. It was regarded as one of the contributions to the imperial court. In the process of picking pearls, many divers lost their lives one way or another deep in the sea. As described, pearls are acquired at the sacrifice of human lives. Pearls are actually tears and drops of blood!

It was after the founding of the People's Republic of China that the south pearl genuinely came back to Hepu. In 1957, under the personal concern of Premier Zhou Enlai, the natural picking of pearls that had lasted for thousands of years was transformed into artificial cultivation. The year 1958 witnessed the setup of the first base of artificial cultivation of sea pearls in Hepu.

海上丝路处女地

The Starting Point of the Silk Road on the Sea

再识北海是缘于这里曾经是孕育中华民族海洋文明的起始地。

中国南方是南岛人种的发源地。先秦时代称之为百越民族，是世界上分布最广的民族之一，他们拥有优秀的航海经验和冒险精神，足迹遍及太平洋和印度洋，史前时代起即开始了远洋迁徙，马达加斯加、夏威夷和新西兰均有分布。

两千多年前的秦汉时期，一艘艘满载瓷器、丝绸、食糖和五金等货物的商船，在合浦港集结列队，扬帆远航，架起了中国与东盟乃至世界众多国家经贸文化的桥梁。这条古代海道交通大动脉，早于两千多年前张骞通西域、陆地丝绸之路出现之前，成为中国与西方跨海交流的主要通道和门户，这就是闻名海内外的海上丝绸之路。

西汉朝廷派出驿使率领的船队，沿着先前民间贸易开发的海上航线，到达中南半岛、南洋群岛、印度东南海岸和斯里兰卡等地。公元前1世纪，中国丝绸已成为地中海沿岸各国最珍贵的衣料，其中部分衣料由海上“丝路”运达这里。外国的香料、金银器、宝石、琉璃器等货物亦从海路运来中国。同时，也为中国这个历来以农耕文明为主导的文明古国，带来了十分或缺的海洋文明的信息。

中国东南部沿海山多平原少，且内部往来不易。因此自古以来，百姓为生计所迫，积极向海上发展。中国东南海岸夏、冬两季皆有季风助航，因此也增加了由海路通往欧陆的可能性。海上丝绸之路主要有东海起航线和南海起航线，形成于秦汉时期，发展于三国隋朝时期，繁荣于唐宋时期，转变于明清时期，是世界上已知的最为古老的海上官方往来航线，与陆路丝绸之路共同形成了中国与域外贸易往来的完整体系。

作为古代中国与外国交通贸易和文化交往的海上通道，随着时代的变迁，始发港和贸易重点有所不同。船运起始点逐渐北移，包括徐闻、合浦、临海、广州、泉州和漳州等等。汉代海上丝绸之路的始发港为徐闻古港，从公元3世纪30年代起，广州取代徐闻、合浦成为主港。宋末至元代时，泉州超越广州，并与埃及的亚历山大港并称为“世界第一大港”。明初海禁，加之战乱影响，泉州港逐渐衰落，漳州月港兴起。在隋唐时运送的主要大宗货物是丝绸，海上丝绸之路由此得名。到了宋元时期，瓷器出口渐渐成为主要货物。因此，人们也把它称作“海上陶瓷之路”，还由于输入的商品历来主要为香料，因此也把它称作“海上香料之路”。

海上丝绸之路的发展也几经沉浮。在隋唐以前，海上丝绸之路曾辉煌一时，是陆上丝绸之路开通后中外贸易的另一种重要补充形式。隋唐时期，由于西域战火不断，陆上丝绸之路被战争所碍，海上丝绸之路又代之兴起。到唐宋两代，伴随着北方少数民族的活跃以及中国造船、航海技术的长足发展，中国通往东南亚、马六甲海峡、印度洋、红海，以及非洲大陆的航路纷纷开通与延伸，海上丝绸之路又再一次替代了陆上丝绸之路，成为中国对外交往的主要通道。

两千多年以来，海上丝绸之路为沟通中外各国的友好交往，促进中外各国的社会、经济和文化的繁荣发展，做出了永不磨灭的贡献，被世界各国人民传为佳话。

北海市尤以北面临海由此得名，因其地处中国大陆最南缘，南濒北部湾，这种独特的地理位置，使北海市在海上丝绸之路诸航线中夺得先机。

“自日南障塞、徐闻、合浦，船行可五月，有都元国……黄支之南，有已程不国，汉之译使自此还矣。”这段出自《汉书·地理志》的记载，是史籍中关于中国官方商船从中国南部港口至东南亚各国进行商贸活动和海上航路的最早记载，也是有关海上丝绸之路的最早记载。

北海合浦自西汉元鼎六年（前111年）设置合浦郡，是汉朝南海对外海上贸易的中心和枢纽，向来为云、贵、川、桂、湘、鄂等省与海外贸易的主要商品集散地之一，也是中国从海上走向东南亚、南亚、欧洲的最便捷的海上通道。

近年来在北海出土的一大批与海上丝绸之路有关的文物，印证了北海合浦作为海上丝绸之路始发港昔日的繁华。

合浦汉代文化博物馆内陈列的数百件汉墓出土文物，很多是海外舶来的奇珍异宝：一尊波斯陶壶，通体涂着产自波斯的湖蓝色釉料；几枚缠花金球，工艺造型带有明显的希腊风韵；大量琥珀饰品，产于斯里兰卡、欧洲和非洲等地；蓝色玻璃杯和大量玻璃珠，来自东南亚、印度和罗马等地；一尊胡人俑座灯，面貌服饰都为海外民族；一座铜熏炉，残存香料原产地来自马来西亚一带。其中，黄泥冈一号墓的陪葬品，就占据了该馆的“半壁江山”。该墓主人是汉代徐闻县令陈褒。一个小小的县令就拥有龙首金带钩、玉璧等多种奢侈品，合浦当年海上贸易之繁盛、豪商巨贾之多可窥一斑。

草鞋村汉城遗址是北海合浦成为汉代中国“海上丝绸之路”繁荣兴盛的又一重要见证。位于廉州镇西南侧，其一面临江，另三面有护城河相通，

相机：尼康 NIKON D70S，镜头：尼康 18–55mm，光圈：f/3.1，快门：1/100秒，曝光补偿：0EV　**北海市城市广场**

外形清晰，总面积约九千平方公里。这一带是平坦的台地和宽冲积形成的南流江平原，土壤肥沃，利于耕作，对于人口增加后的郡城，是颇为理想的居址。又由于这里的河道更为宽阔深邃，距离汉代的海岸线不足三公里，对外的海上贸易更为便利。据专家推测，它是西汉晚期和东汉时期的合浦郡城遗址，继承和发展了大浪古城遗址的城市功能。其丰富的遗存要素，如此大规模、完整的汉代古城遗迹，在我国汉代考古上十分罕见。

历史和文化，总是在昭示一个地区未来的发展走向。两千多年以后的今天，一条新的海上丝绸之路正从北海向外延伸，中国唯一一条国际海上旅游航线在此诞生。更为重要的是，持续升温的不仅仅是单纯的“邮轮经济”，而是昭示了中华民族走向海洋、走向未来伟大复兴之路的宏大气魄。

Beihai enjoys our attention because it is the original place that gave rise to the sea-and-ocean civilization of the Chinese people.

South China is the place of origin for the Indonesians, who were referred to as the Baiyue people in pre-Qin times, one of the most widely spread peoples in the world. With rich sea-faring experience and adventurous spirits, they went to various places around the Pacific and Indian Oceans. Even in the prehistoric age, they began to migrate to faraway places such as Madagascar, Hawaii, New Zealand, etc.

In the Qin and Han Dynasties about 2,000 years ago, merchant ships laden with porcelain, silk, sugar and hardware arrayed in the Hepu Port set sail for distant lands. They functioned as bridges for the economic trade and cultural exchange between China and southeast Asian nations as well as other parts of the world. This ancient sea-faring artery was 2,000 years prior to the Silk Road that Zhang Qian, who was an eminent adventurer, traveler and diplomat of the Han Dynasty as well as the pioneer of the Silk Road on land, took to the West. Therefore, it was the main thoroughfare and passage for the exchanges between China and the West, thus named the Silk Road on the sea a name well-known all over the world.

The starting port and the trade along the Silk Road on the sea have changed with the lapse of time. The starting point for the ships moved northwards, from Xuwen to Hepu, to Linhai, to Guangzhou, to Quanzhou, to Zhangzhou, etc. During the Han Dynasty, the starting point of the Silk Road on the sea was the ancient Xuwen Port. In the third decade of the third century A.D., Zhuangzhou replaced Xuwen and Hepu, and became the major port. By the time of the end of the Song Dynasty and the beginning of the Yuan Dynasty, Quanzhou surpassed Guangzhou. And Quanzhou, as well as Alexandia of Egypt, was referred to as the world's largest port. At the beginning of the Ming Dynasty, due to the wars then, Quanzhou Port declined; consequently, Zhangzhou Port thrived. The major freight transported in large quantities during the Sui and Tang Dynasties was silk, thus the name the Silk Road on the sea. In the Song and Yuan Dynasties, however, the major freight was porcelain. For this reason, it was also called the Porcelain Road on the sea. And also because of the transportation of spices, it was known as the Spice Road on the sea.

For over 2,000 years, the Silk Road on the sea, in spite of ups and downs, has made indelible contributions to international communications and social, economic, and cultural prosperity in China and foreign countries. It was highly praised by people of various countries.

相机：尼康 NIKON D70S，镜头：尼康 18–55mm，光圈：f/10，快门：1/400秒，曝光补偿：0EV **北海冠头岭海滩**

Beihai City, which means North Sea City, was so named because it is attached to the sea on the north. Its unique location, i.e. at the southernmost tip of Mainland China and bordering Beibu Gulf on the south, enabled the city to take priority in all the seaward routes of the Silk Road on the sea.

Hepu of Beihai City became a county in 111 B.C., i.e. in the West Han Dynasty. It served as a trading center and hub of the South China Sea during the Han Dynasty. It was one of the collecting and distributing places of the major goods of the sea trade for such provinces as Yunnan, Guizhou, Guangxi, Hunan, Hubei, etc. It started the shortest passage on the sea towards Southeast Asia, South Asia, and Europe.

In recent years, large quantities of cultural relics related to the Silk Road on the sea have been unearthed in Beihai, thus proving the then prosperity in Hepu of Beihai, the then starting port of the Silk Road on the sea.

History and culture always reflect the future development of the area concerned. Today after over 2,000 years, a new Silk Road on the sea is extending out from Beihai, and the only worldwide tourist route on the sea will come into being in China. What's more important, what is getting warmer is not only the 'ocean liner economy', but also the great enterprising outlook with which theChinese people will stride toward the seas and into the future.

Tips 寻访者须知

佳境指数 Scenery Index：★★★★

备选序列：海上丝绸之路——中国世界文化遗产预备名单第16号（国家文物局2012年11月版）

List Number: Silk Road on the Sea, No.16 in the preparatory list for Chinese World Heritage (November,2012 Edition by the State Cultural Relics Bureau)

寻访提示：北海市银滩素有“中国第一滩”之誉，游客到此要充分享受明媚的阳光、蔚蓝的大海、洁白的沙滩等大自然给予的优厚馈赠。同时，这里有我国最大、最年轻、有大量火山遗迹的涠洲岛，有罕见连片红树林和珍稀动植物生存的合浦县山口红树林湿地自然保护区，这些人文和自然景观不可错过。

Location Notes: The Silver Beach of Beihai City has long been known as China's No.1 Beach. Tourists that come to the beach will fully indulge themselves in the bright sunshine, blue sea, and white grains of sand. On Weizhou Island, where there are the largest, youngest remains of volcanoes, can be found stretches of mangrove trees and rare flora and fauna species. It is a mangrove tree wetland, a natural reserve. You should not miss it.

摄影提示：北海的摄影创作尤以海滨风光为主。蓝天白云、碧海银沙、椰树婆娑、海岛湿地、火山遗迹等均可成为创作主题。利用海平面反射天空光影的绚丽变化，是在银滩进行摄影创作的要诀之一。根据海平线为基准完成富有特色的构图以后，在日出、日落时有意识地利用水面的反光，会使作品收到意想不到的效果。涠洲岛是用火与水精雕而成的作品，其因火山喷发而被烧灼、积压而成的石壁、石台、石洞、石崖等景观，壮观怪诞，色彩绚丽，最佳的摄影创作

相机：尼康 NIKON D70S，镜头：尼康 18-55mm，光圈：f/4.5，快门：1/60秒，曝光补偿：0EV **北海市避风港**

时间在日落时分，因色温变化而使岩礁呈现耀眼的赤红色，绚烂多姿。在构图上要处理好岩嶕、海礁、海平面和渔舟之间的关系。

Tips for Photography: Photography in Beihai should focus on the scenery of the sea beach. White clouds in the blue skies, the silver beach along the blue sea, the graceful coconut trees, and the remains of volcanoes could all be themes for photographic creation.

民俗提示：疍家风情为北海市一道民俗风景线。疍家作为“以舟楫为家，捕鱼为业”的水上人家，其居住一般在傍岸临水架设的棚户里，人称“疍家棚”。疍家在历史上被看做是“愚蠢不谙文字，不记岁年，朝夕惟局促舟中，所得鱼仅充一饱的蛮民”，有“男女衣不盖肤，婚时以蛮歌相迎”等习俗。可见当时的疍家生活是何等艰辛。如今这种情况早已不复存在。疍家的婚嫁仪式颇有情趣。闺女出嫁前要例行“哭嫁”，男女对答，哀婉动听。

Brief Introduction to the Local Culture: The Dan people form a folk scene in Beihai City. They live in boats and make a living by fishing. The huts erected along the banks of the sea are referred to as Dan Huts.

美食提示：北海是中国四大渔场之一，海产丰富，是吃海鲜的好地方之一。当地民间素有“第一芒，第二鲳，第三马鲛郎”之说。芒鱼是一种生活在江河入海口咸淡水中的鱼类，肉质尤其腴美。体色灰白，状如小狗。这种鱼用八角、南乳红焖，香嫩异常。鲳鱼有白鲳、黑鲳和花鲳三种，以白鲳为上。白鲳中又以鹰鲳味道最好，价格也比其他鲳鱼高得多。鲳鱼巴掌大小，一般姜丝清蒸。一块入口，细、嫩之感油然而生。马鲛鱼肉质弹性特别好，切片油煎或者煎焦黄后用葱花闷熟，好看而且爽脆。马鲛鱼也可做鱼丸，煮汤汤白清甜，老少皆宜。其他比较著名的佳肴有：鸡饭、老虎鱼汤、椒盐弹虾、清蒸笠鱼、白灼沙虫、姜葱花蟹、白灼中虾、清蒸插螺和梅子蒸普鱼等。

Food Tips: As one of the four fishing areas in China, Beihai is rich in seafood products. Therefore, people go and enjoy seafood delicacies there.

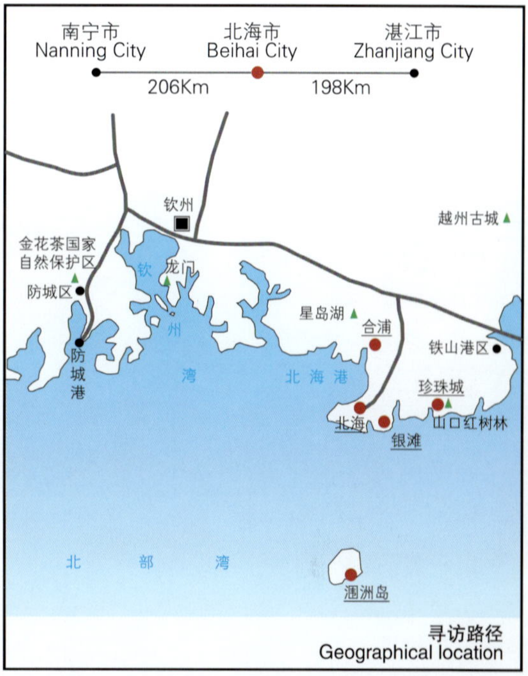

寻觅备选世遗佳境 1
福建省宁德市闽浙木拱廊桥
Pingnan County, Ningde, Fujian

14 虹之桥 Rainbow Bridge

深藏闽浙腹地木拱廊桥之“侏罗纪公园”
世界桥梁史上之孤本范例

Jurassic Park of Wooden Covered Bridges Hidden Deep in Interior Fujian and Zhejiang;
Only Example of its Kind in World History of Bridges

北宋张择端名画《清明上河图》中横跨汴水的虹桥，千年之后在闽浙腹地重放异彩。

木拱廊桥也称贯木拱风雨桥，俗称“厝桥”，是我国传统木构桥梁中技术含量最高的一个品类。著名桥梁专家唐寰澄先生所著的《中国科学技术史·桥梁卷》中，称廊桥“在世界桥梁史上惟中国有之”，而著名桥梁专家茅以升则赞其为中国桥梁史上的“侏罗纪公园”。

The rainbow bridge across the Bianshui River in the famous painting *Riverside Scene at Qingming Festival* relived its glorious life in interior Fujian and Zhejiang.

Among the traditional wooden bridges in China, the wooden arch bridge is the type that is of top technology. Mr. Tang Huancheng, the famous bridge specialist, once said that the wooden arch bridge can be found only in China in the world history of bridges. Mr. Mao Yisheng, the eminent bridge specialist, referred to such bridges as the Jurassic Park in the Chinese history of bridges.

长虹卧波飞古渡

Rainbows Soaring over Rivers and Valleys

中国木拱廊桥现尚存一百三十余座，且主要分布于闽东北和浙西南地区，包括福建省的屏南、寿宁、周宁和政和县，以及浙江省的泰顺、庆元和景宁县等。其中在福建省宁德境内就有五十余座，而集大成者主要在屏南和寿宁县。

屏南县治县于翠屏山之南，双溪交汇之地，境内山高林密，溪多涧深，迁自中原地区的屏南先民中的桥梁工匠，根据屏南地区这种特殊的地理环境和当地森林资源丰富的特点，充分施展聪明才智，精选经得起风雨侵蚀的杉木为建桥材料，数百年间，在屏南境内修建了五十多座形式各异的木拱廊桥，成为与外界沟通的重要纽带，大大改善了屏南地区的交通状况。

相机：尼康 NIKON D700，镜头：70–200mm f/2.8，光圈：f/11，快门：1/80秒，感光度：ISO200，曝光补偿：–1EV **屏南县长桥镇万安桥**

在屏南地区，木拱廊桥大多为古代乡绅行善积德出资建造，变溪涧为通途，造福一方，世代受益。数百年来，廊桥既是当地民众便捷出行、乘凉歇息、躲避风雨、观光浏览、社交贸易的重要场所，同时也是村民祭祀的载体之一，廊桥上都设有神龛供乡民祭祀。有的桥屋内设多个神龛，可同时供奉多组神灵。供奉的神像很广泛，祭祀的对象有为屏南民众崇拜的观音菩萨、临水夫人陈靖姑、五显灵官大帝、真武帝、齐天大圣孙悟空等，甚至连乡村肇基始祖也摆上神龛。不同族群的民众，把各自不同的宗教信仰神像供奉在廊桥里，显示了当地村民宗教信仰的多样性和融合性。每年的农历五月初五，屏南地区在端午节都有廊桥走桥祭祀习俗，祭祀的对象不仅有桥神以及桥头庙神灵，还有历史人物屈原，寄托了村民对家族幸福安康和来年风调雨顺的期盼，称屏南为中国廊桥文化博物馆一点不为过。

屏南木拱廊桥还具有与众不同的特点：一为量多类广，在保存至今的近百座古代桥梁中，有木拱廊桥13座、平梁式木构廊桥22座、石拱廊桥18座；二为年代久远，现存廊桥建造历史最远的可追溯至北宋。始建于宋代的有万安桥、千乘桥、百祥桥、龙井桥、广利桥等，始建于元代的有广福桥等；三为桥长形美，万安桥是我国现存最长的木拱廊桥；四为人文璀璨，许多古廊桥在碑记、桥屋梁、桥面、桥墩等处记载着建（修）桥的时间和筹建者、捐款人、建桥工匠等人的姓名，有的还在屋梁或亭柱上书写着对仗工整、充满诗情画意的对联，不仅增添了古代廊桥的艺术魅力，也为今天研究廊桥文化留下了珍贵的文字依据；五为便于修缮，木拱廊桥设计精巧，不费寸钉片铁，只凭榫卯衔接，结构严密，稳固耐用，日常维护也非常方便，稍具木工常识的工匠都能胜任维修工作，确保了古桥完好且延续至今。

相机：尼康 NIKON D70S，镜头：18–55mm，光圈：f/13，快门：1/800秒，感光度：ISO1000，曝光补偿：0EV **屏南县棠口乡千乘桥**

相机：尼康 NIKON D70S，镜头：18-55mm，光圈：f/10，快门：1/250秒，感光度：ISO1000，曝光补偿：0EV **屏南县白水洋双龙桥**

Up to now, there are still some 130 wooden arch bridges in China, and most of them are found in the northeast of Fujian and the southwest of Zhejiang. In the Ningde area of Fujian alone there are still over fifty such bridges, most of which are located in Pingnan and Shouning Counties.

Pingnan County is located on the south side of Cuiping Mountain and at the meeting place of two rivers, where there are high mountains and thick forests, numerous streams and deep ravines. Among the people that migrated from the Central Plains to Pingnan, the bridge builders fully displayed their ability and wisdom to build bridges in accordance with the special geographic environment and by means of the rich forest resources. They deliberately chose weather-resistant Chinese fir trees as the building material. Over the coures of several hundred years, more than fifty wooden arch bridges that are unique in style were erected. They served as important links with the outside world and greatly improved the transportation status of the Pingnan area.

In this area, most wooden arch bridges were built with funds donated by the local gentries that cherished the intention to do good deeds for society. They aspired to make thoroughfares over streams and rivers, thus benefiting the local people and their descendants generation after generation. For hundreds of years, these bridges have been performing several functions: convenient for local people to come and go, easy for passers-by to take a rest, possible for travellers to get shelter from wind and rain, plausible for visitors to do sightseeing, and important for social exchanges and trades.

相机：尼康 NIKON D70S，镜头：18-55mm，光圈：f/9，快门：1/100秒，感光度：ISO100，曝光补偿：0EV **屏南县棠口乡金造桥**

Meanwhile, they also served as a means for local villagers to offer sacrifices to ancestors and deities; therefore, such bridges had shrines for people to offer sacrifices. The images of different religions put in the shrines by people of different families and clans reveal the diversity and reconciliation in their religious beliefs. On every 5th of the 5th lunar month, people in Pingnan hold a variety of activities to celebrate the Dragon Boat Festival, wishing happiness and prosperity in the year to come. Therefore, Pingnan deserves the name Museum of Wooden Arch Bridge Culture in China.

Such bridges bear quite a number of special features. First of all is the number and variety. Among all the hundred-odd ancient bridges that have been preserved up to now, there are 13 wooden arch bridges, 22 flat-beam wooden bridges, and 18 stone arch bridges. Second, all of them were built a long, long time ago. The earliest of the existent bridges were built back in the northern Song Dynasty. Third, they are all long and beautiful. The Wan'an Bridge is the longest wooden arch bridge in China. Fourth, they boast literary brilliance. In one way or another, many of them show records of construction time, sponsors, donors of funds, and bridge builders. The couplets left on the beams and pillars were so well composed and hand-written that they not only add artistic charms to these ancient bridges but also offer invaluable verbal records for the research of such bridges. Fifth, they are easy to repair and renovate. The meticulous design and superb craftsmanship make the bridges withstand wear and tear. At the same time, it is not difficult to carry out routine maintenance. People

新春走桥

with a little knowledge of carpentry could manage to do the repair and maintenance work; that's why, they remain in pretty good shape even today.

架木凌空峙千秋

Wooden Bridges Suspended High in the Skies

从屏南县城古峰镇往南驱车三十余公里，便到了长桥镇。走街过巷，再穿过一处人流熙攘的集市，似长虹卧溪的万安桥，静静的展现在眼前。

始建于北宋元祐五年（1090年）的万安桥，又称长桥、龙江公济桥，是我国现存最长的木拱廊桥。据史料记载："长桥宋时建，两溪相接，亘如长虹，叠石为墩，五构亭其上。"现能证明宋代遗构的，是正中桥墩上存有一块嵌入桥墩的石碑："弟子江稹舍钱一十三贯又谷三十四石，结石墩一造，为考妣二亲承此良因，又为合家男女及自身各乞保平安。元祐五年庚午九月谨题。"后桥几毁几建，现存桥为民国二十一年（1932年）重建。听当地老人说，在这次重建过程中，有一位工匠不慎从拱架上跌落溪中，却毫发无损，安然无恙，所以更名为"万安桥"。现桥长98.2米，宽4.7米，桥屋杉木立柱152根，37开间，双坡单檐悬山顶。桥面用杉木板铺设，两旁设长凳、靠背栏杆，外置挡雨板。桥墩前尖后方呈半船形，桥堍、桥墩均用块石砌筑，可御洪水冲击。该桥跨度大，桥孔多，技术性强，用材量大，仅拱与立柱就使用杉木长料达四百三十多根，充分体现了古代造桥工匠的高超技艺和智慧。

达才溪上，视野开阔，树木青翠，风光秀丽。遥望长桥，恰似长虹卧波。此景正如清贡生江起蛟诗中描写的美景："千寻缟带跨沧州，阳羡桥应莫比幽。月照虹弯飞古渡，水摇鳌背漾神州。汉家墨迹留中砥，秦洞桃花接上流。锦渡浮来香片片，令人遥想武陵游。"此景还为屏南昔日"龙江八景"之一："桥接溪渠畔，遥瞻似彩虹。横村连左右，隔水渡西东。雁齿休专美，鳌梁岂羡工。济人

相机：佳能 Canon Eos-1DX，镜头：24-70mm f/2.8，光圈：f/3.5
快门：1/125秒，感光度：ISO800，曝光补偿：0EV **泰顺县泗溪镇北涧桥**

相机：佳能 Canon Eos-1DX，镜头：24-70mm f/2.8，光圈：f/11
快门：1/100秒，感光度：ISO800，曝光补偿：0EV **庆元县阜梁桥**

传旧政，今日不须蒙。"

棠口乡棠口村水尾的千乘桥，是屏南县形态最美的廊桥。千乘桥又名祥峰桥，是屏南境内长度仅次于万安桥的木拱廊桥。始建于南宋理宗年间（1225—1264年），同样也是屡毁屡建。现桥为清嘉庆二十五年（1820年），由当地乡绅、秀才周大权等人募捐复建。当时召集能工巧匠精心设计，将桥梁建成形似一只昂首展翅的雄鸡。桥长62.7米，宽4.9米，一墩二孔，单孔跨度27米。桥墩用块石整齐叠砌，呈船形。为确保桥梁永固，墩尖端雕成鸡头形状，上面压着重石，寓意镇水。桥中设神龛，祀五显灵官大帝。屋面为单檐悬山顶，中脊置风狮爷，翘角呈燕尾式，线条自然流畅。

千乘桥横跨棠口溪上，北连祥峰寺，南临八角亭，两岸风景秀丽。桥上两边有条板椅，供行人憩息。两旁尚存档风板，以御风雨侵袭。距桥十米处，有清乾隆四年（1739年）的石坊一座和八角亭、林公庙、祥峰寺和两口龙井，附近还竖有新四军三支队六团北上抗日纪念碑。桥西端有四通碑记，其中三通记载着捐款人姓名和金额，一通为周大权撰写的千乘桥记，碑文中云："临渊累石，下同鼎峙千秋；架木凌空，上拟云横百尺。"此为赞美千乘桥的最好写照。

金造桥是屏南县最为险峻的木拱廊桥，始建于清嘉庆十三年（1808年），民国三十七年（1948年）重建。清进士张正元曾诗云："廿文桥横两岸边，眼看鱼戏浪三千，前村犬吠花间客，隔水牛耕屋上田。双涧波光摇远权威，四山峰影倒长川，彩虹斜波浮云去，风约潮平镜里天。"原址在屏南县一座有千年历史的古村落棠口乡漈头村旁，2005年5月，为配合当地水库建设，金造桥原拆原装，全部构件被搬运到漈头村附近的屏宁二级公路旁的新址复建。桥长41.7米，宽4.8米，单孔跨度32.5米，桥面距水面高度12米，桥屋建15扇64柱。"两岸锁云烟波上彩虹长挂，双溪流壁玉潭中新月半钩"，这是书写在廊屋梁木上十三副对联中最为出彩的

相机：佳能 Canon Eos-1DX，镜头：24-70mm f/2.8，光圈：f/5，快门：1/80秒，感光度：ISO800，曝光补偿：0EV **泰顺县泗溪镇永庆桥**

相机：佳能 Canon Eos-1DX，镜头：24-70mm f/2.8，光圈：f/8，快门：1/125秒，感光度：ISO800，曝光补偿：0EV **庆元县举水乡如龙桥**

一副。桥上还有建桥首事题写的一首七律："昔日溪洪客不前，汪洋长叹有谁怜。去年议砍群山木，今夏欢联两岸烟。胜似彩虹低渡水，翻教新月与钩弦。我偕弟侄同题柱，永镇川流亿万年。"如此丰富的诗文题咏，表明漈头村千年来浓郁的人文气息。新建的廊桥离溪面约二十米，谷底深邃，四周群山环抱，地势险峻，不愧为屏南境内"险桥之一"。

屏南县还有广利桥、广福桥、百祥桥、龙井桥等众多形态各异的木拱廊桥隐藏在乡野之中，这些散落于山川之间的遗珠，风采依然。其独特的历史文化、科学技术和审美价值，已蜚声中外，要让更多的国人，来此领略这项珍贵中国优秀文化遗产的神采。

Driving for about 30 km southward from Gufeng Town of Pingnan County, you would find yourself in Changqiao Town. Walking through streets and lanes as well as a crowded fair, you will see right in front of you the Wan'an Bridge standing there quieltly like a rainbow over a stream.

The Wan'an Bridge, which began to be built in the 5th year (1090) of Emperor Yuanyou of the northern Song Dynasty, is China's longest wooden arch bridge that has survived to this day.

Above the Dacai Stream, the panoramic view includes verdant trees and beautiful landscapes. The bridge, looked at from a distance, resembles a rainbow reclining over the waves.

The Qiancheng Bridge in Tangkou Village of Tangkou County is the most beautiful wooden arch bridge, and second in length only to the Wan'an Bridge in Pingnan. Built during the years (1225-1264) of Emperor Lizong of the southern Song Dy-

相机：佳能 Canon Eos-1DX，镜头：24-70mm f/2.8，光圈：f/11，快门：1/250秒，感光度：ISO800，曝光补偿：0EV **庆元县濛洲桥**

nasty, this bridge experienced repeated destruction and reconstruction.

Lying above the Tangkou Stream, the Qiancheng Bridge spans Xiangfeng Temple on the north and Bajiao Pavilion on the south. Both banks boast exquisitely charming scenery. On either side of the bridges there is a bench for the passers-by to take a rest. Moreover, there are still boards along both sides of the bridge which protect passengers from rain and wind.

The Jinzao Bridge is the most precipitous wooden arch bridge in Pingnan, whose construction began in the 13th year (1808) of Emperor Jiaqing of the Qing Dynasty and was reconstructed in the 37th year (1948) of the Republic of China.

Besides, a variety of wooden arch bridges unique in style are hidden in the rural areas of Pingnan County. Scattered like pearls among the mountains and rivers, these bridges remain elegant and charming. The unique historic culture, science and technology, and esthetic values of these bridges enjoy a worldwide reputation. Therefore, it is a must for more and more compatriots to come and appreciate this treasure of the excellent Chinese cultural heritage.

Tips 寻访者须知

佳境指数 Scenery Index： ★★★★

备选序列： 闽浙木拱廊桥——中国世界文化遗产预备名单第19号（国家文物局2012年11月版）

List Number: The Wooden Bridges of Fujian and Zhejiang — No.19 in the preparatory list for Chinese World Heritage (November 2012 Edition by the State Cultural Relics Bureau)

寻访提示： 屏南县位于宁德市西部，东临福安、寿宁和周宁县，北与浙江省庆元县相连，周边旅游资源十分丰富，除了木拱廊桥外，屏南县地质奇观白水洋、鸳鸯溪，周宁县鲤鱼溪、九龙漈、霍童古镇、支提山，福鼎县太姥山，浙江省庆元县月山村、百山祖，以及霞浦县海滩养殖、天光云影可顺道寻访。闽浙地区及屏南县境内廊桥分布较为分散，建议出行前做好案头工作，按计划逐一寻访。

Location Notes: Pingnan County is located in the west of Ningde City, bordering Fu'an, Shouning and Zhouning Counties on the east, and Qingyuan County of Zhejiang on the north as well. Its vicinity is rich in tourist resources. In addition to the wooden arch bridges, many other natural scenic spots and cultural sites are worth visiting.

摄影提示： 木拱廊桥为摄影创作的主要对象，但作为古建筑的木拱廊桥元素比较单一，在摄影创作过程中，最好在构图上结合当地的民俗民风、劳作场景、天光云影、春花秋色、河流溪水、峡谷山峦等元素，既可增添作品的信息量，也可提升作品的内涵和感染力。

Tips for Photography: The wooden arch bridges are, of course, the major theme of photography. Mere bridges may look quite monotonous; therefore, in the process of taking photos, other elements, such as folk culture, laboring peo-

相机：佳能 Canon Eos-1DX，镜头：24-70mm f/2.8，光圈：f/10，快门：1/160秒，感光度：ISO800，曝光补偿：0EV **庆元县兰溪桥**

ple, skies and clouds, spring flowers and autumn scenes, rivers and streams, valleys and mountains, could all be included in the pictures one way or another.

民俗提示：屏南地区木拱廊桥在每年农历正月初一至十五、五月初五端午节等，一般会有比较隆重的走桥祭祀活动。除了春节、元宵灯节、端午节、中秋节外，屏南每月皆有一两次传统节日，尤为隆重的是农历十月廿七的齐天大圣孙悟空诞辰之日。届时请神祭神，祈愿风调雨顺，人寿年丰，成为远近闻名的民俗文化节日。村中锣鼓、民乐、腰鼓、舞龙（布龙、香龙）、武术、花灯、八仙、杖头木偶等表演队伍轮番上场；诸多平时秘不示人的楹联、古牌匾、古石坊上的古圣旨等“传家宝”相继亮相；业余剧团老艺人演出的已有三百余年历史的平讲戏《马匹卜换妻》，不断引来台下如雷鸣般掌声；还有踩街活动也令人眼界大开。

Brief Introduction to the Local Culture: From the 1st through 15th of the first lunar month, i.e. the Spring Festival, and on the 5th of the 5th lunar month, i.e. the Dragon Boat Festival, some grand ceremonies and activities such as walking through the bridges and offering sacrifices are usually held on the wooden arch bridges in Pingnan.

美食提示：屏南饮食文化在清乾隆年间就闻名遐迩。最为出名要数漈头扁肉（云吞），扁肉的皮、馅都为家传秘技现场制作，皮薄、柔韧、润滑。汤汁都要用鸡鸭、猪骨等现场熬制而成，再配以佐料，肉馅色艳透亮，入口爽滑，鲜美无比。米烧兔也是当地特色美食，兔子宰杀后，烧谷米壳熏制而成，表皮呈暗红色，肉质香甜软糯，表皮脆且口感柔韧。较为出名的糕点有七层糕、根豆糕、雪片糕、喷糕。比较有名的饼类有咸馅、葱肉饼、炸蛎饼、光饼。颇受欢迎的米粿类有秋菊粿、煎黄粿、七重粿等。香糯可口的粽子类有粮粽、肉粽、豆粽等。还有花生炒米、肉包、鸡髻包、烧卖、水

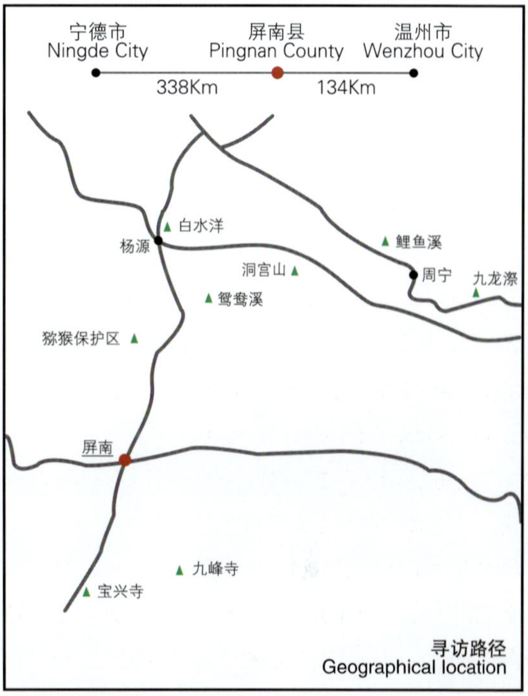

粉、拌面等也远近闻名。

Food Tips: The food of Pingnan was already well known far and wide as early as the reign of Emperor Qianlong of the Qing Dynasty. The best known dish is the wonton, which is unbelievably and unforgettably tasty. There are, of course, many other delicious snacks as well.

寻觅备选世遗佳境 1
福建省泉州市南安红砖建筑
Old Red-brick Houses of the Cais, Guangqiao Town,
Nan’an Town, Quanzhou, Fujian

15 故土的呼唤 Summons of Hometown

中原移民南迁出洋脉络之印证
中西合璧闽南红砖文化之大成
Migration from Central China to the South and Abroad; East–West Red–brick Culture

就瑰丽的色彩而言，中国所有的乡土建筑，在闽南红砖厝面前，都会黯然失色。当2013年元旦第一缕煦阳铺洒在闽南大地时，我来到了南安市官桥镇漳里村寻访蔡氏红砖大厝，一股浓郁的乡土芬芳扑面而来，沁人心脾。

厝，在闽南语中意为房屋。全村十余座气势恢宏的闽南红砖古厝错落有致，在旭日的照射下，墙体似火如焰，这些色彩艳丽的红砖赤瓦，俗称“胭脂红”，全由取之于当地富含氧化铁的红土壤烧制而成。与红得耀眼的砖瓦形成强烈色彩反差的，是家家户户门前房后大大小小竹匾中晾晒的白薯粉，晶莹如雪，白得抢眼，它们同样源自闽南大地的红土壤。

这些代表闽南“红砖文化”巅峰之作的蔡氏古居，为何从里到外都传递出一种与乡土密不可分的信息呢？除了具有强烈视觉冲击力的外在形态和美轮美奂的物理空间外，更难能可贵的是其蕴藏着一种中华民族千百年来一脉相承的集体人格和人文精神。

When the first ray of sunlight shone on the land in south Fujian on New Year's Day of 2013, I came to the old residence of the Cais in Zhangli, Guanqiao Town, Nan'an City. I was immediately greeted by a rich rural aroma, which was quite refreshing.

About a dozen ancient red-brick houses, high and low, are well arranged in the village, grand and imposing. In the morning sun, the walls look like frolicking flames. These bright red bricks and tiles are nicknamed Rouge Red, and are made from the local red clay rich in iron oxide. In sharp contrast to the dazzling red bricks are the white potato powders in bamboo trays, large and small, basking in the sun. As blindingly white as snow, they are also the local products from the red earth in south Fujian.

The former residence of the Cais represents the best work of art in the red-brick culture in

相机：佳能 Canon Eos-1DX，镜头：24-70mm f/2.8，光圈：f/11 快门：1/2000秒，感光度：ISO500，曝光补偿：0EV **蔡氏红砖厝村民晒秋**

south Fujian. How is it that it sends out a message that is inseparable from the local culture? It makes a strong visual impact and offers a physical space of extreme beauty. What's more, it embodies the collectivism and literary spirit that have been passed down for thousands of years in China.

泥土芬芳叶归根

Roots in the Earth

中华民族素有眷恋故土、叶落归根的人文情结。

蔡姓为福建省大姓之一，按最新权威统计数据，蔡姓在福建省排行第11位，在全国排行第44位。若从历史人文的角度看，福建蔡姓折射出了中原移民南迁的历史脉络。

蔡姓的始祖，可追溯到西周初年的蔡叔度。据《史记·卷三十五·管蔡世家第五》：叔度乃周文王第五子，周武王之弟。武王克商后，叔度受封于蔡(今河南上蔡县)，史称蔡叔。武王去世，成王继位，蔡叔等反叛，被周公平定后放逐。此后，周成王仍将蔡叔之子胡封于蔡。

春秋时，蔡姓主要繁衍于现在的河南省境内，其间因受楚国相逼，曾先后迁徙于新蔡（今属河南）和州来（今安徽凤台，时称下蔡）。西晋惠帝时，曾将蔡氏聚居的河南陈留郡的一部分划出设置济阳国，后改济阳郡，辖地相当于今河南兰考、民权一带。故蔡姓族人大都以“济阳”作为郡望或堂号。

至两晋时期，战乱频发，迫使蔡姓族人随同中原士族大举南迁，辗转定居于江浙各地。至唐初时，蔡姓宗族始迁闽、桂等地。安史之乱爆发后，中原蔡姓族人又一次大举南下，与唐初先入闽之蔡姓合为一体，逐渐发展成为福建大姓，并成为当今台湾和广东蔡姓的主要来源。

宋朝时期，中原外族入侵不断加剧，尚留北方的蔡姓族人，不得不再次大规模南迁，进入江浙、

相机：佳能 Canon Eos-1DX，镜头：24-70mm f/2.8，光圈：f/14，快门：1/500秒，感光度：ISO500，曝光补偿：0EV **蔡氏红砖厝**

相机：佳能 Canon Eos-1DX，镜头：24-70mm f/2.8，光圈：f/24，快门：1/11秒，感光度：ISO1600，曝光补偿：0EV **蔡氏红砖厝晒秋**

皖南、闽粤等地，使南方蔡姓人口大幅增加。至北宋蔡襄时，已是名扬天下的望族。现今晋江青阳蔡氏祠堂正厅遗存的一副对联便是最好的印证，上联是“裔出周代，肇基唐代，官封宋代，长绵百代振家声”；下联为“脉映济阳，支分莆阳，派衍青阳，好就三阳开泰运”，涵盖了青阳蔡姓繁衍的源流和脉络。官桥镇漳里村的蔡氏堂号，也属“济阳衍派”，正是源于蔡襄这一支脉。

到了明清时期，蔡姓已迁衍各地，并远赴海外。南安紧邻宋元泉州海上丝绸之路起始点，自宋以来，历代都有人自此出海谋生，明清时期出洋者更甚，其中不乏功成名就者。蔡氏古居的始创者蔡启昌、蔡资深父子，就是其中的佼佼者。

据民国四年（1915年）《南安县志》中《蔡启昌》一文记载：“蔡启昌，名树清，三十五都漳里人。商于吕宋，积资甚裕，量宏好善。捐修文庙考棚，筑造寺院桥路，恤孤怜贫，施茶舍药，倡设拯婴堂，靡不踊跃乐输。”

另据菲律宾柯蔡济阳公所《蔡永明翁传略》记载：蔡资深于清后期与其父南渡菲律宾，父子同心协力，在岷市后街仔开设晋益小烛铺子。1850年蔡启昌回国，铺子交由蔡资深经营。蔡资深克勤克俭，取信于当地百姓，在岷市广置产业，经营范围和规模盛极一时，先后涉及百货、布匹、木材、房地产、家具、大米、纺织和铁器等。积累起雄厚财力的蔡资深乐善好施，办学兴教，收养弃婴，修桥造路。光绪三十一年（1905年），时逢安徽、浙江、江苏等遭受水涝，他捐金万两，又集资数百万两赈灾济民。为表彰义举，清廷曾封其为“资政大夫”。蔡资深还曾资助过菲律宾民族独立运动，当过菲律宾第一届国会议员，这在国内其他古民居建造者中并不多见。

千百年来，中华民族传统的耕读传家和重农轻商的观念可谓根深蒂固。蔡氏父子也不例外，深

相机：佳能 Canon Eos-1DX，镜头：24-70mm f/2.8，光圈：f/14，快门：1/250秒，感光度：ISO500，曝光补偿：0EV **蔡氏红砖厝院落**

信“久远之业，商不如农”，深感经商犹如水中浮萍，转眼易逝，全然没有土地的那种厚重与坚实，故应“士农工商全面发展”。长期漂泊海外，与积累巨额资财形成强烈反差的是内心深处日思夜想的乡土情结和民族归属感。

于是，蔡氏父子便在故土闽南泉州一处称“漳州寮”的地方广置荒地，组织族人开垦种植，择地建祠，祭祀先祖。然后，帮助族人先后在此建起带有中原文明、闽南文明和南洋文明鲜明印记的十多幢红砖大厝。

The Chinese people have always been known to be nostalgic, and they believe in returning to hometowns wherever they might have been.

The earliest ancestor of the Cais can be traced back to Cai Shudu in the first year of the western Zhou Dynasty. Historically speaking, Cai Shudu was the fifth son of King Wen of the Zhou Dynasty, and the brother of King Wu. After King Wu conquered the Shang Dynasty, Shudu was appointed the governor of Yucai, what is now Shangcai County of Henan. From then on, historical records referred to him as Cai Shu. After King Wu died, King Cheng succeeded. Cai Shu and some others rebelled, but were suppressed by the king and exiled. Later on, however, King Cheng appointed Hu, Cai Shu's son, the governor of Yucai.

During the Spring and Autumn Period, the Cais multiplied in what is now Henan. However, because they were driven out of the Chu Kingdom then, the Cais moved to Xincai (now in Henan) and Zhoulai (now Fengtai of Anhui, and then called Xiacai). Later on, they gathered and lived in Lankao and Minquan of Henan.

Up to the West and East Jin Period, when

闽南红砖大厝

wars broke out frequently, the Cais were compelled to move southward together with many people from the center of China, and finally settled down in various parts of Jiangsu and Zhejiang. In the early Tang Dynasty, the Cais began to move to Fujian and Guangxi. After An Lushan and Shi Siming started a rebellion, many of the Cais fled to the South once more. They merged with the Cais that came to Fujian in the early Tang Dynasty. Gradually Cai became a big name in Fujian, and that also explains the reason why there are people of the Cais in Guangdong and Taiwan nowadays.

During the Song Dynasty, because of the ever increasing invasion of middle China by alien nationalities, the remaining Cais in the North had to migrate to the South in large numbers. They entered Jiangsu and Zhejiang, south Anhui, Fujian and Guangdong; thus the population of the Cais drastically increased. Up to the northern Song times, the Cais had become a noble family known all over the world.

During the Ming and Qing Dynasties, the Cais moved and settled down in different parts of China, and even migrated abroad. Nan'an is close to Quanzhou, one of the starting points of the Silk Road on the sea in the Tang and Song Dynasties. Therefore, from then on, people from generation to generation went abroad for a living, especially an increasing number of people in the Ming and Qing Dynasties. Among them, quite a few were successful in business and reputation, such as Cai Qichang and Cai Zhishen, father and son, who were the pioneers of the construction of the Cais' old house.

It is said that father and son went the Philippines, where they started their business running a small candle shop. In 1850, the father returned to China and entrusted the shop to his son. Cai, Jr. worked very hard with frugality and diligence; what's more, he won the trust of the local people. Gradually he accumulated a lot of wealth and involved himself in a series of industries like general merchandise, cloth, timber, real estate, furniture, rice, textiles, ironware, etc. Meanwhile, he made great contributions to the local society by running schools, adopting abandoned children, and building bridges and roads.

It is a deep-rooted belief among Chinese people for hundreds of years that emphasis should be devoted to farming and that agriculture should be preferred to commerce. Father and son of the Cais were no exception. Holding the idea that "For an eternal family glory, commerce is inferior to farming", they deeply felt that doing business is just like a lotus leaf floating on the water, by no means immortal and utterly less solid and sustainable than the farmlands. In spite of the huge amount of wealth they had amassed, they seemed to be tortured by lack of the sense of belonging and by strong nostalgia.

Therefore, the father and son returned to their hometown, Quanzhou of south Fujian, where they purchased vast stretches of wasteland. Then they organized their family members to exploit the wastelands and build up their family temples where they offered sacrifices to gods and ancestors. Finally they built up more than ten red-brick houses which bear the obvious mixed characteristics of middle China, south Fujian and south Asian culture.

相机：佳能 Canon Eos-1DX，镜头：24-70mm f/2.8，光圈：f/14，快门：1/500秒，感光度：ISO500，曝光补偿：0EV **蔡氏红砖厝院落**

相机：佳能 Canon Eos-1DX，镜头：24-70mm f/2.8，光圈：f/10，快门：1/125秒，感光度：ISO500，曝光补偿：0EV **蔡氏红砖厝街巷**

红墙赤瓦皆传情

Red Bricks and Tiles: Everlasting Emotions

土楼、土堡、灰砖和红砖民居为福建四大民居，其中尤以红砖民居最为靓丽奇特。其浓缩了闽南人坚韧、开朗、沉稳和豁达的性格，表达了他们对美好生活的憧憬和向往。

蔡氏古居集闽南高超的建筑工艺之大成，并发扬光大了中国传统建筑文化的理念。而且，其建筑元素还兼容并蓄了印度佛教、伊斯兰教及南洋文化和西方建筑艺术的精华，极富历史文化内涵。

蔡宅其营造时间之长，做工布局之精实属罕见。蔡资深自清同治四年（1865年）开始斥资建造这一民居建筑群，直至清宣统三年（1911年）才竣工，耗时44年，十余座红砖大厝共有大小房间近四百间，占地面积三万多平方米。其不仅依靠群体布局、空间变化和外在形态，来传达和表现外在的神韵和精彩，更是运用雕刻、楹联、书画、色彩等多种装饰艺术，来提升其超凡脱俗的内在精神境界。

整个建筑群因地制宜，气势恢宏，布局严整，充分考虑了风水、防火、排水、日照、通风和防震等因素。在整体设计上更是独具匠心，用心良苦。每座大宅屋脊高翘，红墙赤瓦，雕梁画栋。门前墙砖浮雕，立体感强，窗棂镌花刻兽，装饰巧妙华丽。门墙厅壁书画点缀，情趣盎然，篆隶行楷，各具韵味。走进每一座大厝，令人眼界顿开，仿佛进入了一座建筑艺术博物馆。

蔡宅其装饰品味之高，类别之多，反映了闽南地区多种文化共生共荣的特色。蔡氏古宅的众多建筑元素中，大多展现了中国传统的儒、道、释理念，这在国内古民宅中不足为奇，而其独到的红墙赤瓦与燕尾翘脊的运用，却在中国民居史上独树一帜。千百年来，中国封建社会房屋的建造延续着一套等级森严的规制，红、黄两种色彩为皇宫和庙宇专用，而绿、青、蓝等艳丽色彩则属达官权贵的专有，普通百姓均不得染指。因而民间住宅大多只能使用黑、灰、白三种单调的色彩。敢于开风气之先，冲破这种死气沉沉

相机：佳能 Canon Eos-1DX，镜头：24-70mm f/2.8，光圈：f/11，快门：1/2000秒，感光度：ISO500，曝光补偿：0EV **蔡氏红砖厝晒秋**

的建筑规制的禁忌和束缚，赋予更为艳丽大气，包容开放的建筑理念，要归功于闽南这片热土上的百姓较早地接纳和融入了蓝色文明的种子。

泉州在宋元时期，为海上丝绸之路的始发港，中外文明在此交汇互通，而闽南大厝成为展现中西文明成果的最好载体。红墙赤瓦，再加上燕尾翘脊式的瓦顶，使闽南古厝有了皇城的气势。而许多带有印度佛教文化的辉绿岩连珠饰柱础、伊斯兰教艺术风韵的火焰形山花、西方建筑常见的蓝釉式葫芦栏杆和南洋文化特征的鱼尾狮雕塑等外来文化元素，在蔡氏古居中均可找到清晰的印记，凸现着闽南地区独有的中西合璧、文化交融的特征。

蓝天、碧海、白云、红砖，这是闽南红厝的关键词。这处色彩瑰丽、和谐大气的中国古民居瑰宝，现已蜚声中外。如今，蔡氏后裔仍然守护着自己的祖屋，述说和延续着荣耀，同时也敞开大门，迎接来自世界各地的宾客，展现中华民族包容并蓄、进取开放的心态和气度。

Earthen building, earthen fortress, gray-brick house and red-brick house are the four types of civilian residence in Fujian. Among the four, the red-brick house is most strikingly beautiful. In a condensed way, it fully embodies the typical dispositions of southern Fujian people: firm and tenacious, open and clear, deep and steady, and straight and optimistic. They always look forward to a good life in the future.

The buildings of the Cais symbolize the great achievements of superb architecture and carry forward the cultural conceptions in traditional Chinese architecture. Moreover, these buildings consist of the elements of Buddhism of India, Islam, and the essence of southeastern Asian culture and Western architectural arts, thus very rich in historical and cultural connotations.

It is definitely rare that the construction of the Cais' houses took so long a time and demonstrated such detailed craftsmanship.

The whole group of the imposing and magnificent buildings was built in adaptation to the local conditions and in terms of rigorous layout, taking into consideration such factors as geomantic omen, fire safety, water drainage, sunshine, ventilation, quakeproof measures, etc. The general design was so artistic that every house is actually a museum of architectural arts.

The use of red bricks and tiles as well as swallow-tail roofs is unique in the history of Chinese civilian residence.

As the starting port of the Silk Road on the sea in the Tang and Song Dynasties, Quanzhou, which was the mustering place of Chinese and foreign culture, boasted the south-Fujian houses that served as the best vehicle to show the achievements of Chinese and Western civilization.

Blue skies, blue seas, white clouds, and red bricks are all key words for the red houses in south Fujian. The use of beautiful colors and the harmonious atmosphere are treasures of traditional Chinese civilian residence well known all over the world. Nowadays, the descendants of the Cais are still safeguarding the houses of their ancestors, narrating and continuing the glories of their families. At the same time, they open their houses and welcome, with open arms, guests and visitors from all parts of the world.

Tips 寻访者须知

佳境指数 Scenery Index： ★★★★

备选序列： 闽南红砖建筑——中国世界文化遗产预备名单第22号（国家文物局2012年11月版）

List Number: Red-brick Houses in south Fujian — No.22 in the preparatory list for Chinese World Heritage (November 2012 Edition by the State Cultural Relics Bureau)

寻访提示： 南安市紧邻国家历史文化名城鲤城泉州，曾因是宋元海上丝绸之路的始发港，因而遗存众多极富审美价值的自然和人文景观。主要有道教名山清源山、海上丝绸之路名山九日山，以及开元寺、崇福寺、承天寺、天后宫和“海内第一桥”洛阳桥等名胜。

Location Notes: Adjacent to Quanzhou City, a national historic and cultural city, and once the starting port of the Silk Road on the sea in the Tang and Song Dynasties, Nan'an City is rich in extremely valuable natural scenes and cultural sites. Among them are Qingyuan Mountain, a famous mountain of Taoism, Kaiyuan Temple, Chengtian Temple, Heavenly Queen Palace, and the Luoyang Bridge.

摄影提示： 南安市蔡氏古居当仁不让地成为摄影创作的最佳主角。最好选择日出日落时分前往开展创作活动，此时为扫地光，光线柔和，色温较高，可突出表现蔡宅艳丽动人的红墙赤瓦。在构图上除了考虑建筑本身的各种元素外，还应注重捕捉古厝房前屋后当地居民展开的晒匾、晒谷等辛勤劳作和日常生活的场景，可为作品增添不少闽南地区的人文神韵。蔡氏民居均为一层建筑，平视的角度较难表现古厝的丰满和气势，拍摄位置最好选择临近的制高点，蔡氏古居入口处及村东头，尚有几处略高的民宅，可上门征得主人同意后登临屋顶拍摄。

Tips for Photography: The old houses of the

相机：佳能 Canon Eos-1DX，镜头：24-70mm f/2.8，光圈：f/14，快门：1/200秒，感光度：ISO500，曝光补偿：0EV **蔡氏红砖厝院落**

Cais in Nan'an City are, of course, the best views for photography. The best time for taking photos is at sunrise and sunset, when the touchingly beautiful color of the red bricks and tiles can be fully presented.

民俗提示：泉州是著名的石雕之乡，石雕多以花岗岩和辉绿岩为材，采用透雕、浮雕、平雕等多种手法，作品传神动人。南安古民宅中除了当地常见的精美石雕外，还采用了木雕、泥灰雕和砖雕等多种雕刻工艺，表现主题多为飞禽灵兽、花草虫鱼、山水人物、戏剧故事、博古图案和民俗民风。无论你身处南安何处，众多精彩纷呈的雕刻作品都会映入你的眼帘。

南安市有正月二十一“攻炮城”的习俗，寓意新的一年万事皆成。此习俗源于当年郑成功在福建厦门一带操练水师的娱乐活动。部将为防士兵过年思乡开小差，想出此策，订造大量鞭炮，扎成一个个“炮城”，再发给士兵部分鞭炮，鼓励官兵全力以赴“攻炮城”，攻下者给予重赏。此法既可消除士兵的思乡之情，又可操练瞄准技巧，有助提高部队的实战能力。

Brief Introduction to the Local Culture: Quanzhou is home to stone carving. The products are carvings on granite and diabase, which are vivid and life-like. Besides stone carvings, there are wood carvings, cement sculptures and tile carvings in the local residences in Nan'an.

美食提示：南安的餐饮以闽南风味为主。生猛海鲜以当地产的黄鱼、甲鱼、鱿鱼和对虾等闻名。素菜坚持素料、素做和素名，如“满园春色”“香妮藏珍”“竹荪如意”“莲中圣果”和“鸳鸯菜卷”等，色、香、味、行和名俱佳。风味小吃香醇甘美、清淡爽口，为南安一大特色，较知名的有蚵仔煎、烧肉粽、牛肉羹、面线糊、卤料、黑粿、麻糍、九重粿和肉圆等。

Food Tips: Nan'an food is chiefly of west Fujian cuisine, offering people a large variety of fresh seafood. Besides, lots of vegetarian food, famous for color, flavor and taste, is available.

寻访路径
Geographical location

寻觅备选世遗佳境 1
江西省赣州市龙南县客家围屋群
Groups of Kejia Circular Houses,
Longnan County, Ganzhou, Jiangxi

16 凝固的记忆 Fossilize Memories

客家文化鲜活的实物载体 中原远古习俗凝固的历史

Rich Artifacts of Kejia Culture;
Fossilized History of Ancient Customs

赣南围屋与北京四合院、陕北窑洞、闽西土楼并称中国“四大古民居”。一踏入赣州市龙南县，仿佛走进了一座露天的赣南围屋博物馆，一座洋溢浓郁文化风情的客家园。

The Gannan Enclosed Houses, as well as Siheyuan (i.e. Chinese quadrangles) in Beijing, Caves in north Shaanxi, and Tulou (i.e. earthen buildings) in west Fujian, are referred to as the four typical residential buildings for ancient Chinese people. As soon as you step into Longnan County of Ganzhou City, you feel you have entered an open-air museum of the enclosed houses and enjoy a strong flavor of rich Kejia culture.

客家风情活标本

Living Samples of Kejia Ambience

赣南现存五百多座客家围屋中面积最大、结构功能最为齐全的当属龙南县关西新围。始建于清嘉庆三年（1798年），围主徐名钧为关西名绅，靠经营木材生意掘得“第一桶金”，后又开药铺、当铺，资产越滚越大，成为一方富豪。因为子女增多，原围屋日显拥挤，于是斥资十万余银两、历时29年建起这座新屋。赣南围屋通常都有一个围名，但这座围屋完工时，徐名钧来不及起名就过世了，所以相对老围来说，将此称为新围。关西围占地七千七百余平方米，与之配套的附属设施达万余平方米。围屋整体结构形似巨大的“回”字形，围屋的核心建筑就处于中间的“口”字部位，此围是在客家民居“三进三开”特征基础上扩充为“三进六开”，从而形成“九栋十八厅”大型客家民居的建筑典范，共有主房124间。

“三进”即从大门进来为下厅，往上走则依次为中厅、上厅，层层递进，层层增高。而“六开”则是以正厅为中轴线往左右均衡延伸，两边院落、房屋和门窗对称。而以中轴线往左右延伸的结构，又使正厅成为整座围屋的核心，体现着一种极

相机：索尼 Sony Nex-7，镜头：18-55mm，f/2.8，光圈：f/8，快门：1/80秒，感光度：ISO100，曝光补偿：0EV（照片经后期处理） **龙南县关西新围**

强的向心力和凝聚力。关西围不仅处处体现着巧妙构思的建筑美，而且体现客家风情的绘画、装饰之美也令人赞叹不已。其正厅大门前有一对雕刻精美栩栩如生的石狮，左边的公狮昂首张口凶猛威武，右边的母狮雍容大度端庄肃穆，显示出工匠精湛的雕刻技艺；大门框上八卦中乾、坤两卦的圆柱形石雕，厅内十多根大木柱下的石墩上都雕刻着各种各样的图案或文字；厅堂偏院以及厢房都镶嵌有许多龙、虎、麒麟、凤凰等动物木雕，栩栩如生，雕工精湛。此围是赣南地区最有特色、最为珍贵的客家民居建筑，被誉为“东方古罗马城堡”。

龙南最高大的围屋为“燕翼围”，又称“高守围”。据《太平志》载：此围屋由赖福之及其长子赖从林所建。始建于清代顺治七年（1650年），历经27年，占地面积为1,367平方米，围高15米，是赣南众多两层结构客家围屋中最高的一座围屋。其主要特色在于所有房屋都依四面高墙而建，围屋中间本应是主房的位置，却是一大片空坪，这种独特的布局别有一番风味。直至三百多年后的今天，它仍然是杨村圩镇上的最高建筑，登高可以饱览周边山水景色和田园风光，感受淳朴浓郁的客家风情。

当时慕名前来登高望远的乡邻络绎不绝，清道光年间，时任赣州知府的殿试钦点探花周玉涵来此赏景，他在围顶上纵览云飞，赏月观霞，把酒临风，吟诗作赋，并挥毫题写了围名，流连数日不忍离去。1937年秋，刚任国民党赣南行政公署专员不久的蒋经国先生也慕名而来，并在围里住了三天，他对三百多年前能在深山密林中建起如此高大壮观的围屋赞美有加，对当地淳朴的客家民俗兴致极高，并将此行的所见所闻收入《本区的真面目》一书中。另据《龙南县志》和《太平志》载：1938年9月15日，日寇三架轰炸机成品字队形气势汹汹向杨村扑来，当飞机掠过杨村圩上空时，对下方突兀的一幢高耸坚固的古堡甚为疑惑，日寇判为重要军事设施，于是飞机在围屋上空低空盘旋数周后投下数枚炸弹。据地方志记载：炸毁民房10间，杨村小

相机：索尼 Sony Nex-7，镜头：18-55mm，f/2.8，光圈：f/4.5，快门：1/60秒，感光度：ISO100，曝光补偿：0EV（照片经后期处理） **关西新围粮库**

相机：索尼 Sony Nex-7，镜头：18-55mm，光圈：f/5.6，快门：1/80秒，感光度：ISO100，曝光补偿：0EV（照片经后期处理） **龙南县杨村燕翼围**

学教室1间，炸死居民和学生共18人。其中有一枚炸弹落在燕翼围西面围顶处爆炸，仅在一角炸开一处2.7米宽的V形缺口，围体丝毫不为所动，至今在西面外墙处仍留有当年日机扫射未能洞穿墙体的弹孔。

赣南最大、最早的围屋是龙南里仁镇的栗园围。占地45,328平方米，始建于明弘治辛酉年（1501年），迄今已逾五百年。四周围墙均由毛石砌造，几百间民房错落有致，密布其间。围内三口鱼塘并列成湖，翠竹柳影，散落沿岸。虽说是典型的客家围屋，却有着江南景物的韵致。

围内居民都姓李，相传是明代大将军李清公的后人。李将军曾追随著名的儒将王阳明统军平叛，战功卓著，还乡后就用赏赐的土地修建了围屋，据说“栗园围”这三个字为王阳明亲笔题写。栗园围建筑尤为出彩的是“一祠三厅”，即纪缙祖祠、栊梃厅、新灶下厅和梨树下厅。其中纪缙祖祠是整个围屋的主祠，族人集会议事、婚丧嫁娶都要来这里举行。新灶下厅竣工于嘉靖末年（1820年），出了两位五品大夫，成了围里著名的“大夫第”。第二位五品大夫李遇汉在95岁高龄之时又喜得重重孙，“五世同堂”一时传为佳话。据传，在围屋建造之前，这里是一片数百亩的板栗林，名为“栗树园”。板栗林西边长有数十棵枝繁叶茂的梨树，形成了一大片天然梨园，当地人称之为“栗树园”中的“园中园”。有一年夏天非常炎热，李家很多人得了肺热病，久治难愈。有位过路的高人指点迷津，说梨园中的梨果能清热排毒润肺，再取树根与梨果同时煎水熬膏，便能治好疾病。村民依言而行，果然灵验。但由于挖了太多的树根，梨林中的梨树慢慢全部枯死了。但这片“梨园”却永远驻入李家人的心中，在扩建栗园围时，就在“梨园”的原址上建起一座“围中围”，起名为“梨树下”，祠堂里也供起了梨山老母的牌位，以谢对李氏家族

相机：索尼 Sony Nex-7，镜头：18-55mm，光圈：f/6.5，快门：1/80秒，感光度：ISO100，曝光补偿：0EV（照片经后期处理） **龙南县杨村燕翼围内景**

的救助之恩。

赣南围屋中客家文化底蕴最深厚的为杨村乌石围。此围因门前有一块大乌石而得名，建于明代万历三十九年（1611年）。其特色在于围屋以前方后圆，而呈现半圆形，是赣南众多围屋中独一无二的半圆围。据有关资料显示，自明代万历年建围至清末的三百多年间，乌石围家族中有七十多人经乡试、会试得中举人和进士，并有两人得授三品大夫衔；新中国成立至今，有三十余人考入高等学府获学士、硕士和博士学位。

客家围屋是赣南地区独具特色的民居建筑，是中华民族建筑中的一枝奇葩。赣南现存客家围屋多达五百多座，其中376座分布在龙南县，其余一百多座散落在赣南的定南、全南、大余、信丰、安远和寻乌等县。龙南是典型的客家县，又因保存客家围屋数量之多、风格之全、保存之完好，被誉为“客家围屋之乡”。

Among the over 500 enclosed houses still in existance Gannan, the one found in Longnan County is the largest in area and most complete in structural functions. The owner, by the name of Xu Mingjun, began the construction of his enclosed house in the third year of Emperor Jiaqing of the Qing Dynasty (i.e. 1798 A.D.). Xu made his first "barrel of gold" in his lumber business, with which he ran pharmacies and pawn shops, and made more and more money. He became the wealthiest man in his place. Because of his large number of children, the old enclosed house gradually felt rather crowded. So he invested more than 100 thousand taels of silver in the construction of a new enclosed house, which lasted 29 years. Every enclosed house in Gannan usually had a name. Upon the completion of the new house, Xu passed

东方城堡

away. He didn't live long enough to name the new house. Therefore, in contrast to the old house, it was named New House. It covers an area of over 7,700 square meters and reaches an area of over 10,000 square meters with the attached facilities included. The whole structure of the enclosed house is in the shape of a small square inside a larger square. The core structure of the house is located in the small square, and the whole house consists of 124 rooms.

The largest and tallest enclosed house in Longnan is the Swallow-wing Enclosed House. Its construction began in the seventh year of Emperor Shunzhi of the Qing Dynasty (i.e. 1650 A.D.). It covers an area of 1,367 square meters and its circular walls are 15 meters high. Of the many two-story enclosed houses in Gannan, it is the tallest. Its major characteristic is that all the buildings were constructed along the high walls and that the center of the house, which ought to be occupied by the master's building, is a vast open space. Even today after more than 300 years, it still remains the tallest structure in town. At the top of the house, one can not only enjoy the beautiful scenery of the surrounding mountains and rivers as well as the rustic atmosphere around, but also savor the simple but rich Kejia flavor.

The largest and earliest enclosed house in Gannan is the Chestnut Garden Enclosed House in Liren Town of Longnan County. Covering an area of 68 mu (approximately 45,350 square meters), its construction began during the reign of Emperor Hongzhi of the Ming Dynasty, about 1501 A.D. It is already over 500 years old. The enclosed walls were built of rocks, and the several hundred rooms are well arranged high and low inside. Within the

相机：佳能 Canon Eos-1DX，镜头：24-70mm f/2.8，光圈：f/10，快门：1/60秒，感光度：ISO100，曝光补偿：0EV (照片经后期处理) **燕翼围外墙**

enclosed walls are three parallel fish ponds making up a lake with willow trees and bamboo scattered along the banks of the ponds. A typical Kejia enclosed house, it boasts the charm and beauty of the scenery on the south side of the Yangtze River.

The enclosed house that shows the richest flavor of Kejia culture is the Wushi (meaning black stone) Enclosed House in Yang Village. It was thus named because of a huge piece of black stone in front of the entrance. Its construction started in the 39th year (1611 A.D.) of Emperor Wanli of the Ming Dynasty. Its characteristic lies in the fact that the front part of the house is in the shape of a square and the rear part is in the shape of a circle. It is the only semi- enclosed house out of so many enclosed houses in Gannan.

The Kejia enclosed houses are unique residential constructions in the Gannan area, and make up a rare species in the national architectures of China. To date, there still exist more than 500 Kejia enclosed houses, out of which 376 are located in Longnan County while the rest are scattered in such counties as Dingnan, Quannan, Dayu, Xinfeng, Anyuan, Xunwu, etc. of Gannan. Longnan is a county typical of Kejia culture. Besides, because of the largest number of the Kejia enclosed houses, completeness in Kejia style and good conditions of the preservation, the county is honored with the name of Hometown of Kejia Enclosed Houses.

传承中原细无声

Unnoticeable Passing down over the Years

赣南围屋是中国特殊历史环境下的产物，是了解明清时期赣南及整个客家民系社会历史极其宝贵的实物载体。

一千六百年前，为躲避兵燹战祸，客家先民不得不离开中原故土，走上了艰难且前途未卜的南迁之路。在漫漫岁月中，他们曾遭遇过何等的磨难已经不重要了。重要的是，在中国汉民族的谱系中，自此又多了一个优秀的民系——客家；在中国南部蛮荒的山林之中，从此又多了一支勤劳奋进的拓荒者——客家人。当他们的足印踏遍南方广袤大地，汗水洒落在南方群山密林的同时，也把中原先进的生产力、优秀的中原文化传播到了南方的山山水水。

赣州城池构建在千里赣江的源头。在古城的制高点郁孤台下，章江和贡江在此汇合成了滔滔北流的赣江。赣江是中国南部唯一南北走向的长江支流，赣州是客家祖先南迁途中最早的落脚地、集散地和聚集地。客家先民自中原沿长江顺流而下，在南昌城下转舟自赣江溯流而上，行至赣州城下便弃船登岸。客家先祖就是从这条通道进入赣南山区，然后再辐射进入福建闽西的龙岩、广东的梅州等地。至11世纪以后，当客家人在中国南部偏僻山区逐渐安定下来的时候，赣州成为中国南部通往广州地区的交通枢纽和工商要地之一。

说到赣南，说到客家，龙南围屋便成为一个无法回避的话题。它是客家历史最鲜活的载体，更是客家文化最生动的物证。围屋几乎就是客家人的象征。客家人可以不住围屋，但住在围屋中的人，一定是客家人。

据考证，客家人构筑的围屋，源于东汉的坞堡。这种建筑形式在两晋南北朝时曾盛行于中原广大地区。客家人聚族而居、耕战结合的习俗，也基本源于此。围屋具有坚固封闭的外围，以及严密的防御体系，对于天灾人祸有着极其周密精细的应对措施和防备手段。围屋的外墙高大厚实，没有窗户，只有对外射击的枪孔。围屋四周建有像碉堡一样的角楼。围屋整体坚固高大，门却很小很窄，第一道外包铁甲，第二道设木栅栏，第三道才是住家日常进出的木门。

客家人至今还过着一种聚族而居的生活。这是一种有别于中国其他地区汉民族的传统生活习俗。在过去的千年岁月中，当正常的生活和劳作被战乱或宗族之间的资源争夺威胁时，围屋就立刻成为保护族人生命和财产安全的军事要塞。楼上房屋之间，连通着许多小门，平时各过各的日子，紧急之下，家家后门敞开就连成了一条抵抗外来入侵的大回廊。围屋因其特有的封闭性和独立性，很少受到当地社会文化、习俗、语言等影响和同化，虽然历经沧桑世变，但仍保持其固有的社会生态。

一座大围屋，通常住有几百，甚至上千人，他们同源同宗同姓，有的还是同一祖先的直系血缘后代。当围屋容纳不下住家时，长子这一支就被留在老围屋内，而次子等则分离出去，再建新的围屋。春秋更替，日月轮回。一代代的客家人就在围屋中繁衍生息；一则则客家风情故事就在围屋里天天上演。尽管远逝的历史已遥不可及，但客家围屋将其凝固成为永恒的记忆。寻访围屋，我们仿佛触摸到了客家历史的体温；亲近围屋，我们似乎发现了客家千百年来的人文脉络。

进入民国以后，由于封建专制的衰亡和民主文明体制的兴盛，社会日趋安定，土匪盗寇和宗族势力大大削弱，百姓生活状态有了基本保障，这种集家、祠、堡诸功能于一体的围屋也就随之停建了。

龙南围屋就像一部厚重的史书，人们可以从不同的侧面，去回味客家人曾经有过的生存状态，去探究它的军事、建筑、民俗和美学价值。今天，已有越来越多的客家人走出了围屋，走出了大山深处。同时，也有更多的四方宾客千里迢迢来此探访，领略世代客家人创造的宝贵人文遗产。

The enclosed house in Gannan is a product of the special historical environment of China. They serve as the valuable artifacts by which the social history of the Kejia people as a whole and specifically in Gannan in the Ming and Qing Dynasties can be learned.

About 1,600 years ago, with the intention of escaping the wars, the Kejia people had to leave their hometowns in the middle of China and start trekking southward without knowing what was waiting for them. In the years to come, the difficulties they encountered when crossing rivers was no longer important. What's important is that in the family trees of the Han nationality in China, there appeared one more tree of excellent family, i.e. Kejia. In the barbarous mountains and forests of South China, there appeared one more group of hardworking and enterprising exploiters, i.e. the Kejia people. When they walked all over the broad lands in the south and sweated in the mountains and forests, they were actually introducing the advanced productivity and superb culture of the middle of China to all parts of South China.

Whenever Gannan or Kejia is mentioned, the topic of the enclosed houses in Longnan cannot be avoided. The enclosed houses serve as the vehicle of the lively Kejia history and as the most vivid artifacts of the Kejia culture. An enclosed house is a symbol of the Kejia people. Some Kejia people may not have lived in enclosed houses; however, those that live in them must be Kejia people.

The Kejia people live a gregarious life, which is a different life style from those of the Han people in other parts of China. In the past thousand years, when the normal life and labor were threatened by wars and clashes for resources among clans, the enclosed houses immediately became the military fortresses that protect the lives and properties of the families. The rooms upstairs are connected through many small doors. In time of peace, the families live their respective lives. In time of urgency, all the small doors can be removed, making the upper part of the house a circular corridor used for resistance against alien invasions. Because of its special closeness and independence, the enclosed house is less likely to be influenced or assimilated by the local social culture, customs or dialects. In spite of the vicissitudes of time, the Kejia people still maintain their social biology.

Several hundred, or even about one thousand people, who are direct descendants of the same forefathers, thus sharing the same family name, usually live in one large enclosed house. When the enclosed house can no longer accommodate all the family members, the eldest son and his family remain in the house, but the younger sons and their families have to leave to build new enclosed houses. With the passing of time, the Kejia people live, generation after generation, in the enclosed houses, repeating their life stories day by day. Even though the bygone history is far away and even out of reach, Kejia houses fossilize their memories. By visiting the enclosed houses, we seem to be able to take the temperature of Kejia history. By dropping in the enclosed houses, we seem to be able to discover the thousand-year-old traces of the Kejia people.

The enclosed house is like a thick history book. From different angles, we could relive the life that the Kejia people have lived, exploring their military, architectural, folk and esthetic values. Today, more and more Kejia people have stepped out of the enclosed houses and out of the mountains. Meanwhile, however, more and more people make light of thousands of miles to come and visit so as to appreciate the valuable cultural heritage that the Kejia people have built up one generation after another.

相机： 佳能 Canon Eos-1DX，镜头：24-70mm f/2.8，光圈：f/6.3，快门：1/25秒，感光度：ISO100，曝光补偿：0EV (照片经后期处理) **关西新围内景**

Tips 寻访者须知

佳境指数 Scenery Index： ★★★★

备选序列： 赣南围屋——中国世界文化遗产预备名单第23号（国家文物局2012年11月版）

List Number: Enclosed Houses in Gannan — No.23 in the preparatory list for Chinese World Heritage (November 2012 Edition by the State Cultural Relics Bureau)

寻访提示： 赣州是中国文化名城，客家集居地之一，"江南第一石窟"通天岩、八境台和西津门等处保存完好的三千余米宋城墙、用百舟连接的古浮桥等人文和自然景观可游览。红都瑞金当年苏维埃临时中央政府旧址、于都长征第一渡等红色遗迹也可探访。另外龙南境内形制独特的廊桥太平桥、丹霞奇山小武当山和原生态名山九连山等也可顺道寻访。

Location Notes: Ganzhou, historically a famous city of culture in China, is one of the residential areas for the Kejia people. In such places as Tongtian Rock, Bajing Terrace, and Xijin Gate, there is the 3,000-meter-long city wall, which was erected in the Song Dynasty but is still relatively intact. The ancient floating bridge, made up of over one hundred boats linked together, is a cultural site and natural scene to see. Some historical sites like the former site of the then Provisional Soviet Central Government in Ruijin, the red capital then, and Yudu, where the Red Army made their first crossing during the Long March, are all worth visiting. Besides, the Taiping Bridge, a specially built corridor bridge, in Longnan, the lesser Wudang Mountains, and the Jiulian Mountains are also are also worth visiting in passing.

摄影提示： 龙南摄影创作活动的主要创作对象

相机：佳能 Canon Eos-1DX，镜头：24-70mm f/2.8，光圈：f/14，快门：1/80秒，感光度：ISO100，曝光补偿：0EV（照片经后期处理） **杨村太平桥**

以分布在各乡镇的围屋为主。在视角上多以45度角拍摄，能体现景物的立体感，但要处理好主体与陪体的关系，不能喧宾夺主。在构图上尽量采用黄金分割线原则，以使画面的比例更显和谐。拍摄位置可多项选择，以登临制高点为佳，更能体现围屋的气势和全貌。在用光上以自然的顺光和侧光为好。

Tips for Photography: The enclosed houses located in various towns and villages in Longnan are excellent subjects for photography.

民俗提示：客家民俗文化以其古朴和充满浓郁的乡土气息而别有情趣。客家民俗活动一年四季均有举行。春节期间有龙灯、蛇灯、鲤鱼灯、马灯、狮灯等各种彩灯的表演；端午节有龙舟竞渡；中秋节有“放孔明灯”“请月光姑姐”等活动。除外赣南地区还有一些其他汉族地域所不见的大型民俗活动。如上犹“九狮拜象”、宁都竹篙火龙节、于都唢呐等等。另外民间文艺也很丰富，如客家山歌、赣南采茶戏和歌谣等。

Brief Introduction to the Local Culture: The folk culture of Kejia is especially interesting for its old, simple and rich flavor and rustic atmosphere. Folk activities are held all seasons of the year. During the Spring Festival, there are lots of lantern performances like lion lanterns, snake lanterns, carp lanterns, horse lanterns, lion lanterns, and so on. During the Dragon Boat Festival there are dragon boat races. During the Mid-autumn Festival, people hold activities such as lighting Kong-ming lamps, etc. Besides, some large-scale activities held in Gannan are not likely to be seen elsewhere.

美食提示：赣南客家饮食种类繁多，丰富多彩，既继承了中原祖居地的特点，又具有客家的鲜明特色。其主食、副食、菜肴和小吃均就地取材，采用南北相兼的制作方法，风味独特。赣南人以大米为主食，仅以大米做成的美食有捞饭、焖饭、煮饭包、竹筒饭、钵子饭等。粥的品种有甜粥、盐粥、什锦粥、苦瓜粥、蛋粥等。各类米制品有粉

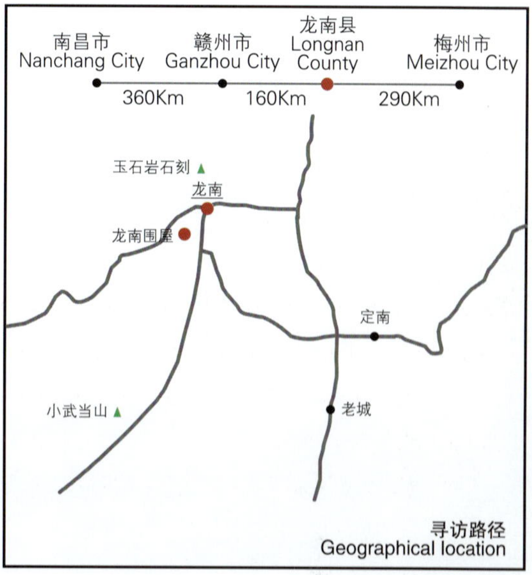

干、沙河粉、艾米馃、烫皮、麻糍、黄元米馃等。赣南盛产番薯芋头，有番薯粉、番薯片、番薯干、炸芋包等。传统名菜佳肴主要有三杯鸡、小草鱼、荷包胙、米粉肉、粉蒸鱼、红烧狗肉、肉丸、鱼丸、酿豆腐等。菜肴烹调制作注重主料和佐料的搭配，炒、煎、炸、熘、烩、蒸、炖、烧、卤等方法独特，风味也独特。

Food Tips: The Kejia cuisine in Gannan boasts a great diversity. It has inherited the special features of the ancient hometown in central China and to demonstrate unique Kejia characteristics. The main foods, side dishes and snacks are mostly made of local ingredients. The cooking methods stem from northern and southern cuisines, thus making up a unique taste.

護國門

寻觅备选世遗佳境 1
重庆市合川区钓鱼城遗址
Diaoyu Town Ruins, Hechuan District, Chongqing

17 远逝的硝烟 Bygone Smoke of Gunpowder

冷兵器时代山城防御体系之典范
改变欧亚历史进程之古战场遗址

Cold Weapon Era Model Defense System;
Former Sites of Battlefields that change Euro-Asian History

在这座方圆2.5平方公里的红色“弹丸”之地上构筑的古代城堡，七百年前曾历经腥风血雨、你死我活的殊死拼杀，是迄今中国保存最为完好的古代战争遗址。

这里作为冷兵器时代山城防御体系的典型代表，在世界和中国古代的战争史上均占有重要地位。以此处山形地势为依据制作的“攻防战”沙盘模型，至今仍在中国人民革命军事博物馆古代战争馆向观众展示其不凡功绩。

这里被西方称为“东方麦加城”和“上帝折鞭处”。1259年7月，强悍的蒙古大军核心人物元宪宗蒙哥汗和名将汪德臣在此城下的激战中殒命，致使蒙古诸汗王之间兵连祸结，最终造成所向披靡的蒙古铁骑，在众多对手毫无招架之力的情况下却全线退兵，无力继续向欧洲和埃及扩张，成为改变欧亚历史进程的一个重要转折点。

这里也大大影响了中国历史的发展进程，一方面使南宋政权又向后延续了二十多年，另一方面也促成倾慕汉唐文明的开明之士忽必烈，成为蒙古统治集团的核心人物。

这座城堡，就是位于重庆市合川区城东五公里处雄居一方的钓鱼城。

The old tower on the tiny 2.5-square-km area witnessed bitter and desperate battles some 700 years ago. It is, to date, the best-preserved remains of the battlefields of ancient China.

This representative example of how the defensive system of a mountain city worked during the period of cold-steel weaponry takes a significant position in the history of wars in China and in the world.

In July 1259, Möngke Khan, Emperor Yuanxuan of the Yuan Dynasty, and Wang Dechen, a famous general, led their army to fight here. They both died in the fierce battles outside the city. Their failure was actually a turning point in the history of

相机：松下 Panasonic GF3，镜头：14mm f/2.5，光圈：f/2.8，快门：1/125秒，感光度：ISO160，曝光补偿：0.3EV **重庆市合川区钓鱼城悬空卧佛**

Asia and Europe.

Besides, what happened in this part of the world greatly influenced the developmental process of Chinese history. On one hand, the regime of the southern Song Dynasty lasted some 20 more years; on the other hand, Kublai Khan, who cherished a strong admiration of the culture of the Han and Tang Dynasties, became a core member of the Mongolian ruling class.

This tower is located in Diaoyu Town, some 5 km in the east of Hechuan District of Chongqing.

一

从合川南岸相继渡过涪江和嘉陵江大桥，转瞬间即到了钓鱼城。自1243年始，钓鱼城攻防战历经两百余次殊死搏杀，持续时间长达36年之久。最终以守城六万多军民，对抗数十万蒙古铁骑而屹立不倒，在中外古代战争史上写书了重彩浓墨的一笔。

登高凭望，思绪万千。只见城下嘉陵江、渠江和涪江三江汇流，滚滚向东，奔腾不息，周围山色凝重，雾气蒸腾。一部封尘了七百余年的历史之书，仿佛在我面前徐徐开启。

钓鱼城海拔约三百米。城南、城北和城西三面江水环绕。此地恃山水之险，易守难攻；又兼交通之便，经水路及陆上道，可通往蜀中各地。因其占尽天时地利，成为兵家必争之地。

1234年宋、蒙联合灭金后，南宋出兵欲收复河南失地，却遭蒙军伏击而兵败。自此南宋转入防御态势，再也无力发动对蒙军的攻势。

1235年，宋蒙战争全面爆发，蒙古铁骑在西起川陕、东至淮河下游的数千里战线上同时对南宋发动大规模进攻。1241年，蒙军蹂躏南宋大片疆土。也就是在这一年，蒙古帝国元太宗窝阔台汗去世，其内部政争不断，对南宋的攻势稍有减弱。利用这天赐良机，南宋对南方各战场的防御阵地进行充实和调整。彭大雅任四川制置副使期间（1239—

相机：松下 Panasonic GF3，镜头：14mm f/2.5，光圈：f/2.8，快门：1/125秒，感光度：ISO160，曝光补偿：0.3EV **钓鱼城悬空卧佛局部**

相机：松下 Panasonic GF3，镜头：14mm f/2.5，光圈：f/5.6，快门：1/400秒，感光度：ISO160，曝光补偿：0.3EV **钓鱼城古炮台**

1240年），曾命甘闰初筑钓鱼城。南宋淳祐二年（1242年），宋理宗派遣在两淮抗蒙战争中战绩显著的余玠入蜀，出任四川安抚制置使兼知重庆府，以期扭转四川战局的颓势，巩固川南防线。1243年，余玠采纳播州（今遵义）贤士冉琎、冉璞兄弟“择险、任人、积粟、驻兵、徙城”的良策，遣冉氏兄弟复筑钓鱼城，并移合州治及兴元都统司于其上。“春则出屯田野，以耕以耘；秋则运粮运薪，以战以守”，做好应对长期战争的准备。

至1251年，战势骤变。成吉思汗之孙、拖雷之子蒙哥登上蒙古大汗宝座，元英宗大权在握，很快稳定了蒙古政局，并积极谋划再次发动全面的攻宋战争。第二年，蒙哥汗命其弟忽必烈率师灭亡大理，对南宋形成南北夹击之势。1254年，合州守将王坚进一步完善城筑，并召集流民，秣马励兵，积蓄力量，枕戈待旦，使钓鱼城与神臂、云顶等城堡一起，成为兵精食足的坚固堡垒，从川北到川南构筑了多道屏障，以阻挡蒙古大军东犯长江中下游地区。

1257年，蒙哥汗亲率蒙军主力猛攻四川。意欲发挥蒙古骑兵善于陆地野战之长，而避于不善水战之短，以其精锐先声夺取四川后，再顺江东下，与诸路蒙军会师，横扫江南，最后直捣宋都临安（今杭州）。1258年，蒙哥挟西征欧亚非四十余国的威势，分兵三路侵宋。除京湖和两淮战场外，四川则是宋蒙三大战场中遭蒙军攻势最为猛烈的一个地区。1258年秋，蒙军相继占据剑门苦竹隘、长宁山城、蓬州运山城、阆州、大获城和广安大良城等，迫近合州。1259年2月，蒙哥汗亲率精兵十万，兵临合川钓鱼城下。然而在钓鱼城主将王坚与副将张珏的率领下，全城军民凭借天险顽强抗击，一次又一次击退蒙军的猛攻。尽管钓鱼城似铁桶般被围数月之久，但城中依然物资充裕，守军将士斗志昂扬，蒙军在此始终不能越雷池半步。而城外蒙军的状况却每况愈下。蜀南地区酷暑时节天气闷热

相机：松下 Panasonic GF3，镜头：14mm f/2.5，光圈：f/4，
快门：1/250秒，感光度：ISO160，曝光补偿：0.3EV **钓鱼城三圣岩**

相机：松下 Panasonic GF3，镜头：14mm f/2.5，光圈：f/4，
快门：1/250秒，感光度：ISO160，曝光补偿：0.3EV **钓鱼城摩崖石刻**

潮湿，蒙古人本来就畏暑恶湿，因水土不服导致军中暑热、疟疾、霍乱等疾病流行。据《元史》和拉施特《史集》记载，蒙哥在此得了疠疫，不久在金剑山温汤峡（今重庆缙云山北温泉）含恨离世。而《马可·波罗游记》和明万历《合州志》，及城中于1517年明正德年间所立的《新建二公祠堂记》石刻碑文记载，1259年7月，蒙古蒙哥汗在攻城时“中飞矢而死”。不管怎么说，蒙军上下无心再战，世界历史进程由此改写。

一

After crossing the Fujiang River and then crossing the Jiangling River Bridge, the tourist finds himself at Diaoyu Mountain. Starting in 1243, Diaoyu City experienced more than 200 desperate defensive and offensive battles, which lasted 36 years. Finally, the 60,000 soldiers and citizens won over the 10,000 Mongolian mounted soldiers. It deserves everlasting attention in the history of wars in China and in the world.

Diaoyu City is about 300 meters above sea level. It is encircled by rivers on the south, north and west. With mountains behind and waters in front, the city is quite easy to defend but very difficult to attack. What's more, because of the convenient transportation by water and by land, the city is connected to various places in Sichuan.

二

除了金戈铁马、刀光剑影之外，钓鱼城独具特色的自然和人文风光也可圈可点。

早在唐宋时期，合州石头和尚就建护国寺于此，此为合州四大名刹之一，精美绝伦的悬空卧佛、千佛石窟的摩崖造像，使此地成为驰名巴渝的信徒朝拜圣地。

最为罕见的是一座“一卧千古”的悬空卧佛。此佛雕刻于唐代，横卧在赤红峭壁之上，身长11米，肩宽2.2米，双脚宽1.2米。卧佛背北面南，头西脚东，袒胸露肌，面额丰满，神态端庄慈祥。其娓娓动人的摩崖造像，充分展示了古代劳动人民精湛的石刻艺术造诣。清代诗人胡德琳有诗赞云：“千尺高岩瀑布流，振衣五月讶深秋。莫言此子津梁倦，卧听沧江日夜流。”

三圣岩因其刻有“西方三圣”摩崖造像而得名。“弥陀三圣”是指阿弥陀佛和观世音、大势至菩萨。此造像刻于清代道光二十三年（1843年）间，由护国、白塔两寺住持智慧和尚及众门徒捐资刻造。在长4米，高3米的石龛中，端坐于莲台上的“三圣”栩栩如生。正中主位上的佛祖，高2.5米，肩宽0.6米，发式为螺髻，头顶有高宽的肉髻，身着通肩式袈裟。他右手施莲花印，左手托如意宝珠，表情怡淡，慈祥壮观。佛祖两边的菩萨头戴宝冠，身着天衣，卷发披巾，胸前饰以璎珞，腕有环钏。一个怀抱沉香，一个手抚净瓶，含蓄温柔，亲切而恬雅。尤其令人赞叹的是这龛造像，通肩佛衣折褶，线条明快自然，给人以软而薄，轻欲飘的感觉。

钓鱼城是改写世界中古历史的中外名城，因此在数平方公里的城池之上，自然和人文景观不胜枚举，令人目不暇接。现存有“一字城”等城垣八公里、“护国门”等城门八道，以及炮台、栈道、暗道出口、军营、帅府、天池等南宋军事及生活设施遗址；有千年古桂树、护国寺、鱼山八景等名胜古迹；还有文天祥、刘克庄、陈毅、郭沫若、张爱萍、刘白羽等历史名家的诗咏及蒋介石、何应钦、张治中等国民党军政要员的摩崖题记。

游罢古城，正值夕阳落辉，古城四周紫霞弥漫，此奇景为“西市晚烟”。眼前仿佛又出现了昔日鏖战正酣的战争场面。岁月如逝，如今战争的烟云早已离我们远去，江山依旧，城池依然。今天有

相机：松下 Panasonic GF3，镜头：14mm f/2.5，光圈：f/5.6，快门：1/400秒，感光度：ISO160，曝光补偿：0.3EV **涞滩二佛寺石佛造像**

多少人还曾记得七百年前发生在此地的那场惊天地泣鬼神的著名战役呢?

II

Diaoyu City is well known for its natural scenic spots and cultural sites.

As early as the Tang and Song Dynasties, a monk built the Huguo Temple here. One of the four famous temples in Hechuan, it is best known for its suspended Reclining Buddha and the thousand-Buddha Grotto, which has long been the Mecca for the Buddhist disciples from Chongqing and elsewhere. The reclining Buddha, 11 meters long, 2.2 meters wide at his shoulders and 1.2 meters wide at his feet, is suspended from the red cliffs high above.

As a city well-known for rewriting the history of China and the world, Diaoyu City has numerous natural scenic spots and cultural sites within its several-square-kilometer area, far too many for ordinary tourists to enjoy.

At the end of the sightseeing in the old city, it is almost sunset. The city is pervaded with purple twilight. The tourist can't help feeling that he is facing the scenes of battlefields where fierce battles are being fought. Gone are the days together with the fire and smoke of wars; however, the city still remains, permanently glorious.

相机：松下 Panasonic GF3，镜头：14mm f/2.5，光圈：f/5.6，快门：1/500秒，感光度：ISO160，曝光补偿：0.3EV **涞滩二佛寺佛事**

Tips 寻访者须知

佳境指数 Scenery Index：★★★★

备选序列：钓鱼城遗址——中国世界文化遗产预备名单第33号（国家文物局2012年11月版）

List Number: Former Sites of Diaoyu City — No.33 in the preparatory list for Chinese World Heritage (November 2012 Edition by the State Cultural Relics Bureau)

寻访提示：重庆西北部群山迭起，有一条"温泉故里，石刻之乡"的游览路线，人文和自然景观十分丰富。钓鱼城、"小峨眉"缙云山、长达十公里的天府溶洞群、北温泉、金刀峡、胜天湖等秀美壮丽。涞滩、路孔和偏岩古镇等是寻访重庆民俗民风、品尝美食的上好去处。我国石刻造像艺术的巅峰之作大足石刻、二佛寺等石窟蜚声海内外。

Location Notes: With range after range of mountains, lying to the northwest of Chongqing is a long sightseeing route, known as "Hometown of Hot Springs and Village of Stone Carving", where there is an abundance of natural scenic spots and cultural sites.

摄影提示：钓鱼城三江汇流，城池凸兀，山势险峻。古城墙、古城垛、古城楼等高耸挺拔，为摄影创作的主要元素，若再与彩霞落晖、晨雾浮云相遇，那就幸运至极。古城内雕刻在丹霞赤壁之上的摩崖造像和题记，也不失为摄影创作的极好元素。另渝北"三江号子"等民俗活动极富地域特色，为不可多得的人文摄影题材。

Tips for Photography: Located at the meeting place of the three rivers, the city stands out conspicuously. The ancient city walls, battlements, and towers are all good themes for photography. If the photographer can chance upon either the colorful rays of sunrise and sunset or the morning fog and thin clouds, that is the best luck for being able to produce ideal pictures.

民俗提示：合川古为巴国别都，民俗文化风情怡人，乡土气息浓郁。

龙舟竞渡：合川地处嘉陵江、涪江、渠江三江汇合之处，自古有划龙船的习俗。每逢农历五月初五，城区及涞滩等地处江边的乡镇都要举行龙舟竞赛活动。参赛龙舟多达二三十支。同时，须用大木船或囤船扎以彩绸，做成数艘花船。花船亦称彩龙舟，有供抛奖和游江观赏两种。龙舟竞渡时，花船伴以武术演出、民族乐器演奏助兴；有的花船上还由一些儿童扮成各种戏剧人物，伴以川剧锣鼓助兴。

架香童子舞：流传至今已有三百多年历史。源于观音菩萨的父亲妙庄王因火烧白雀寺而病，为消灾而组建架香队去南海朝拜观音菩萨而延续至今。架香会之所以在巴蜀地区盛行，其主要原因是朝山拜佛，祈求风调雨顺，国泰民安，五谷丰登，六畜兴旺，人和家兴。内容有宗教祭祀仪式，有唱赞及佛歌，伴有童子舞蹈、龙舞、狮舞等文娱表演，加上传统架香乐器的伴奏，其内容丰富多彩。道具有香架、香盘、香烛等。舞蹈的基本特征是庄严、肃穆、文静、虔诚，基本动作都是以过堂、搭架、上香的内容进行变化表演。在历次的朝山拜佛活动中，跳架香童子舞都是活动的最重要项目之一，形象地体现了人们内心对神佛的虔诚，有浓郁的地方特色。

三江号子：这是嘉陵江、涪江、渠江的船工们在长期推船拉纤的艰辛生产斗争中，为协调全船操作步伐，鼓舞大家劳动情绪，战胜凶滩恶水，保证船只航行安全而谱写的船工劳动歌曲。三条江各河流行驶的大小船，都配有号子头，在航行中领唱号子，遇到什么水势就喊什么号子，指挥全船工人操作步伐，与险滩急浪搏斗。三江号子的格调和曲牌，是船工根据江河沿岸的自然景色、风土人情、航道水流缓急和船只载重情况，应时即兴呼喊出来的。在过险滩急流时，所喊号子雄伟浑厚高亢，短促有力，使大家精力集中，用力猛拉猛划。在水流平缓之处，则又唱出轻柔婉转，节奏缓慢的号子，用以缓和过滩的紧张情绪，消除疲劳。三江号子属于民间歌谣的一种，具有巴渝文化的鲜明特色，其内容极为丰富。

大田薅秧：为当地广泛流传的劳动歌曲，产生于春夏田间的薅秧劳动之中，劳动场面大，男女老少都可以参加。可领唱、对唱、合唱；艺术形式丰富多样，内容生动活泼，长期以来深受广大群众喜爱。

Brief Introduction to the Local Culture: Hechuan used to be the capital in the ancient times. Therefore, the whole city is submerged in the ambience of folk culture and the strong local flavor.

Dragon Boat Race: Located at the meeting place of the three rivers, Jialing, Fujiang and Qujiang, Hechuan has always had a tradition of dragon boat racing. On the 5th day of the 5th lunar month every year, almost all the towns and villages along the rivers hold dragon boat races.

Incense Dance: This kind of activity has lasted for over 300 years. It began when the local populace sent teams of people to burn incense and pray to Avalokitesvara (Guanyin) in order to save her father, King Miaozhuang, who had fallen ill after he burnt down Baique Temple.

Three-river chants: In their year-after-year labor to push and pull the boats on the rivers, the boatmen chanted to synchronize their steps, to boost their morale, and to overcome difficulties. These were the songs composed and sung by the boatmen to ensure safety during the voyages.

Seedling planting songs: These songs are very popular. When men and women, young and old, plant rice seedlings in the fields in spring and summer, they all join in and sing these songs.

寻访路径
Geographical location

美食提示：重庆有的美食合川都有，但合川有的美食，重庆不一定有。“合川肉片”是川菜菜谱之一，为合川传统名菜，至今已有一百多年历史。据说，此菜是当地一家饭店的厨师无意中创制的。一日，饭店打烊后，厨师将卖剩的肉片用鸡蛋、淀粉包裹后，用少量油煎至两面金黄，再加多种辅料和调料烹炒，供自己下饭吃。没想到此菜竟然呈橘红色，甜酸带辣，外脆里嫩，鲜美可口，并在四川和全国广泛流传。

羊杂米粉与羊杂汤：合川人熬羊杂汤，可以追溯到宋元时期。其主要原料是：猪骨头、羊头肉、羊脑花、羊肠肚与羊心肺。汤汁洁白而爽口，养神保胃。

Food Tips: Hechuan offers a rich variety of good food. As is said locally, all the delicacies that can be found in Chongqing can be definitely found in Hechuan. However, what can be found in Hechuan may not be found in Chongqing.

寻觅备选世遗佳境 1
四川省甘孜州丹巴县甲居藏寨
Jiaju Tibetan Village, Danba County, Ganzhizhou, Sichuan

18 空谷佳人 Beautiful Valley

东女故国之都城　嘉绒藏居之典范

The Capital of the Women's Kingdom;
An Exemplary of Tibetan Residences

阳春的一天日暮时分，当我一踏上甲居藏寨的土地之时，天空中最后一缕阳光将大金川河谷两岸抹成一片金色，一弯硕大无比的彩虹自谷底凌空飞渡，高耸入云的卡帕纳群峰时隐时现，墨尔多神山仿佛一位慈母，敞开宽大温柔的胸襟，将散落在绿荫丛中星罗棋布的多彩藏居搂抱于怀中，这种酷似艺术品形态展现在世人眼前的绝美村寨，可谓举世无双。

At dusk on an early spring day, I set my feet on the soil of the Jiaju Tibetan Village. Just at that moment, the last beam of sunshine rendered the banks of the valley of the Dajinchuan River into a golden world. A gigantic rainbow arch soared from the bottom of the valley high into the skies. Mount Kapana loomed in the floating clouds. The sacred Moerduo Mountain opened her arms, like a benevolent mother, to embrace the colorful Tibetan houses dotting the green landscape. What a peerlessly fantastic view, in which the breathtakingly beautiful villages unfold themselves in front of the people like artwork!

此地源自东女国

Formerly the Women's Kingdom

这里是嘉绒藏族的聚集地，“嘉绒”意为“女王的谷地”。这里有女王的神山，墨尔多神山自古就被中外宗教信徒虔诚崇拜；这里有女王的汗水和泪水汇成的河流，大小金川汇流后称为大渡河；这里有以女人智慧建成的十三角碉，女性文化的流风遗韵一直绵延至今；这里也曾是东女国都城的核心区域，历史上神秘消亡的东女国故都遗址就在丹巴中路乡。

这个由女性主宰一切的神秘王国，曾经在中国历史上几度活跃，一度辉煌。这个如梦一样的国度、谜一般的王朝，像流星般划过历史的夜空，渐渐淡出了世人的视野，留下的是无尽的遐想与神秘

相机：尼康 NIKON D700，镜头：尼康 70-200mm f/2.8，光圈：f/9，快门：1/80秒，感光度：ISO200，曝光补偿：0EV **甲居藏寨彩虹凌空**

的传说。

东女国是公元六七世纪出现的部落群体及地方政权，是昌都地区及整个藏族历史上重要的文明古国之一。据《旧唐书》卷197《南蛮西南蛮传》记载："东女国，西羌之别种，以西海中复有女国，故称东女焉。俗以女为王。东与茂州、党项接，东南与雅州接，界隔罗女蛮及白狼夷。其境东西九日行，南北二十日行。在大小八十余城，其王所居名康延川，中有弱水南流，用牛皮为船为渡。"据考证，"康延川"即今昌都一带，"弱水"即今之澜沧江，所谓"大小八十余城"，谓其国辖有八十余"纵"，即农业聚邑，包括了今四川阿坝州茂汶以西，甘孜州巴塘、理塘（白狼夷故地）以北及整个昌都地区，范围十分广大。

东女国时期，昌都地区及四川西北藏区已有较发达的文明。当时东女国人口四万余户，胜兵一万余人，散布于山谷之间的八十余座聚邑之中，东女国文化最突出的特点之一，就是以女性为中心和女性崇拜的社会制度，《旧唐书》称该国"俗重妇人而轻丈夫"，《新唐书》卷146《西域传》上"东女国"条则记载东女国"俗轻男子，女贵者咸有侍男"。东女国以女性为国王，"女王号为'宾就'，有女官，曰'高霸'，平议国事。在外官僚，并男夫为之。其王侍女数百人，五日一听政。女王若死，国中多敛金钱，动至数万，更于王族求令女二人而立之。大者为王，其次为小王。若大王死，即小王嗣立，或姑死而妇继，无有篡夺"。由此可见，东女国王位继承采取了女王终身制与家族垄断制相结合的方式，男子无权参与。

松赞干布于641年统一了西藏，建立了吐蕃王朝。据《旧唐书》记载，670年，唐、蕃"大金川役"爆发，吐蕃"尽收羊同、党项诸羌之地，东与凉、松、茂、嶲等州相接"。783年，双方订立"清水会盟"，明确"蕃国守镇在兰、渭、原、会，西至临洮，东至成州，抵剑南西界磨些诸蛮，大渡水西南为蕃界。"此界包括了丹巴在内的嘉绒

相机：尼康 NIKON D700，镜头：尼康 70-200mm f/2.8，光圈：f/5，快门：1/100秒，感光度：ISO200，曝光补偿：0EV **甲居藏寨大渡河谷**

相机：松下 Panasonic GF3，镜头：14mm f/2.5，光圈：f/4.5，快门：1/400秒，感光度：ISO160，曝光补偿：-0.3EV **甲居藏寨晚霞**

地区。

在以后的岁月中，吐蕃对所辖区域采取民族“融合”政策，使嘉良夷，即南北朝时中路人和古羌人、东女国、外来的吐蕃人互相融合，逐渐演变为现在的嘉绒藏族。作为康巴藏族的一个分支，嘉绒藏族拥有了与其他藏族不同的特征。头帕、绣花鞋和腰带等装饰与羌族相似，以农业为主的生产模式又似于汉族。

东女国虽亡，但其文化却为吐蕃所吸收，成为吐蕃文化暨藏族文明的重要组成部分。作为“东女国”后裔，藏族的一支，由于自然环境以及社会、经济等因素，构成了金川人勤劳、勇悍、豪爽热情的秉性，形成独具魅力的东女国后裔特色。

数千年前，中路人到西羌，再到东女国，接着是吐蕃。今天的丹巴女子就是土著中路人、藏、汉、羌等民族相融合的结晶。遗传基因学证明，这种结合往往使人类无论在智力上还是在身材和容貌上更胜一筹。

今天，当我们漫步于滔滔大金川河谷两岸时，深感金川这块浸润千年文明的热土风采依旧，美丽依然。丹巴的女子楚楚动人，雍容大气，让每个到达这里的访客深感惊艳和震撼。她们自幼喝着雪山的甘露长大，天生的冰肌玉肤吸取了日月精华，身着华丽无比的百褶裙风韵顿生，言行举止间有着城市女子无法比拟的天然高贵之美。

This place used to be the congregation site for the Jia Rong Tibetans. Jia Rong means the “Queen’s Valley”. Here, the queen’s sacred mountain, Moerduo Mountain, has been piously worshipped by religious disciples at home and abroad. Here is the river, which is said to be the collection of the Queen’s sweat and tears. The Dajinchuan River and Xiaojinchuan River merge into the Dadu River. Here is the thirteen-angle castle,

相机：尼康 NIKON D700，镜头：70-200mm f/2.8，光圈：f/8，快门：1/60秒，感光度：ISO200，曝光补偿：-0.3EV **甲居藏寨碉楼**

which is said to have been built according to women's wisdom. Therefore, the tradition and romance of feminine culture have stayed intact even up to today. Here used to be the core area of the capital city of the Women's Kingdom. The remains of the former capital of the kingdom, which mysteriously disappeared in at some point history, are what is now the Zhonglu Town of Danba County.

The mysterious kingdom, where women used to hold sway over almost everything, enjoyed glory quite a few times in Chinese history. As a land of dreams and a dynasty of riddles, the feminine kingdom, similar to a meteor that sweeps over the night sky of history, gradually faded away, leaving behind only people's endless imagination and mysterious legends.

The Women's Kingdom, the tribal groups and local administration that came into being in the 600s and 700s AD, used to be one of the important ancient kingdoms in the Changdu area and in fact all of Tibetan history.

In the times of the Women's Kingdom, the Changdu area and the Tibetan area in the northwest of Sichuan boasted a rather developed civilization. At that time, it had more than four million families with an army of about ten thousand soldiers. The most prominent feature in the culture of the Women's Kingdom is the social system of matriarchy and worship of women. In AD 641, Songzain Gambo unified Tibet and established his Tubo Dynasty.

Despite the extinction of the Women's Kingdom, its culture was absorbed into Tubo culture, which is an important component of Tibetan cul-

岩巅之城 （毛时惕 作品）

相机：尼康 NIKON D700，镜头：70-200mm f/2.8，光圈：f/5.6，快门：1/200秒，感光度：ISO200，曝光补偿：0EV **甲居藏寨藏族女子**

ture. As the descendants of the Women's Kingdom, one group of Tibetans, the Jinchuan people, are industrious, brave, straightforward and enthusiastic, fully demonstrating their uniquely charming characteristics as descendants of the Women's Kingdom.

Today, as we saunter along the banks of the turbulent Dajinchuan River, we fully realize that the charm and beauty of the thousand-year civilization remain intact. The Danba women, who are beautiful, attractive, graceful and dignified, usually leave a very deep impression on visitors and guests. They have been drinking the spring water from the Snow Mountains ever since childhood, and their complexion that has been exposed to the sun and the moon is attractively tender and smooth. Attired in their gorgeous pleated skirts, they look so elegantly beautiful that no women in cities can ever compete with them.

别有天地非人间

A Paradise on Earth

"天人合一"的丹巴地理环境十分独特，其位于四川横断山脉峡谷地带，是甘孜州的东大门，大金川、小金川、革什扎河、东谷河与大渡河五条河流在此汇聚。蓝天白云，高山峡谷，河流纵横，草木茂盛，牛羊遍地，风景如画。

丹巴藏居全部依山取材，木石为构，依起伏的山势迤逦连绵，隐没在高山之上、田野之中、密林深处和蓝天之间，与充满灵气的山谷、清澈的溪流、皑皑的雪峰水乳交融。

阳春三月是丹巴最迷人的季节，人和藏居都融入了花的海洋。冰川雪线下的大小金川两岸，梨花、桃花、油菜花漫山遍野竞相怒放，色彩缤纷娇艳诱人。田野里还没有收割的冬小麦，呈现一片片嫩绿色，藏寨就掩映在灿烂的梨花丛中，偶尔有一两枝娇艳欲滴的桃花，在初春轻浮的薄雾之中探出头来，更增添了一份如梦如幻的感觉。东谷天然盆景区山体陡峭，奇峰如林，激流一路往南倾泻狂奔，高山植被生态原始，由大片红石滩形成的自然奇观，令人眼界大开。

每临春节前夕，当地藏民依照传统习俗，以当地的"白泥"为主要原料，通过配方制成白色染料，精心涂染寨楼的墙面。甲居藏寨中每一座藏居都是一件艺术品，房子外墙用色大胆鲜明，红、白、黑的搭配藏风浓郁。寨楼是古碉式的建筑，旧称碉楼寨房。碉楼和寨房，原本是两种不同性质的建筑形式，随着时光流逝，如今两者已完美融合于一起。既有寨房的特征，又有碉楼的形态，整个建筑物外形犹如虔诚的佛教徒盘腿打坐诵经。房顶的四角分别代表山、树、水、地，耸立着的4座白色小石塔代表四方神祇，将屋顶装饰成半月形，上插经幡，迎风招展。每当春祈秋报或者年节祭祖之时，嘉绒人都要对着白石塔祭祀。虽然有些老屋已有数百年的历史，但经历代主人的精心呵护，依旧呈现勃勃生机。

走进藏居家中，藏画的热烈与绚丽迎面扑来，浓艳得无法化解。鲜艳的红、黄、绿、蓝化身为莲花、树木、河流、山川、鸟虫和僧侣，布满房间的墙壁、柜门、桌椅和床榻。每个房间的装饰都很精致，角角落落雕刻着鲜艳且藏风浓郁的图案，让你感觉仿佛走进了艺术殿堂。楼顶上、阳台边、院落内种植的各式花卉争奇斗艳，让人赞叹主人对生活的热爱。

到了秋天，藏居山寨周围又呈现一派色彩斑斓的七彩世界。漫山遍野的树叶渐次变色，分别呈现黄、橙、金、赤、红和紫色，灿烂可人；藏寨的房顶则铺满了金黄的玉米棒和火红的辣椒干；寨前房后的果树枝头挂满香气四溢的累累果实；起伏的坡地上，望不到尽头的包谷田中色块明亮、线条流畅，一个一个吐出暗红色穗须的包谷，仿佛在引吭欢唱丰收的田歌。

桃花流水窅然去，别有天地非人间。甲居藏寨的每一幢房子，都恰到好处地犹如撒落在山间的一颗颗珍珠；每一幢房子，都隐藏着一则委婉曲折的动人故事。秀丽大气的自然风光，悠久神秘的人文历史，使之无愧于“中国最美乡村”的称谓。

Geographically and environmentally unique, Danba is located in the cross-sectional area of the mountains and valleys in Sichuan. It is the east entrance of the Ganzi Autonomous Prefecture, where the Dajinchuan River, Xiaojinchuan River, Geshenzha River, Donggu River and Dadu River merge. With white clouds floating in the blue skies, high mountains and deep valleys, rivers crisscrossing each other, luxurious grass and abundant trees, and cattle and sheep roaming and grazing everywhere, what picturesque scenery it is!

March is the most charming season in Danba. People and the Tibetan residences are all submerged in a sea of flowers. Pear flowers, peach flowers and rape seed flowers all burst into a prism of bewitching colors all the way along the river banks. The verdant fields are still covered with winter wheat that is waiting to be harvested. The Tibetan residences are hidden among the brilliant pear trees in blossom interspersed with the occasional blossoming peach tree. Emerging in the thin spring mist, they add a fanciful dreamlike feeling. In the Dong Valley area, the mountains are precipitous, and grotesque peaks form a stone forest. The river waters flow torrentially southward. The mountain vegetation remains primitive. The vast stretches of red stone beaches make up a natural miracle. What a view to remember!

When autumn comes, the surroundings in the vicinity of the Tibetan residences become a col–

相机：尼康 NIKON D700，镜头：70–200mm f/2.8，光圈：f/4.5，快门：1/200秒，感光度：ISO200，曝光补偿：–2EV **夏诺多吉峰夕照**

orful world. The leaves of the trees all over the mountains change color gradually: yellow, orange, golden, red, crimson and purple. Quite a feast for the eyes. The roofs of the Tibetan houses are covered with golden corn ears and scarlet dried peppers. Before and behind them are fruit trees laden with fragrant fruits. And in the endless undulating fields are the numerous corn ears with darkish red tassels sing the song of harvest.

All the houses of the Tibetan villages are just like pearls scattered amidst the mountains. Every one of them has a touching story to tell. For the fantastic natural scenery and mysterious age-old culture, the Jiaju Tibetan Village deserves the title of Most Beautiful Village in China.

相机：尼康 NIKON D700，镜头：尼康 70-200mm f/2.8，光圈：f/13，快门：1/640秒，感光度：ISO200，曝光补偿：-1EV **剪子弯山巅玛尼堆**

Tips 寻访者须知

佳境指数 Scenery Index： ★★★★★

备选序列：藏羌碉楼与村寨——中国世界文化遗产预备名单第36号（国家文物局2012年11月版）

List Number: Castles and Villages in the Tibetan and Qiang Area— No.36 in the preparatory list for Chinese World Heritage(November 2012 Edition by the State Cultural Relics Bureau)

寻访提示：丹巴位于中国最美的景观大道——138国道（川藏线）北线中段，沿途分布众多自然和人文品位极高的绝美景观，东有四姑娘山、日隆镇和西岭雪山，北有马尔康米亚罗和羌族碉赛，南有康定海螺沟、贡嘎山和木格措，西有八美塔公草原、新都桥等，为摄影和徒步客的旅行天堂。百花争艳的春季和层林尽染的秋季为最佳出游季节，雨水充沛的夏季和冰雪消融的初春易发山洪和泥石流等自然灾害，不宜出行。另318国道路况险峻，事故易发，建议租赁越野车且请驾技好、路况熟的司机同行。沿途海拔高度在三千米以上，需做好防寒保暖及预防高原疾病的措施。

Location Notes: Danba Prefecture is located in the middle of the northern section of State Route 138, China's most beautiful scenic highway. All along the highway are numerous natural scenes and cultural sites. To the east are the Four-girl Mountain, Rilong Town, and West-ridge Snow Mountain; to the north are Maerkang, Miyaluo and the Qiang people's castles; to the south are the Conch Channel of Kangding, Minya Konka and Mugecuo; and to the west are the Bamei Tagong Prairie and Xindu Bridge. This is a paradise for photographers and hikers. Spring, when hundreds of

相机：尼康 NIKON D700，镜头：尼康 70-200mm f/2.8，光圈：f/10，快门：1/400秒，感光度：ISO200，曝光补偿：-1.3EV **理塘藏寨秋色**

flowers blossom, and autumn, when all kinds of trees are dyed a variety of colors, are the best seasons for tourists. However, summer, when it rains too plentifully, and early spring, when the melting snow might cause mountain torrents, mud slides and other natural disasters, are not suitable for tourism.

摄影提示：甲居藏寨是摄影创作出大片和佳作的首选地之一。拍摄题材和元素十分丰富，藏寨、碉楼、河川、谷地、田园、高山、森林、草甸、天光云影、云雾、彩虹等自然景观及民俗人文均令人陶醉。在构图上尽量摄入更多的元素，并考虑近、中和远景景物的比例。拍摄位置以制高点为佳，寨子北面有多处观景平台可俯视全寨，寨门前有一高坡可俯视大渡河沿岸。拍摄角度应根据被拍摄物的特点，可采用平视、俯视和仰视等角度；拍摄景别上视被拍摄物与周围环境的关系，拍摄自然景观和藏居可采用远景、中景，拍摄民俗及人物风采可用特写。

Tips for Photography: The Jiaju Tibetan Village tends to be the first choice for photographers to work out their miraculous photos, for this place is rich in a variety of subject matter and elements; Tibetan villages, castles, rivers, valleys, fields, mountains, forests, prairies, clouds in the skies, mists, rainbows, and other natural scenes and cultural sites that intoxicate the viewer. Spring and autumn are the best seasons of the year for photography, and sunrise and sunset are the best times of day for picture-taking.

民俗提示：特定的地理、社会背景，形成了甲居藏寨独具特色的文化内涵，丰富的民族歌舞是东女国古老文化的载体。《金川琐记》记载："俗喜跳锅庄，嘉会日里，党中男女各衣新衣，合色巾帕之属，罄家所有，杂俩其身，以为华赡，男女纷沓，连臂踏歌，俱欣欣有喜色。"跳锅庄一般逢喜庆佳节时跳，如看花节、藏历年、婚礼乃至丰收喜庆或春耕下种等。锅庄多与酒相关，跳时置青稞酒于圆圈中，随饮随跳，愈饮愈欢，酣畅淋漓。由德高望重者执串铃领舞，领舞者起调，随者应和，其动作亦随领舞者。兴起时，领舞者将圈缩小，快捷轻灵，抒胸中快意，举手投足中展豪情壮志。

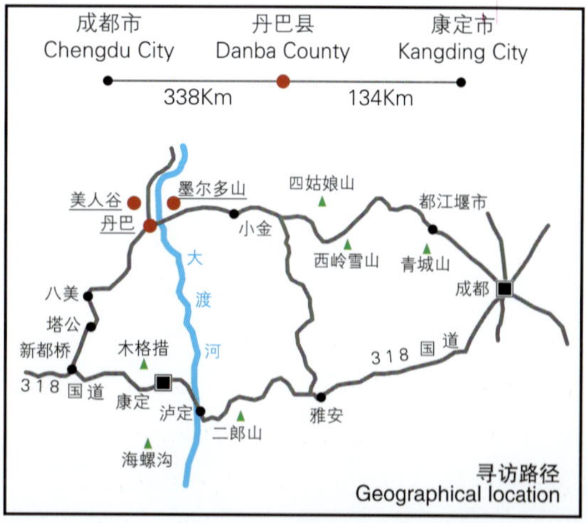

寻访路径
Geographical location

Brief Introduction to the Local Culture: The unique geographical location and social background result in the special cultural connotations of the Jiaju Tibetan Village, and the rich ethnic dancing serves as the vehicle for the ancient civilization of the Women's Kingdom.

美食提示：丹巴在饮食上兼有四川和藏族风味。川味饭馆以冷锅鱼出名。如果住在藏家，一定会品尝到正宗的酥油茶。丹巴的水果资源十分丰富，春天有樱桃，秋天有梨子和苹果，收获时节可进入村寨的果林大快朵颐。

Food Tips: Danba is characteristic of Sichuan and Tibetan cuisine. Sichuan-style restaurants are well known for their cold fishes. If you live in a Tibetan home, you will definitely have a chance to try butter tea. Danba is rich in fruits: cherries in spring and pears and apples in autumn. During the harvest days, you are welcome to the gardens to enjoy the fruits to your heart's content.

寻觅备选世遗佳境 1
云南红河州元阳县哈尼梯田
Hani Terraced Fields,Yuanyang County,
Honghe Prefecture, Yunnan

19 哈尼，哈尼 Hani, Hani

人工湿地的典范　稻作文明的杰作

A Typical Artificial Wetland; A Masterpiece of Paddy Civilization

一

一把短柄铁锄
在茶马古道的雾霾中
终日缥缈
舞动千年
红河之滨的哀牢山
从此放歌大地

A sickle has been dimly floating for a thousand years amidst the hazy fog along the ancient Chama Road in the Ailao Mountains by the side of the Honghe River. Ever since, it has been singing out all over the wide expanse.

二

敬畏的种子
在你的心中开出鲜艳的木棉花
黑夜中的一轮明月
那是神灵通透的慧眼
生存和春天
永远发生冲突
文明与自然
笑着签下协约
放弃征服，这是和解的价码
绿色的履带碾过大地
一路播撒收获的信念

The awesome seeds have burst into brilliant kapok flowers deep in your heart. A bright full moon shedding light late at night is actually the penetrating eye of a deity. Existence and spring are always in direct confrontation. Civilization and nature have smilingly signed an agreement, i.e. giving up conquest, which is the price for reconciliation. Caterpillar belts of tractors are rumbling over the green fields, sowing along the rows of land the seeds that will definitely bring in a bumper harvest.

相机：佳能 Canon Eos-1DX，镜头：24-70mm f/2.8，光圈：f/19.9，快门：1/200秒，感光度：ISO320，曝光补偿：0EV **多依树梯田日出**

相机：佳能 Canon Eos-1DX，镜头：24-70mm f/2.8，光圈：f/14，快门：1/320秒，感光度：ISO320，曝光补偿：0EV **大鱼塘梯田**

相机：佳能 Canon Eos-1DX，镜头：24-70mm f/2.8，光圈：f/10，快门：1/160秒，感光度：ISO320，曝光补偿：0EV **坝达梯田日落**

老虎嘴夕照 （孙磊 作品）

三

风景就等在大山之上
葱郁的黄草岭上探出一束光
多依树的脸上，慢慢荡起了笑意
拨开层层迷雾，铺晒一路斑斓
坝达，孤岛般在浩瀚的大海中摇曳
唯见波涛汹涌，却不闻浪花拍岸
日落余晖，斜照在老虎嘴湖水般清澄的双眼
闪着蓝光的骏马，在破碎的镜面中驰骋
骑上一头耕牛
轻轻犁过，龙树坝螺丝田的心房
静心等待，藏匿大山深处的处子
舒展迷人的曲线
牵着莫名的悸动
悄然潜入菁口的蘑菇房
一行乘风破浪的帆船，直冲云外
山水，欲沉似浮
心绪，已在天上

Beautiful scenery awaits visitors among the big mountains, which emit rays of light from the thriving yellowish grass. The trees, slowly and smilingly, are driving away the fog and showing wonderful colors all along the paths. Bada, like an isolated island rocking in a vast sea, could only hear the roaring torrents of waves but not see any wave splash against the banks. The sunset sheds twilight on the lakes, which resemble crystal and bright eyes. And, meanwhile, horses of twinkling blu-ish color gallop on the broken mirrors. The farmer on top of a bull is gradually plowing the terraced fields of Longshu Ba. Waiting patiently, the virgin hidden deeply in the mountains is stretching her body, displaying her bewitching curves. Naturally aroused and somewhat excited, they sneak into the mushroom hut nearby. A fleet of sailing boats are moving upward against the wind and waves.

相机：佳能 Canon Eos-1DX，镜头：24-70mm f/2.8，光圈：f/11，快门：1/500秒，感光度：ISO320，曝光补偿：0EV **龙树坝梯田**

相机：佳能 Canon Eos-1DX，镜头：24-70mm f/2.8，光圈：f/16，快门：1/200秒，感光度：ISO200，曝光补偿：0EV **红河谷木棉花**

相机：佳能 Canon Eos-1DX，镜头：24-70mm f/2.8，光圈：f/11，快门：1/500秒，感光度：ISO320，曝光补偿：0EV **哈尼村庄**

相机：佳能 Canon Eos-1DX，镜头：24-70mm f/2.8，光圈：f/13
快门：1/125秒，感光度：ISO100，曝光补偿：0EV **元阳村民**

相机：佳能 Canon Eos-1DX，镜头：24-70mm f/2.8，光圈：f/20
快门：1/40秒，感光度：ISO320，曝光补偿：0EV **元阳村民**

相机：索尼 SONY-Nex7，镜头：16mm，光圈：f/9，快门：1/100秒
感光度：ISO100，曝光补偿：0EV **元阳村民**

相机：索尼 SONY-Nex7，镜头：16mm，光圈：f/5.6，快门：1/80秒
感光度：ISO100，曝光补偿：0EV **元阳村民**

相机：佳能 Canon Eos-1DX，镜头：24-70mm f/2.8，光圈：f/10，快门：1/50秒，感光度：ISO200，曝光补偿：0EV **元谋土林余晖**

The passengers in the boats, who see the mountains and waters going into the river but actually still floating backward, are so thrilled, feeling as if they were high above in the sky.

四

哈尼，哈尼
活力，是你千年如一的驻颜术
生机，是你畅行天下的二维码
文明与自然的联姻
成为所有生灵永恒的光彩
三千年光阴
始终讲述一个故事
三千米高度
无法丈量一座丰碑
大地艺术家
这是上苍对你的最高褒奖

Hani, dear Hani,

Vitality is how you have remained permanently young and beautiful for thousands of years. Virility is the QR code that enables you to be known all over the world. The wedlock between civilization and nature has become the everlasting brilliance for all beings. For over three thousand years, the same story has been narrated. The height of three thousand meters fails to match a glorious monument. For artists of the world, Hani is the best award from heaven.

Tips 寻访者须知

佳境指数 Scenery Index：★★★★★

备选序列：哈尼梯田——中国世界文化遗产预备名单第39号（国家文物局2012年11月版）

List Number: The Terraced Fields of Hani — No.39 in the preparatory list for Chinese World Heritage (November 2012 Edition by the State Cultural Relics Bureau)

（作者注：本篇在发稿付印前，欣闻元阳哈尼梯田于2013年6月22日在柬埔寨召开的第37届世界遗产大会上正式入选联合国教科文组织《世界遗产名录》，成为我国第45项世界遗产。）

(Author's Note: Before the present writing went to print, the present writer was gladly informed that the terraced fields of Hani at Yuanyang County were officially selected and listed among the World Heritage at the 37th World Heritage Conference held in Cambodia on June 22, 2013, thus becoming the 45th in the list of world heritage in China.)

寻访提示：元阳哈尼梯田已成为向全世界展现中国农耕文明、稻作文化的一张名片，境内分布的19万亩哈尼梯田依山顺势，布满高山河谷，不仅体现自然之美，更蕴含着深厚的哈尼农耕文化习俗，成为稻作文明的独特景观存在于世，尤其是多依树、老虎嘴、坝达、箐口、龙树坝等点位景色变幻无穷，宛如置身仙境之中。每年的11月至次年的4月为寻访的最好时间，但尤以1至2月为最佳。在这一季节出游的同时，可顺道寻访元谋土林、东川红土地、罗平油菜花、澄江抚仙湖、建水孔庙等品位上乘的人文和自然景观。

Location Notes: The terraced fields of Hani in Yuanyang are a symbol to demonstrate Chinese agricultural culture and paddy culture to the world. Naturally downward along the mountains in this region, the 19,000-mu Hani terraced fields that cover the high mountains and deep valleys not only display the natural beauty but also embody the profound agricultural culture and customs of the Hani people. It is a unique type of paddy culture in the world. Facing the ever-changing views of such places as Duoyishu, Tiger Mouth, Bada, Jingkou, Longshu Dam, etc., visitors cannot help feeling that they are in heaven. The time from November of one year to April of the next, especially in January and February, is the best for sightseeing. There are many other excellent natural and historic sites in the neighborhood, such as the Dongchuan Red Lands, Luoping County rapeseed fields, the Earthen Forest of Yuanmou, Fuxian Lake, the Confucian temple at Jianshui, etc, and all are particularly worth visiting at the same time of year as the terraced fields.

摄影提示：元阳哈尼梯田是摄影者的天堂，自然和人文题材众多，也是出好作品的地方。箐口和坝达一线，最能直观展现哈尼梯田森林、村寨、梯田、水系四要素同构的区域，同时也是进行梯田、云海、蘑菇房、人文风俗摄影创作的理想点位；坝达和多依树方向，多为近距离拍摄梯田的区域，多依树以拍摄日出景观名闻天下，是拍摄云海、梯田和村寨的最佳点位；箐口和老虎嘴一线风景优美，老虎嘴以拍摄日落而著名，是地势最为险峻的点位；多依树与老虎嘴一线全长15公里，拥有122个弯道，可拍摄硐浦、一碗水村寨、螺丝田等景观。摄影者除备妥广角、长焦、三脚架等摄影器材外，徒步走入梯田之中进行创作，会有意想不到的收获。

Tips for Photography: The Hani terraced fields of Yuanyang are a heaven for photographers, who work out many good pictures in view of such a large number of historic sites and natural scenes. The four elements of forests, villages, terraced fields and water conservancy systems in the area of Jingkou and Daba could best directly manifest the Hani terraced fields. Meanwhile, this is an ideal spot for the photography of terraced fields, seas of clouds, mushroom huts and folk customs. There are quite a few places where wonderful photos of sunrise and sunset as well as bewitching scenery could be produced. Besides having the wide-angle lenses, telephoto lenses, tripods and other apparatuses ready, the cameramen could simple walk into the terraced fields, where they would acquire unexpected harvests.

民俗提示： 元阳民俗多姿多彩，民族风情绚丽宜人。主要的民俗活动有农历正月初二的苗族“踩花山节”；农历正月属龙日哈尼族“昂玛突节”，这是哈尼人一年中最盛大的节日，当天要在山寨摆上酒席，祭护寨神，拜龙求雨；农历三月初三壮族的“三月三节”；农历四月十二日傣族的“泼水节”；农历六月二十四日彝族的“火把节”；农历七月十四日瑶族的“盘王节”；农历十一月十八日元阳梯田旅游文化节。

Brief Introduction to the Local Culture: In Yuanyang, the folk arts are very colorful and the ethnic customs quite pleasant. All the year round, there are a series of celebrations and ceremonies either for religious worships or for get-togethers.

美食提示： 元阳哈尼美食主要有哈尼沾水鸡、豆豉和虫宴；梯田鱼、泥鳅、黄鳝和鸭蛋；原生态山鸡、牛肉和猪肉；野生紫山药、山茅野菜。“昂玛突节”期间，长街宴是哈尼族一种传统习俗，家家户户要做黄糯米、三色蛋、猪、鸡、鱼、鸭肉、牛肉干巴、麂子干巴、肉松、花生米等近四十种哈尼族风味菜肴，备上好酒，抬到指定的街心摆放，一家摆一两桌，家家户户桌连桌，沿街摆成一条长长的街心宴（当地人也称长龙宴或街心酒），这也是中国最长的宴席。

Food Tips: The major delicacies of Hani in Yuanyang include feasts of chicken, fermented soya beans and even insects. Besides, local people offer fish, loach, and eel from the terraced fields as well as duck eggs, pheasants, beef, pork, purple yam, wild vegetables, etc. On occasions, long-street banquets would be held, when all the families bring out their best dishes, usually some 40 kinds. Each family will set one or two tables in the designated street with self-brewed rice wine and dishes. Table after table in the street, it makes the longest feast in China.

寻访路径
Geographical location

寻觅备选世遗佳境 1
四川省甘孜州丹巴县梭坡碉楼
Suopo Watchtowers, Danba County,
Ganzhi Prefecture, Sichuan

20 耸立天空的族谱 Outstanding Family Tree

石头写就的羌族人文史书

The History of Qiang People, Written in Stones

自丹巴县城沿大渡一路溯流而上，但见河谷两岸地势险峻雄奇，抬首仰望，山脉逶迤，奇峰连绵，云遮雾绕，俯瞰河谷纵横，河床陡狭，激流险滩，惊涛拍岸，疑为天堑。

行至梭坡乡莫洛村时，一道气势逼人的奇异景观映入眼帘，蓝天白云之下，数十座高低错落的碉楼拔地凌空，蔚为壮观。这些灰黑色的高大石头杰作，棱角分明，巍然屹立。隔江远眺，疑为天国。在这每一座都历经百年风雨的碉楼面前，我的思绪瞬间穿入了历史隧道，失去了方向，迷失了自我。

The Town of Danba spreads upward along the Dadu River. The river is flanked by towering mountains. Upward, there are the meandering tall mountains, peak after peak in the clouds; and downward, the river waters crisscross and flow torrentially between precipitous banks. The river is usually referred to as natural chasm.

At the Moluo Village of Suopo, an imposing view comes into sight. Right below the white clouds in the blue skies, dozens of watchtowers, high and low, soar into the skies. Spectacular-looking, isn't it? Standing in front of each of the watchtowers, my thoughts fly through the tunnel of history. I've lost both my sense of direction and my own ego.

攻碉难于克城池

Unconquerable Watchtowers

清乾隆十三年（1748年）底，乾隆以“当失误军机律”为由，问斩了两年多来在平定大、小金川土司叛乱中屡战不克的川陕总督张广泗。

1746年，这是乾隆皇帝登基后的第十一个年头，在他统驭下，大清国已有十几年无大的战事。这年3月，一个有关大、小金川土司叛变的消息传入紫禁城内。大、小金川位于四川西北部，历来均为多个少数民族混居之处。自元朝以来，中原王朝授予当地的部族首领以土司之职，负责行使当地行政管理权，主政赋税、官司和募兵等，职位并可世袭。清雍正

相机：尼康 NIKON D700，镜头：尼康 70-200mm f/2.8，光圈：f/6.3，快门：1/60秒，感光度：ISO200，曝光补偿：0EV **丹巴梭坡碉楼**

曾试图用汉族的流官代替土司，但未果。自1737年起，大、小金川之间内讧频发，四川地方官员曾不断上奏朝廷，乾隆下谕只要他们不干扰内地，乐得隔岸观火。

但这场火很快就烧得控制不了局面。1746年3月，大、小金川将战火烧到了明正土司所辖的鲁密、章谷等地，距离打箭炉（今康定）仅四天路程，南方岌岌可危。乾隆方才重视，速调云贵总督张广泗为川陕总督，以川贵之兵，进剿大、小金川。乾隆判断，大、小金川方圆不过数百里，壮丁仅七八千人，难敌数万精锐清兵。且张广泗在前不久在平定苗民起义中战绩非凡。但是，随着战事的发展，很快证明乾隆过于自信了。8月间，张广泗不断向乾隆上奏战事不利的消息。大、小金川群峰耸立，山势陡峻，羌人在要道及地险处皆建一种独特的防御性建筑——碉楼，形成一个个易守难攻的军事要塞。“其扼要处必有战碉，于墙垣间以枪石外击，旁既无路，进兵必须从枪石中过，故一碉不过数十人，万夫皆阻。”清军“或穴地道，以轰地雷，或挖墙孔，以施火炮，或围绝水道，以坐困之，种种设法”，却损兵折将，收效甚微。

更令清军无奈的是，每座碉楼的入口皆离地面数米高，遇有敌情守方即刻将活动的独木梯抽至楼上。碉楼的入口十分矮小，门板坚实厚重，木制门闩带有保险，攻方极难攻破。守方将碉楼最下层的开口盖住后，碉楼底部就成为一个狭小封闭的空间，清军若用火攻，产生的浓烟因无法消散反而呛了己方。

清军对此只能“半月旬日攻一碉，攻一碉难于克一城”。直至1748年7月，清军兵马损失过半，大、小金川平定仍遥不可及。张广泗再次上疏朝廷，“乃议令官军筑碉，谓与贼共险。上以为非策，责广泗附和推诿，严谕诘难”。张广泗建议以守代攻，以碉楼对碉楼，但被乾隆斥责为本末倒置，成本太高。清廷上下一时对大、小金川碉楼束手无策。令人匪夷所思的是，乾隆听说御史王显绪父子熟悉金川情形，则命王显绪征询其父王柔破金川之策，王柔竟建议请终南

相机：尼康 NIKON D700，镜头：尼康 70-200mm f/2.8，光圈：f/5，快门：1/100秒，感光度：ISO200，曝光补偿：0EV **丹巴墨尔多神山晨曦**

相机：尼康 NIKON D700，镜头：70–200mm f/2.8，光圈：f/7.1，快门：1/200秒，感光度：ISO200，曝光补偿：–1EV **梭坡碉楼春色**

山道士用五雷法术以击贼碉，让乾隆哭笑不得。

情急之下，乾隆突然想起祖辈的攻城之策："开国之初，我旗人蹑云梯肉搏而登城者不可屈指数，以此攻碉，何碉弗克？"于是，他下旨命工部在京城西山脚下修筑数座类似大、小金川的碉楼，从京城八旗内选拔两千精锐，组成香山健锐云梯营，每日演练攻打碉楼的技能。

1748年底，乾隆处斩了剿叛不力的张广泗，以傅恒为经略大臣，率包括健锐云梯营在内的两万五千名清军再次入川平乱。至次年年初，大、小金川土司溃败乞降，头顶佛经立誓决不再叛。

大、小金川的战争让乾隆这位"十全武功"的皇帝颜面无存。双方相峙八年，历经大小战争百余场，用兵四万有余，耗国库银两七千余万两，付出了巨大的代价，而对手只不过是小小的土司。最后，乾隆以张广泗的项上人头，平息了朝廷内外的非议。

现在看来，张广泗并非无能之辈，而是碉楼强大的防御能力，在冷兵器时期确实占据了一定的优势；而清廷也不是毫无所得，这种碉楼建筑样式在后来被直接引用于中原王朝的防御体系，在湖南以制苗、滇边以制"倮夷"、四川以制"生番"和川甘以制"回乱"中，均发挥了重要的作用。

In the 13th year (1748 A.D.) of Emperor Qianlong of the Qing Dynasty, the emperor had Zhang Guangsi, the then governor of Sichuan and Shaanxi, beheaded. Zhang had failed to quench the constant rebellions staged by the chieftains of Jinchuan repeatedly in the past two years.

In 1746, the 11th year after the emperor mounted the throne, the Qing Dynasty had seen no serious wars for more than a decade under his rule. In March of that year, however, the news that the chieftains of Jinchuan launched rebellions thronged to the Forbidden City. Jin–chuan was located in the northwest of Sichuan, where

相机：尼康 NIKON D700，镜头：70-200mm f/2.8，光圈：f/8，快门：1/60秒，感光度：ISO200，曝光补偿：-1EV **大渡河谷藏家碉楼**

people of different nationalities lived together. Starting from 1737, strife frequently occurred among the people there. The local magistrates reported to the imperial court time and again. The emperor ordered that as long as the chieftains did not molest the internal areas, he preferred to adopt a "wait–and–see" attitude.

Unfortunately, however, the war fires soon spread beyond control. In March 1746, it approached Lumi, Zhanggu and other places, only about four days' distance from Jianlu, which is Kangding today. South China was in imminent danger. With due attention, Emperor Qianlong dispatched Zhang Guangsi, the then governor of Yunnan and Guizhou, to take the position of Governor of Sichuan and Guizhou to attack Jinchuan. In the emperor's opinion, Jinchuan, with an area of some hundred mu and a population of 7 or 8 thousand able–bodied men, could never be able to resist the imperial army. Yet, Governor Zhang, who had made glorious achievements in the suppression of the uprisings by the Miao people, failed to go forward because of the watchtowers on the precipitous mountains. A few dozen people in one tower warded off thousands of soldiers. The Qing army made no progress.

The imperial army found that it took them ten days to half a month to conquer one tower and that it was more difficult to crack a tower than a city. Until July 1748, the imperial army suffered serious casualties, almost more than half; nevertheless, the victory in the suppression of Jinchuan rebellions was still beyond reach. The imperial court was at a loss over what to do.

At the end of 1784, Emperor Qianlong sentenced Zhang Guangsi to death, for having failed in the suppression. In the following year, another army of 15,000 soldiers was dispatched to Sichuan. In early 1749, the

四姑娘山秋色 （丁言纲 作品）

chieftains of Jinchuan were defeated. They begged to surrender and swore never to rebel.

The war in Jinchuan made the omnipotent Emperor Qianlong lose face completely. The two sides confronted over eight years, during which they fought hundreds of battles. The imperial court dispatched over 40,000 soldiers and used up 70 million taels of silver from the national treasury. Such an exorbitant cost, and the opponents were merely petty chieftains. In the end, Emperor Qianlong had to use Zhang Guangsi's head to pacify the censure within and without the imperial court.

From the present-day point of view, Zhang Guangsi was by no means an impotent person. In the period of cold-steel weaponry, the strong defensive capability of watchtowers did enjoy some advantages. And the imperial court of the Qing Dynasty could not be said to have gained nothing in the war. They made use of such watchtowers in the future suppression of rebellions by minority peoples elsewhere in China.

石头写就千年史

Thousand-year-old History Carved on Stone

在大、小金川战争中声名鹊起的碉楼，羌语称“邛笼”，最早的文字记载见于两千多年前的《后汉书·西南夷传》：“依山居止，垒石为屋，高者至十余丈。”其建筑者就是自秦以来就广泛分布于中国西南地区的羌人，碉楼就是这个古老民族人文遗迹留存至今的鲜明印记之一。

羌族是一个有着古老文明史的民族。据考，羌人祖先原在甘肃、青海一带。炎帝、大禹、夏启、周文王、周武王和姜子牙等中国历史上众多举足轻重的人物皆为羌人。今所说的羌族，为秦汉时迁至岷江上游，并由游牧生活转为农耕定居，自此世代繁衍。羌族有语言而少文字，其民族文化多通过口头传承世代相袭。

相机：尼康 NIKON D700，镜头：70-200mm f/2.8，光圈：f/7.1，快门：1/200秒，感光度：ISO200，曝光补偿：-1EV **四姑娘山双桥沟枯树滩**

羌人好集族而居，数家连为一片，形成羌寨。传说以前凡有男孩的羌人家庭必须修一座碉楼，逐渐形成了“千碉之国”。其实，为应对部落之间的战争，这才是古碉群形成的真正原因。历史上的记载也确实如此。丹巴地处大渡河谷，气候温和，土地肥美，物产丰富，历史上曾经历了多次部落战争和宗族械斗。唐朝反对吐蕃东扩曾经在此发生过战争。西夏王朝败落之后，其中一部顺金川河谷南下丹巴，曾经遭到当地居民的顽强抵抗，故而兵败西行。乾隆年间大、小金川土司两次叛乱，朝廷两次用兵，面对坚如磐石的碉楼损失惨重。从岷江河谷的松潘、茂县、汶川、理县，直到大渡河上游的丹巴、金川、马尔康等地区，高耸入云的碉楼随处可见。这里，曾被史学家视为“民族走廊”，自古以来战争不断。因此，碉楼从诞生之初，就是一个应对战争的防御体系。

碉楼自汉代始在羌族地区发展盛行。至南北朝时期，丹巴周围碉楼林立。到五代之后，碉楼建筑技术已相当成熟。最迟者为清乾隆皇帝平定大、小金川时所建。羌式碉楼主要有四种形式：隘碉往往筑于悬崖险道之上，或者横挡于要冲之间，有一夫当关、万夫莫开的作用；烽火碉多构于山头或高台之上，用以传递战争信息；寨碉是为保护村寨或部落而修建的，一般伫立于村头；家碉多与楼房居所相连，平时作为住家和贮藏室，如遇战事，即可用于战争防御。整个村寨碉楼林立，相依相倚，呈易守难攻之势。碉楼的外形，一般为高状方柱体，有四角、五角至八角的，也有多达十三角的。高度一般不低于十米，多在三十米左右，高者可达五六十米。虽然皆由片石砌成，但墙体表面光滑，缝隙紧密，棱角笔直，整个建筑下大上小，一气呵成，远远望去，宛如一根根顶天立地的擎天巨柱，尽显羌族的雄健、刚毅之气。

由于受到民族历史、居住环境以及生产方式的制约，羌族长期以来形成了一种特殊的民族信仰和生活理念。走进每个羌寨，可以看到各家各户的房顶或碉楼上都有白石英石，那是羌民敬奉的白石神。在此基础上逐渐出现的宗教理念、人生礼仪、社会象征等

相机：尼康 NIKON D700，镜头：70-200mm f/2.8，光圈：f/16，快门：1/100秒，感光度：ISO100，曝光补偿：0EV **四姑娘山双桥沟牛棚子**

相机：尼康 NIKON D700，镜头：70–200mm f/2.8，光圈：f/6.3，快门：1/60秒，感光度：ISO400，曝光补偿：–1EV **木格措七色海秋色**

民族文化内涵，又使得碉楼最终成为羌族人民的民族符号。

如今，刀光剑影和血雨腥风早已成为过眼烟云。但那一座座碉楼，以其伟岸的身躯，依然在默默述说着遥远的故事。它是一部“石头写成的历史”，忠实记录了羌族人民对文化的创造和追求。

随着社会的发展和文明的进步，碉楼的军事意义消失了，而它的人文意义在现代文明的冲击下弥足珍贵，它是中华民族贡献给世界的又一份具有独特文化魅力的文化遗产。

The watchtowers rose to fame in and after the wars in Jinchuan. The builders of such watchtowers were the Qiang people that had been scattered in southwest China since the Qin Dynasty. The watchtower has long been one of the obvious historical remains left by people of this old nationality.

The Qiang people belong to a nationality that has a long history of ancient civilization. Historically speaking, their ancestors used to live in Gansu and Qinghai. Many a famous figure in Chinese history were of the nationality, for example, King Yan, King Dayu, King Xiaqi, King Wen and King Wu of the Zhou Dynasty, Jiang Ziya, etc. The Qiang people today settle down at the upstream of the Minjiang River, and have turned from nomadic to agricultural living. With a stronger oral than written tradition, they have been passing down their national culture from mouth to mouth generation after generation.

The Qiang people are gregarious. Several families live together, forming a stockade. It is said that in the past every family that had a boy or boys must build a watchtower. Consequently, a kingdom of a thousand watchtowers gradually came into being.

相机：尼康 NIKON D700，镜头：70-200mm f/2.8，光圈：f/7.1，快门：1/80秒，感光度：ISO400，曝光补偿：-1EV **木格措七色海秋色**

The construction of watchtowers began in the Qiang areas in the Han Dynasty. In the Northern and Southern Dynasties (420–589 AD), watch-towers encircled Danba. The period of the Five Dynasties (907–960 AD) found maturity in the technology of watchtower construction. The last ones were most probably built in the years after Emperor Qianlong conquered Jinchuan. The most important feature of the watchtower lies in the fact that with one person in the tower, ten thousand soldiers could not break through.

Because of the special national history, people's migration, living environments, and modes of work and ways of life, Qiang people have long established their own national faith and living concept. Stepping into every Qiang stockade, one can't help noticing white quartz stones on the roofs and watchtowers. The white quartz stone stands for the god of white stone for the Qiang people.

Gone are the days when swords clashed and blood dripped in wars. The towers standing aloft are still narrating the by-gone stories. It is a history written in stones, faithfully recording Qiang people's creation and pursuit of culture.

With the development of society and civilization, the military function of the towers has vanished into thin air; however, its literary significance is still highly invaluable in face of the impacts of modern culture. It is another Chinese contribution to the world, unique in cultural charm and heritage.

Tips 寻访者须知

佳境指数 Scenery Index： ★★★★

备选序列： 藏羌碉楼与村寨——中国世界文化遗产预备名单第36号（国家文物局2012年11月版）

List Number: Watchtowers and Qiang Villages in Tibet, No.36 in the preparatory list for Chinese World Heritage (November 2012 Edition by the State Cultural Relics Bureau)

寻访提示： 除了丹巴梭坡碉楼以外，周边还有不少羌族碉楼及人文景观可顺道寻访。如理县的桃坪羌寨、宝殿寺庙，马尔康的松岗碉楼群、卓克基土司宫寨等。其他自然和人文景观及注意事项请参考甲居藏寨篇。

Location Notes: Besides the watchtowers in Danba, many watchtowers of the Qiang people and other cultural or historical sites are worth visiting.

摄影提示： 梭坡碉楼拍摄题材和元素十分丰富，羌寨、碉楼、河谷、山峰、森林和天光云影等自然景观及民俗人文均可入镜。拍摄村寨全景可至隔岸的观景平台，此处可拍摄气势宏大的接片。若要拍摄碉楼的近景及人文民俗风光，则要渡过大渡河，进入梭坡村寨逐个寻访。在拍摄角度上根据被拍摄物的特点，可采用平视、俯视和仰视等角度。在用光方面宜多采用逆光、侧光拍摄，更能突出被摄景物的风采。春天和秋天是一年中最佳拍摄季节，而日出和日落时分为每天最重要的拍摄时间。

Tips for Photography: The Suopo watchtowers are definitely good themes for photography. In addition, Qiang blockades, Qiang watchtowers, valleys, mountain peaks, forests, sunshine and clouds, and other natural scenes and folk culture all have great photographic potential.

民俗提示： 农历十月初一为羌族年节。年节的宴会又称“收成酒”。年节这天全寨人到“神树林”还

相机：佳能 Canon Eos-1DX，镜头：24-70mm f/2.8，光圈：f/8，快门：1/320秒，感光度：ISO100，曝光补偿：0EV **牧民转场**

愿，焚柏香孝敬祖先和天神，要用荞麦粉做成一种馅为肉丁豆腐的荞面饺，有的还要用面粉做成牛、羊、马、鸡等形状不同的动物作为祭品。次日，设家宴，请出嫁的女儿回娘家，进行各项节日活动。祈祷丰收的祭山会是全村寨的一种祭祀活动，除已婚的妇女不准参加外，全寨的人都要带上酒、肉和馍去赴会。由“许”（巫师）主持祭祀，祈求天神和山神保佑全寨人寿年丰，并将山羊宰杀后煮熟，连同其他食品分给各户，过去称“散分子”，最后大家席地而坐，互相品尝各自的祭祀食品。

Brief Introduction to the Local Culture: The first day of the tenth lunar month is New Year's Day for the Qiang people. At the New Year banquet, which is also called Harvest Drinking, all the people of the blockade will go to the Forest of Gods to redeem their vows and offer sacrifices to their dear departed and the gods in heaven. The next day, the married daughters return to their mothers' homes, and participate in various activities.

美食提示：羌族民间大都一日两餐，即吃早饭后出去劳动，要带上馍馍（玉米面馍），中午就在地里吃，称为“打尖”，下午回家吃晚餐。羌族主食大都离不开“面蒸蒸”。常年食用白菜、萝卜叶子泡的酸菜，以及青菜做成的腌菜。肉食以牛、羊、猪、鸡肉为主，兼食鱼和狩猎兽肉。散居在山区的羌族一般不常食新鲜猪肉，都是将猪宰杀后去毛，剖成两半或切成几大块，吊在房梁上熏烤制成“猪膘”，存放时间一般为一年。

Food Tips: Usually, the Qiang people have two meals a day; the first is breakfast, after which they go out to labor and around the noon time they quench hunger with some steamed corn buns they take with them when leaving home in the morning. The second is supper after they get back home. The staple food is steamed flour that goes with some sour vegetables. They eat the meat of cattle,

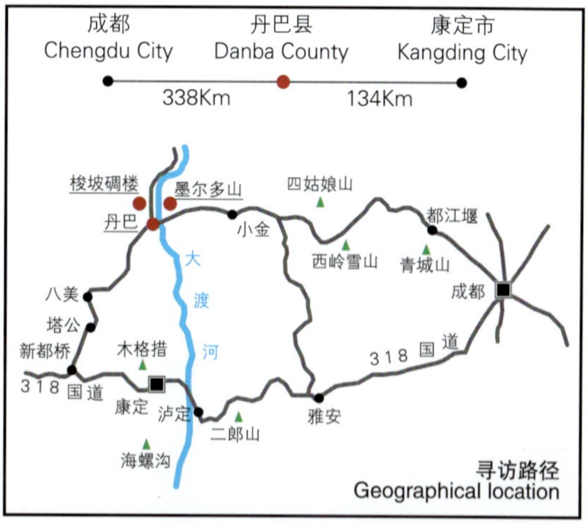

sheep, pig and chicken as well as some fish and animals they have acquired by means of hunting.

微信号：qxqpqwqx

作者简介

About the author

杨永发，上海人，60后，文化工作者。喜爱旅行、摄影和阅读文学。著有《寻觅江南秘境》《寻觅丹霞胜境》。

Yang Yongfa was born in Shanghai in the 1960s. He has long been engaged in cultural work. What's more, he has cherished a zealous interest in traveling, photography, and literature. So far his albums *In Search of the Mystery in the South of the Yangtze River* and *In Search of the Beautiful Landscaping in Danxia* have been published.

译者简介

About the translator

顾大僖，江苏人，40后，上海师范大学英语教授。译著有《巨匠与杰作》《我到我们》《豪情四兄弟》《伦敦浴火战》等。

Gu Daxi was born in Jiangsu in the 1940s. He teaches English at Shanghai Normal University. He has translated *Great Novelists and their Novels, Me to We*, and *London's Burning*.

《寻觅江南秘境》
出版：上海书店出版社
定价：68.00元

江南自古以来人杰地灵，为人们心目中的世外桃源；江南是中国文化中人文精神发生最早、积淀最深厚的地区。如何让更多的人识得这种灵气和积淀？文化摄影旅行家杨永发先生要和读者一起分享自己深入江南城市乡村、青山碧水的二十年旅行故事。

《寻觅丹霞胜境》
出版：上海交通大学出版社
定价：58.00元

分布全世界1200余处丹霞地貌绝美景观中，中国占据了其中的近800处，如果要把它们都放进一本书里似乎是不可能的任务。但是文化摄影旅行家杨永发先生经历十余年穿梭于大江南北、长城内外的丹崖赤壁间，完成了这个“不可能的任务”，将中国丹霞绝美胜境呈现在读者面前。

《寻觅备选世遗佳境 1》
出版：上海科学技术文献出版社
定价：118.00元

从九曲黄河到哈尼梯田，都有一种看得见的自然之美；从玉门雄关到甲居藏寨，都蕴含着一种看不见的人文之美。它们都有一个共同的身份：中国备选世界文化遗产。文化摄影旅行家杨永发先生常年志游于其间，乐此不疲，在这本书里他将与读者一同向未知的自然人文世界伸手、探入。